I0427027

Christian Persecutions in the Middle East

Other works of interest from St. Augustine's Press

George J. Marlin, *The American Catholic Voter:*
200 Years of Political Impact

George J. Marlin, *Narcissist Nation:*
Reflections of a Blue-State Conservative

George J. Marlin, *Fighting the Good Fight:*
A History of the New York Conservative Party

George J. Marlin, *Squandered Opportunities:*
New York's Pataki Years

Rémi Brague, *On the God of the Christians*
(and on one or two others)

Edward Feser, *The Last Superstition:*
A Reflection on the New Atheism

Ernest Fortin, A.A., *Christianity and Philosophical Culture*
in the Fifth Century

H.S. Gerdil, *The Anti-Emile: Reflections on the Theory*
and Practice of Education against the Principles of Rousseau

Marc D. Guerra, *Liberating Logos:*
Pope Benedict XVI's September Speeches

Leszek Kolakowski, *Religion: If There Is No God . . .*

C.S. Lewis and Don Giovanni Calabria, *The Latin Letters of C.S. Lewis*

Gerhart Niemeyer, *The Loss and Recovery of Truth*

Gabriel Marcel, *Man against Mass Society*

Josef Pieper, *The Christian Idea of Man*

Josef Pieper, *Happiness and Contemplation*

Josef Pieper, *In Tune with the World: A Theory of Festivity*

Albert Camus, *Christian Metaphysics and Neoplatonism*

Edward Feser, *The Last Superstition:*
A Reflection on the New Atheism

Karol Wojtyła [John Paul II], *Man in the Field of Responsibility*

James V. Schall, *The Regensburg Lecture*

James V. Schall, *The Modern Age*

Dietrich von Hildebrand, *The Heart*

J. David Woodard, *The Politics of Morality*

Christian Persecutions in the Middle East

A 21st Century Tragedy

GEORGE J. MARLIN

St. Augustine's Press
South Bend, Indiana

My efforts are dedicated to

Father Werenfried van Straaten
(1913–2004)

Founder, Aid to the Church in Need

and

Edward Cardinal Egan

Ninth Archbishop of New York
(1932–2015)

TABLE OF CONTENTS

OTHER WORKS BY GEORGE J. MARLIN

Narcissist Nation: Reflections of a Blue-State Conservative (2011)

Squandered Opportunities: New York's Pataki Years (2006)

The American Catholic Voter: Two Hundred Years of Political Impact (2004)

Fighting the Good Fight: A History of the New York Conservative Party (2002)

The Politician's Guide to Assisted Suicide, Cloning and Other Current Controversies (1998)

The Quotable Paul Johnson (1996) (Co-Editor)

The Quotable Ronald Knox (1994) (Co-Editor)

The Guidebook to Municipal Bonds: The History, The Industry, The Mechanics (1991) (Co-Author)

The Quotable Bishop Fulton Sheen (1989) (Co-Editor)

More Quotable G. K. Chesterton (1988) (Co-Editor)

The Quotable G. K. Chesterton (1986) (Co-Editor)

ACKNOWLEDGMENTS

I am particularly grateful to Aid to the Church in Need. For many years the organization has painstakingly compiled and maintained a record of persecuted Christians throughout world; without those data this book could not have been written.

I am also most thankful to those who assisted and guided me in the preparation of this volume, particularly my loving wife, Barbara, who patiently put up with me during the forging of this work, and Joop Koopman, Communications Manager for Aid to the Church in Need-U.S.A. Without the untold hours Barbara put into the assembling of the manuscript, this book would never have been completed and for that I'm forever grateful.

Also, I would like to thank the following for agreeing to participate in the roundtable on the plight of Christians in the Middle East found in Part III of the book: Melkite Archbishop Jean-Clement Jeanbart, Archbishop Michael Fitzgerald, M. Afr., Bishop Camillo Ballin, M.C.C.J., Bishop Gregory Mansour, Father Samir Khalil Samir, S.J., and Father Paul Karam.

By the same token, my gratitude goes out to those remarkable individuals who agreed to contribute original essays to the book: Bishop Elias Sleman, Bishop Angaelos, Father Wafik Nasry, S.J., Sister Marie Melhem, S.S.C.C., and Father Laurent Basanese, S.J.

I acknowledge my indebtedness to all of the individuals who kindly helped me in the preparation of this volume, yet I alone take full responsibility for any inaccuracies of the work herein.

George J. Marlin
Brooklyn, New York
February 26, 2015

INTRODUCTION

Many Western leaders have insisted, time and again, that religious persecutions are unthinkable in the third millennium. People in the twenty-first century, they proclaim, don't behave in a nineteenth-century fashion. U.S. Secretary of State John Kerry made this very point when he declared that the Islamic State (ISIS) has "no place in the modern world."

The fact is, however, militant Islamic groups have established a significant presence in the twenty-first century and have been accomplishing the unthinkable in the Middle East. According to the 2015 Open Doors International Watch List, radical Islamists were the primary persecutors of Christians in the world in 2014.

"Christians in the Middle East? I had no idea." Sadly, all too often that is the response of the average American Christian to reports of the plight of Christians in the Middle East. And, as this book will demonstrate, the identification of the Arab world with Islam and Muslims is both common and profoundly (and tragically) mistaken. Centuries before Islam appeared on the scene, the Middle East was the historic heartland of Christianity—its birthplace, the context in which its foundational theology and worship were first articulated; the launching pad of its evangelization of Europe and Africa, the land sanctified by the first martyrs and saints.

And Middle Eastern Christianity is not simply a matter of ancient history. Since the Islamic conquest of the region in the seventh century, indigenous Christian communities have remained a vital part of the Arab world, with the faithful among the leading creators of that civilization. In many cities of the region, Christians retained sizable majorities well into the Middle Ages, and Christian artists and masons, in addition to beautifying their own churches, were responsible for the design of many of Islam's most iconic monuments—Jerusalem's Dome of the Rock, for example.

Even when the Middle East became a provincial backwater after the Crusades, the region's Christians, often riled by religious violence, unjust taxation, and discrimination, nevertheless continued to function, through diplomacy and commerce, as the conduit to the wider world. Middle Eastern Christians, hoping for an end to discrimination in modern times, have worked especially since the dawn of the twentieth century for civic change in the Arab world by supporting independence and democratic reform. They have fought to end second-class citizenship for themselves and other non-Muslim minorities.

Many of these reform efforts failed because of competing visions for the region. And, in recent decades they have come up against the rise of an increasingly toxic Islamic militancy, which rejects the modern world and takes its cues from an illusory "golden age" of seventh-century expansionist Islam.

Christians, squeezed between these various forces, have been emigrating for decades. But the recent destabilizing effects of the so-called "Arab Spring" in Egypt and Syria, coupled with the merciless religious cleansing campaigns of ISIS in Iraq, have brought a long-simmering crisis to the point of no return.

In Iraq—ancient home of the Chaldean Church—one of the region's largest Christian communities has been largely expelled. As a result of Syria's chaotic civil war, hundreds of thousands of Christians who have lived in the region since the time of the Apostles are languishing in Lebanon or suffering harsh conditions in refugee camps in Jordan and Turkey. Most Christians who have the financial means or family connections are eyeing the start of new lives in Europe, North America or Australia. Bishops are deeply concerned, not to say traumatized. The prominent Lebanese historian Kamal Salibi famously wrote several years ago: "Each time a Christian goes, no other Christian comes to fill his place, and that is a very bad thing for the Arab world."

Are we witnessing the final act of Christianity's long decline in the very place where it was born? What will it mean for the Middle East and for Christianity itself if this dark scenario is allowed to play out? This is the question *Christian Persecutions in the Middle East* poses. It is my hope that it serves as a wake-up call to Christians in the West to grasp just what is at stake in the current crisis in the Middle East.

In addition to the human tragedy of the devastated lives of more than a million uprooted Christian refugees who lack food to feed themselves and their children; the institutional tragedy of Churches seeing their infrastructure wrecked, ancient manuscripts destroyed, and an ancient patrimony disappearing; there is the inaction and seeming paralysis of the great powers to act decisively in the face of the utter brutality of ISIS and other extremist Islamic groups.

This book opens with a brief overview of the rise of Christianity and of Islam in the Middle East. While in such a sketch many details of this complex history must be passed over, nevertheless, I hope that readers will find it an interesting summary of the historical, religious, and political terrain. Needless to say, very little of what is happening today to Christians in the Middle East can be understood without this background.

The book's second part focuses on the eight countries in the Middle East where Christians have endured systemic persecutions in the twenty-first century. The final section includes comments and reflections by distinguished Churchmen and scholars who have great experience and knowledge of the region and the current crisis. The appendix features two pertinent papal documents, an encyclical by Aram I marking the 100th anniversary of the Armenian Genocide and a statement by Patriarch Louis Sako on Islamist violence. It concludes with the text of the May 2014 Pledge of Solidarity and Call to Action signed in Washington, D.C. by more than 300 Catholic, Orthodox Christians and Protestant leaders.

As this work makes clear, current persecutions inflicted on many Christians in the Arab world is an extension of centuries of Islamic law, discrimination and societal bias, which have relegated Christians, as well as other minorities, to second-class citizenship.

It can't be stressed enough that Christians have long worked for "reform" in the Islamic world, for an evolution that would create the necessary separation between mosque and state, thus removing the barriers that restrict Christians' full participation in government, employment, and society at large. Such a shift will especially require a more critical and less literalist view of the Quran, Islam's holy book, and especially the full admittance of "human reason" in the process, as Pope Benedict XVI suggested in Regensburg. This is a vital task Arab Christians are in a unique position to facilitate.

Christians have had an indispensable moderating influence in the Arab world. On a very personal level, the Christian stands for an openness that translates on the political level into a society willing to embrace and thus benefit from the riches of its many ethnicities and religions. This stands in stark contrast to the Islamist vision of a totalitarian "caliphate" in which not only all non-Muslims have to be removed (or silenced), but in which differences between Muslims themselves must be suppressed in favor of a narrow, life-denying literalism.

Pope Francis wrote in a letter to Christians in the Middle East just before Christmas 2014: "Your very presence is precious for the Middle East. You are a small flock, but one with a great responsibility in the land where Christianity was born and first spread. You are like leaven in the dough." He also told them: "Even more than the many contributions which the Church makes in the areas of education, healthcare and social services, which are esteemed by all, the greatest source of enrichment in the region is the presence of Christians themselves, your presence."

A Middle East without Christians, holy places not surrounded by a living Christian community, would turn the region into a museum of Christianity, maintained by foreign clergy for the benefit of foreign pilgrims. It would become a "Church of stones," in the ominous words of Pope Paul VI.

Christian Persecutions in the Middle East is more than a survey of history and a documentation of Islamist terror, vital as these chapters are: many readers will be surprised to discover the rich history and colorful traditions of these Churches—Melkite, Syriac Catholic, Greek Orthodox, Armenian Apostolic, Maronite, Catholic and Orthodox Coptic and many more; and they will be shocked at the record of their slaughter and abuse in times past and present. Nor is *Christian Persecutions in the Middle East* simply a lament over Christian emigration from the region; nor, finally, does the book presume to come up with ready solutions to the complex circumstances that make life for Christians in the Middle East so difficult.

More importantly, this is a testimonial to the real suffering, courage, and faith of those Christians who have chosen to remain in Syria, Iraq and Egypt, amid the chaos of civil war and in the shadow of the constant and still growing threat of ISIS.

The Church leaders who speak in these pages are risking their lives to remain with their people. The faithful, living under constant threat and in chaotic conditions, often without work or proper sustenance, are choosing to remain where they have lived for centuries, as a witness to the Gospel.

Far more than supplying readers with information and perspective, or even alerting Christians and others in the West to the threat posed by today's ultra-violent expression of Islam, the purpose of *Christian Persecutions in the Middle East* is to enable us to walk the Via Crucis, the "Way of the Cross," with these fellow Christians in the Middle East, to truly stand with them, and to inspire us to provide them with the means to help them continue to bear witness to Christ in the land that gave Him birth.

Above all, this book fervently insists that Christians in the West must never forget their suffering and persecuted brothers and sisters in the Middle East. That sense of abandonment, indeed, is among the greatest crosses they have to bear. "We feel forgotten and isolated. We sometimes wonder, if they kill us all, what would be the reaction of Christians in the West? Would they do something then?" Such was the plea by Chaldean Patriarch Louis Sako I. May these pages serve as a part of the answer he and his flock so desperately await.

George J. Marlin
Brooklyn, New York
February 26, 2015

Part One:
The Middle East: A Historic Overview

CHAPTER 1
THE BIRTH AND RISE OF CHRISTIANITY
IN THE MIDDLE EAST:
AN OVERVIEW

After Jesus Christ's Ascension, the Apostles, the first bishops of the Church he founded, hid at the Cenacle in Jerusalem, fearing they would be hunted down, jailed or executed by the Jewish establishment aided by Roman military might. However, as Christ had promised, the Holy Spirit descended on the Jewish holy day of *Shavuot*—50 days after the Passover—the day Christians would celebrate as Pentecost—giving the Apostles the strength and courage to go out into the world to spread the Good News. It was the beginning of the Apostolic Age.

From that moment on, the Church—with its mostly Jewish adherents—began to grow. Peter and his fellow apostles went on to preach throughout Palestine and the surrounding areas. St. Peter led the way, converting and baptizing 2,000 Jews throughout the region. Before long, Christian cells began sprouting up throughout the Roman Empire.

Alarmed by the growing number of conversions, the chief Rabbi of Jerusalem tried to repress the Church by having Peter and other Christians arrested. Numerous times they were arrested, flogged and forbidden to continue carrying out their mission; but each time after being released they refused to stop.

To help administer the expanding Church, the Apostles appointed the first seven deacons. Stephen proved to be the most dynamic of these earliest deacons, fearlessly carrying out the Church's mission in the face of persecution. Accused of blasphemy, he was stoned to death outside the walls of Jerusalem, going down in the annals of Church history as the first martyr. Continuing persecution drove many Christians throughout Judea and Samaria to flee for their lives, and many sought refuge in the largest city of the time in the region, Antioch—capital of the Roman province of Syria.

Within a generation, the new Church's strongest community was in Syria. The term "Christian," which was originally coined as a pejorative by non-believers, was first used in Antioch. Followers of Christ, however, happily adopted that name. It was first mentioned in the Acts of the Apostles, Chapter 11, Verse 26. Barnabas and Paul "conversed in the church [in Antioch] a whole year; and they taught a great multitude, so that at Antioch the disciples were first named Christians." Calling themselves Christians created a sense of unity among Jewish converts but also particularly among gentiles—people who did not belong to the "Chosen People"—who had joined the Church.

While in the West most Catholics readily assume that, historically, the center of the Church was Rome and that Christendom meant Europe, the fact is that the Church was born and first grew and flourished during the early centuries after Christ in what we today call the Middle East.

St. Barnabas was the first person appointed by the Apostles to guide the Church in Syria. Realizing he needed an assistant, he turned to St. Paul for help in preaching to non-believers. Later, St. Peter, before going to Rome—where both he and St. Paul would meet their death—transferred the Church's headquarters from Jerusalem to Antioch.

St. Peter also met and worked with St. Paul in Antioch and together they developed the decrees of what would become known as the Council of Jerusalem, held around the year 50 A.D. and described in Acts 15. The Council ruled that Gentile converts would not be obligated to follow much of Jewish law, including the rules requiring male circumcision. It also encouraged socializing among Jewish and Gentile converts. St. Paul reports in the Epistle to the Galatians that, after the promulgation of the conciliar decrees, Jews and Gentiles were united.

Reflecting on the history of the early years of the Church, the British Catholic apologist Hilaire Belloc wrote in *The Battleground: Syria and Palestine*;

> The immediate appearance of the Church was a Syrian thing; the whole of that early story, the Apostolic foundation, the missionary journeys, stands in Syria, radiates from Syria, returns to Syria. It is held in the quadrilateral of Syrian places, Antioch and Jerusalem from north to south, Damascus and the sea-coast from east to west. In Syria the thing was rooted, from Syria its influence goes out, to Syria the report of its continued advance returns.

St. Peter named Evodius the first bishop of Antioch, and he was succeeded by St. Ignatius. The letters of St. Ignatius confirm that at the beginning of the second century, episcopal sees were established at Smyrna, Magnesia, Philippi, Ephesus, Trellis and Philadelphia. From Palestine and Syria, the Church also spread to Egypt. St. Mark, who had served as St. Peter's secretary, was named the first bishop of Alexandria.

By the third century, every region in Egypt had a Christian presence. More than 40 sees and 100 bishops reported to Alexandria's patriarch. In addition, Alexandria earned a reputation as a major center of Christian learning. Already in the year 180, a Christian university had been established in the city by the philosopher Pantaenus, a convert. He was eventually succeeded by the renowned exegetes Clement and Origen, who authored the first comprehensive systems of Christian theology. Alexandria's suffragan sees included Cyrene, Ptolemais, Berenice and Arsinoe. By the fourth century, Christianity had such a large presence in the region that it had six metropolitan provinces and more than a hundred diocesan bishops to govern the territory.

By the second century, Antioch had established itself as an important Christian center of early Christian life. Both St. Theophilis and Serapion, who served as bishops of the see between 171 and 203, respectively, were brilliant apologists who fought off various heresies.

The first monasteries were established in Syria in the fourth century. In his seminal work, *The Martyred Church: A History of the Church of the East*, historian David Wilmshurst explains why:

> The conversion of Constantine put an end to the persecution of Christians in the territories of the Roman Empire. For many devout Christians, this was not an unmixed blessing. The example of the emperor made the Christian faith socially acceptable, encouraging social climbers to profess Christianity in pursuit of worldly ambitions. Christian zealots who in earlier decades might have courted martyrdom to demonstrate the intensity of their faith now found in asceticism the challenge they craved. They could not understand that the Church had become a political force, and had to compromise in order to work effectively in the world. As far as they were concerned, it had sold out to ambition. They therefore turned their back on the comfortable life which most Christians now led, and sought in the harsh solitudes of the Egyptian and Syrian deserts a life of endurance which, as in the days of the persecutions, made of Christianity something more than the soft option it had become in the cities.

With the Church growing rapidly in the Syrian region, additional sees were established in the provinces and scores of missionaries from Antioch spread out to preach and convert the inhabitants of such faraway Roman provinces of Armenia as Parthia (in today's northeastern Iran).

While Christian missionaries continued to oppose some pagan elements, overall, by the year 300, as Catholic historian Newman Eberhardt has reported, "the Christianization of the East had gone very far. . . . Christianity . . . constituted a majority or almost a majority in the cities in some parts of the East, and an imposing minority in others."

Christianity's public triumph in the fourth century is perhaps most powerfully symbolized by the conversion of the Roman emperor Constantine in 312, which not only brought an end to the legal persecution of the Church by 324, when Constantine gained control of the eastern provinces, but provided the basis for the spread of the Gospel through all sectors of society.

This rapid growth did, however, cause some problems. Church teachings and forms of worship were not always consistent; there was much internal conflict about various traditions and beliefs. To deal with the threat of a host of heresies in the fourth, fifth and sixth centuries, the bishops with imperial support convened a number of councils.

The Council of Nicea, which was held in 325 AD in Bithynia in present-day Turkey, in the presence of the emperor Constantine, is considered the first council of the whole Church, the first "ecumenical" council. More than 300 bishops attended, the vast majority from the East. It was called for the purpose of settling the growing Arian controversy about the relationship between the human and divine natures of Jesus.

After a priest from Alexandria named Arius explained his position on the finite nature of Christ, the Council rejected this view. The Council concluded that, "Those who say: there was a time when He [Christ] was not before He was begotten, and that He was made out of nothing, or who say He is of another *hypostasis* or another substance, or that the Son of God is created or is susceptible of change or alteration, [them] the Catholic and Apostolic Church anathematizes." To teach the faithful about the nature of Christ, the Council developed a profession of faith, the Nicene Creed, which "affirms the co-essential divinity of the Son, applying to him the term 'consubstantial'."

At the regional Council of Carthage in 412, the Church Fathers, led by St. Augustine of Hippo, rejected the heresy of Donatism, which argued that the validity of the sacraments depends on the moral qualities of the person administering them. Twenty years later, St. Augustine successfully refuted the Pelagian heresy that denied original sin and the necessity of grace for salvation at the Council of Ephesus. At that same council, St. Cyril of

Alexandria refuted the position of Nestorius, patriarch of Constantinople, who held that there were two distinct natures in Christ rather than one nature that is both human and divine—and that Mary was the mother of the *man* Jesus, not the mother of the incarnate God.

And in 451, at the Council of Chalcedon, attended by 600 bishops, St. Flavian, the patriarch of Constantinople, led the charge against Eutyches, who held there was only one nature in Christ—a divine nature. The council decreed that "the same Christ, Son, Lord, Only-Begotten in two natures, without confusion, change, division, or separation; the differences in nature being in no way taken away by the union. On the contrary, the property of each is preserved, and concurs into one person and one *hypostasis.*"

The decisions of these various councils led to a fragmentation of the Christian universe. While the ancient divisions remain to this day, the Christian rites are today more sensitive to the non-doctrinal factors that played a role in the dispute: the difficulty of translating Greek and Latin texts into Syriac and Coptic; Byzantium's use of the military to depose dissenting bishops and persecute so-called monophysite communities, an approach that only hardened resistance and closed off debate. Nevertheless, this first great division in the Church had tragic and long-lasting consequences for the region and only in recent decades have the theological and Christological differences over Chalcedon been bridged.

To fully understand the current situation and the persecuted Christians in the Middle East today, it is essential to have some knowledge of the various rites and traditions that came into being in the early centuries of Christianity. Broadly speaking, they are the Assyrian Church of the East; the Oriental Orthodox Churches, which include the Copts and the Syriac Churches as well as the Armenian Apostolic Church; the Eastern Orthodox Churches. There are a number of Eastern Catholic Churches, which include the Maronites, the Chaldeans, Coptic Catholics, Syriac Catholics, Armenian-rite Catholics, the Melkites, etc., all of whom are in union with Rome but maintain distinct Eastern liturgical traditions. Below is a brief description of these churches.

The Assyrian Church of the East

This church was originally named Nestorian and was renamed centuries later the Assyrian Church of the East. Nestorius, the patriarch of Constantinople, taught that there were two persons in Christ, God the Son and Jesus the man, and that Mary was the mother of Jesus—but not of God. After this position was condemned at the Council of Ephesus in 431, Persian and Syrian Christians who were unable to accept this ruling formed a schismatic Nestorian Church that was later endorsed and protected by the Persian emperor, who viewed it as a smart political move to check the power of Byzantium.

After the Muslim conquest of both Syria and Persia in the seventh century, the Nestorians were generally left alone. As a result, this Church, by the fourteenth century, had more than 20 metropolitan sees in the Middle East as well as in India and China.

Reviewing the rapid growth of the Nestorian Church, historian Philip Jenkins has observed: "Before Saint Benedict formed his first monastery, before the probable date of the British King Arthur, Nestorian sects existed in Nishpaur and Tus in Khurassan, in Northeastern Persia and at Rai. Before England had its first Archbishop of Canterbury—possibly before Canterbury had a Christian church—the Nestorian Church already had metropolitans at Merv and Herat, in the modern nations of (respectively) Turkmenistan and Afghanistan and churches were operating in Sri Lanka and Malabar. Before Good King Wenceslas ruled a Christian Bohemia, before Poland was Catholic, the Nestorian sees of Bukhara, Samarkand, and Patna all achieved metropolitan status."

The Nestorian Church, headquartered in Baghdad as of 766, prospered culturally and intellectually as well. Nestorians in Baghdad and Damascus, Professor Jenkins has noted, "preserved and translated the cultural inheritance of the ancient world—the science, philosophy and medicine. . . ."

The tide turned against the Nestorians in the late fourteenth century when the Tartar, Tamerlane (a/k/a/ Timur) invaded their lands. Born in the city of Kesh—now known as Shahrisabz—in 1336, Tamerlane was allegedly a descendant of Genghis Khan and led armies that conquered Transoxiana, what is today Uzbekistan, Tajikistan, southern Kyrgyzstan and southwest Kazakhstan. After being declared an emir, he went on to conquer most of Central Asia. In 1380, he invaded Russia and fought the Lithuanians. Three years later he conquered all of Persia. Over the next 15 years he took control of Iraq, Armenia, Georgia and Mesopotamia (Persia).

Under Tartar rule, the Nestorians were slaughtered *en masse*. By the sixteenth century, its membership consisted of a small group located in Assyria, which today is a part of eastern Turkey.

Commenting on the plight of the Nestorians, Cardinal Eugène Tisserant (1884–1972), one-time Dean of the College of Cardinals and Secretary of the Congregation of the Oriental Churches, said:

> Tolerated but despised as second-class citizens, rarely persecuted but often harassed and tormented, the Nestorians have suffered a relentless process of attrition over the centuries. So long as there were still fire-worshippers, conversions still took place; but from the closing years of the eighth century in Mesopotamia and western Iran, and a little later in the Caspian and Eastern regions, the Christians maintained themselves only within their own communities, handing down their faith from one generation to the next. Hardly any examples are known of mass apostasies, but many Christians, worn down by incessant attacks of varying severity upon their faith, or tempted by the prospects of marriage with a Muslim, must have abandoned their beliefs. But far more numerous, especially in the wilds of Adiabene, Kurdistan and Adarbaigan, were the Christians who stubbornly remained in their humble villages, at the mercy of their oppressors: bloodthirsty Kurdish tribesmen, who constantly plundered and raided their villages, and grasping Arab landowners, who swindled them out of their best lands or simply stole them from them, killing anybody who stood in their way. They were true martyrs

from the Christian faith, since they could have put an end to their trials by simply converting to Islam.

The membership of the Church further declined when dissident members in 1551 elected a rival patriarch, John Sulaka, who traveled to Rome and converted to Catholicism. Pope Julius III appointed him Catholic patriarch and established the Chaldean Catholic Church, which will be described more fully later in this chapter.

During World War I, the Turks, fearful that the Assyrians would side with the British, murdered about half of the Nestorian Christians—including six bishops and hundreds of clergy.

Many of the survivors escaped to Iraq, seeking British protection. They lived in relative peace in Mosul and Baghdad until the British mandate expired in 1932. A battle ensued between Assyrian and Iraqi troops after the British evacuated. The victorious Iraqi government dispersed the Nestorians and revoked the citizenship of the Assyrian Patriarch Mar Simon XXIII, sending him into exile. He settled in San Francisco, California.

A schism occurred in 1964 over the decision of Patriarch Mar Simon to adopt the Gregorian calendar. The new breakaway group also insisted that the patriarch live in Iraq and elected as their patriarch the Assyrian Metropolitan of India.

After the resignation of Mar Simon in 1973, who was subsequently assassinated in San Jose, California, in 1975, the Bishop of Tehran was elected patriarch. He chose the name Mar Dinkha IV, moved to the United States and established his residence in Chicago.

On November 11, 1994, at the Vatican, Pope John Paul II and Mar Dinkha IV put their signatures to a document called "A Common Christological Declaration." Eastern Church historian Ronald Roberson summed up the agreement this way:

> The statement affirms that Catholics and Assyrians are "united today in the confession of the same faith in the Son of God . . ." and envisages broad pastoral cooperation between the two churches, especially in the areas of

catechesis and the formation of future priests. The Pope and Patriarch also established a mixed committee for theological dialogue and charged it with overcoming the obstacles that still prevent full communion. It began meeting annually in 1995.

Two years later, in November 1996, the Assyrian Church of the East and the Chaldean Catholic Church signed a Joint Patriarchal Statement, pledging to work together on pastoral questions and to strive towards reunion. In 1997 another joint statement committed the two Churches to seeking unity. Guidelines for mutual admission to the Eucharist between the Chaldean Church and the Assyrian Church of the East were approved in July 2001. It permits Assyrian faithful to attend Mass and to receive Communion at Chaldean churches. Also, Chaldean Catholics are allowed to attend and receive Holy Communion in an Assyrian church. The document does describe several issues of contention which prevent a full reunion of the two Churches.

The head of the Assyrian Church of the East is known as "The Reverend and Honored Father of Fathers and Great Shepherd, the Catholikos and Patriarch of the East." The patriarchal family dynasty, which had for centuries been handed down from uncle to nephew, ended with the resignation of Mar Simon in 1973. Today, the patriarch has the power to ordain and depose bishops, and like other Eastern bishops, he must abstain from eating meat and remain celibate. Because the term Nestorian is viewed as pejorative, a synod of bishops has requested that the term not be used. At the turn of the twenty-first century, worldwide membership in the Assyrian Church of the East totaled approximately 400,000.

The Armenian Apostolic Church

The people of ancient Armenia were converted to Christianity in the fourth century by St. Gregory the Illuminator. Theirs was the first nation to embrace Christianity and their king, Tirdates III, built the first cathedral in Etsmiatzin, a structure that still stands today.

In the early part of the fifth century, St. Isaac the Great organized the Armenian Church in accordance with Byzantine traditions. During this same period, St. Mesrop invented the Armenian alphabet and then translated both the liturgy and the Bible into the Armenian language.

When the Council of Chalcedon was convened in 451, the Armenian Church did not send any representatives and took no public position on the council's rejection of monophysitism. However, about 50 years later, the Armenian Apostolic Church broke away from the Chalcedonian consensus and allied itself with the so-called monophysite Churches in opposing the Nestorians—without, however, accepting the arguments of the monophysites. In the end, the Armenian Church supported the decision of the Council of Chalcedon on monophysitism but rejected the Christological formula decreed by the council.

For the next 700 years Armenian Christians were persecuted by Persians and Arabs. The Kingdom of Armenia was dismantled in the eleventh century and many Christians fled to Cilicia, a region located in the south of present-day southern Turkey, where they established the Kingdom of Cilicia. The Crusaders were able to reach Jerusalem thanks to the geopolitical position of this kingdom, which allowed safe passage. The kingdom also encouraged the establishment of relations with the West. In 1375 the Mamluks conquered the kingdom.

The seat of the leader of the Armenian Apostolic Church was Ashtishat in southern Armenia until it moved to Cilicia in 1100. In 1293 it settled north of Adana in Sis and in 1441 it was transferred to Etsmiatzin, the location of the oldest Armenian shrine.

Because the Armenians were persecuted by the Ottoman Turks, historian Donald Attwater has written, the Armenians "naturally supported Russia in her designs upon Persian and Turkish territory." But, he continued, "when the Russians occupied the greater part of Transcaucasia in 1829 the erastianism [the doctrine that the state is superior to the Church in ecclesial matters] of imperial Russian politics was extended to the Catholikate of Etsmiatzin which was completely submitted to the state. This and other vexations caused trouble throughout the century and put an end to any hope of union between the Armenians and the Eastern Orthodox."

The Ottoman Turks continued to seek out and persecute Armenian Christians. In the last decade of the nineteenth century, hundreds of thousands were either massacred or deported. And during the First World War, the Turks, who were desperately trying to preserve their dying empire, slaughtered the Armenians. In 1915, at least 1.5 million died in that genocide and tens of thousands fled to Iraq, Syria, Bulgaria and Greece.

After the war, the Armenians found themselves under the iron fist of the Soviet Union. Attempting to suppress all religions, the Communists closed and destroyed churches and monasteries. Many ecclesiastical structures were turned into government offices.

Shortly after the fall of the Berlin Wall in 1989, the Republic of Armenia was established on September 23, 1991. The Armenian Apostolic Church was declared the state religion. Many new churches and religious facilities were built and in 2001 the nation celebrated the 1,700th anniversary of its conversion to Christianity. Worldwide, the Church has approximately nine million members.

Today, Karekin II is the Catholikos (supreme head) of all the Armenians residing in the Catholicosate of Etsmiatzin. In the wake of the genocide, Armenians sought refuge around the world. They all still fall under the authority of the Catholikos.

Under the Catholikos there are several patriarchs. The patriarch of Jerusalem, who lives in St. James Monastery on Mount Zion, is the spiritual leader of the Armenians in Jordan, Israel and the Palestinian territories. He also oversees the Armenian holy sites in Jerusalem.

The patriarch of Constantinople oversees the faithful in Turkey and the Turkish territory on Crete. Father Ronald Roberson, a specialist in Eastern Catholic and Orthodox Churches, has reported that "this patriarchate [in 1914] included 12 archdioceses, 27 dioceses, and 6 monasteries with approximately 1,350,000 faithful. Today only the Patriarchate itself remains with a flock of about 82,000."

Because of persecution and regional wars, the faithful migrated in different directions and the Church followed them, reconstituting its own structure. One major result of this trend is the existence of a second and equal seat of spiritual authority, the Catholicosate of Cilicia, remnant of the Kingdom of Cilicia, which today is head-quartered in Antelias, Lebanon. The faithful total approximately 400,000 living around the world, including Cyprus, Greece, Iran, Lebanon, Syria and the United States. The two Catholicosates have reunited and eliminated many of their political and religious divisions.

As for the religious dogmas of the Armenian Apostolic Church, they are very similar to the Orthodox Churches. The Eucharistic Liturgy is based on the Greek Liturgy of St. Basil. Communion is under both species and the altar vessels are similar to those used in the Byzantine Rite.

The Armenian Apostolic Church describes itself in matters of dogma and doctrine as being closest to the Syriac Church, the Coptic Church, the Ethiopian Church and the Malabar Malankara Church of India. "These five Churches," the Armenian Church has declared, "are usually referred to as the Oriental Orthodox churches (451) in order to distinguish them from the Eastern Orthodox Churches (1054). Each of these churches has its chief bishop and is independent, yet all five are in close relations with one another."

The Coptic Orthodox Church

Monophysitism, which held that there was only a single, divine nature of Christ, first took root in Egypt. The patriarch of Alexandria, Dioscorus, who promoted the position as propounded by Eutyches, was deposed and his teachings were condemned at the Council of Chalcedon. Many of the faithful and their priests, however, refused to accept the ruling of the Council. By the sixth century, supporters of Chalcedon found themselves in the minority in Egypt and throughout the Middle East. The non-Chalcedonian Coptic Church—Coptic meaning Egyptian—dominated the region.

The Coptic Church, which is the largest minority in Egypt

today, is led by the patriarch of Alexandria who for the first four centuries of the Church's existence (500–900 A.D.) lived in the desert monastery of St. Macarius, located between Cairo and Alexandria.

At the turn of the twenty-first century there were approximately eight million Orthodox Copts. They have many schools, a dozen monasteries and numerous convents and their seminary is near St. Mark's Cathedral in Cairo. The liturgy of the Copts is similar to the Greek liturgy of St. Basil that goes back to the fourth century, and their Mass is celebrated in both Coptic and Arabic.

During the century after the Council of Chalcedon, ecclesiastical battles between pro- and anti-Chalcedonian elements in Alexandria at times led to violence. Finally, in 567, it was accepted that there would be two patriarchs of Alexandria, one Coptic, the other Eastern Orthodox.

After the conquest of Egypt by Muslim Arabs, which took place approximately in 640, Coptic Christians began to suffer persecution. After being dominated for centuries by Arabs, Mamluks and finally the Ottomans, more than 90 percent of Egyptians embraced Islam. The Coptic Church, which was once the religion of a large majority of Egyptians, is today a small and increasingly besieged minority.

The Coptic patriarch is known as "The Most Holy Father and Patriarch of the great city of Alexandria and of all Egypt, of Nubia, Ethiopia and the Pentapolis, and of all places where St. Mark preached." For most of its history, the patriarch was a monk chosen by election. Since 1928, a bishop can be elected by a committee of 96 bishops, clergy and monks.

To be eligible for election, a candidate must be over 50 years old, celibate, and willing to abstain from meat and fish for life. The patriarch of Alexandria also ordains all bishops and is the primate of the Ethiopian Orthodox Church.

Monasticism is an important element of the Coptic Church, for it was in Egypt that monasteries were first established. The first monk, St. Anthony, and the first hermit, St. Paul, and their followers, settled in the barren areas along the Nile River and the Red Sea. Today only a few monasteries remain in the region.

The Syrian Orthodox Church

After the Council of Chalcedon, Syrian Christians who refused to abide by its decrees eventually regrouped under their own bishops. While Syrians and Egyptians shared similar theological objections to Chalcedonian Christology, its leaders were also driven by political opposition to harsh Byzantine rule.

For a time the office of patriarch was claimed by factions on both sides of the dispute. But Byzantine Emperor Justinian I, who supported the doctrines of the Council, condemned the Church in Syria as schismatic and imprisoned its bishops. Non-Chalcedonian communities, however, received new life when Justinian's wife, Empress Theodora, sided with them, engineering the consecration of two of its monks and founding a dissident monastery in Sykae.

The empress urged one of the consecrated monks, Jacob Al-Baradai, to leave his monastery and to lead the non-Chalcedonians in Syria. After being consecrated bishop of Edessa in 541, he anointed more than two dozen bishops and ordained more than 2,000 priests. He established a patriarchate of Antioch but the Church's headquarters was in Eastern Syria. Over time two Churches came to dominate in Syria: those who were pro-Chalcedonian and the monophysites, who became known as Jacobites.

The Jacobite Church expanded beyond Syria into Mesopotamia (Iraq). By the twelfth century, 20 metropolitan sees and more than a hundred diocesan sees in Syria and Asia Minor had been established.

At the 17th Ecumenical Council of the Roman Catholic Church (which commenced at Basel in 1431, then moved to Ferrar in 1438, and then to avoid the Black Plague, to Florence in 1439), efforts were made to establish unity agreements with the Eastern Churches. The Jacobite Metropolitan of Edessa signed the Act of Union but it was rejected and never implemented by the other metropolitan sees because it was not binding on them. The main objection was that the Council had decreed that "the holy Apostolic

See and the Roman Pontiff hold the primacy throughout the entire world."

The Jacobite Church is today known as the Syria Orthodox Church. The head of the Church is known as the "Patriarch of the God-protected City of Antioch and of all the Domain of the Apostolic Throne." He is elected by his fellow bishops and must be celibate and committed to perpetual abstinence.

Prior to World War I, the residence of the patriarch was in the Turkish-dominated area of Dair az-Zafaran which is in the vicinity of Mardin in southeastern Turkey. Due to atrocities inflicted by the Turks on Christians during the war—most infamously the Armenian genocide in 1915—the residence of the patriarch was moved to the third largest city in Syria, Homs. Since 1959 the patriarch has resided in Damascus.

In the post-World War II era, many Syrian Orthodox emigrated from their ancestral homelands in Iraq and Syria to Lebanon. Many also left Mosul in northern Iraq and moved to Baghdad. Very few remain today in southeast Turkey.

Syrian Orthodox monasteries, which were once numerous throughout Syria and Iraq, have largely disappeared during upheavals of the past century. There are just a few left throughout the Middle East and three now operate in Europe: one in Switzerland, the others in the Netherlands and Germany.

The liturgical language of the Syrian Orthodox Church is Syriac, a dialect of Aramaic and Arabic in the vernacular. The Eucharistic Liturgy is generally celebrated only on Sundays and feast days.

The present patriarch is Ignatius Aphrem II. At the turn of the twenty-first century, the Syrian Orthodox Church had approximately five million members worldwide.

The Eastern Orthodox Churches in the Middle East

In the early days of Christianity, the term "Orthodox" applied to those who complied with the decrees of the Council of Chalcedon (451). In later years it was adopted by those Eastern Churches that were no longer in communion with the Roman Catholic Church (1054).

Today, the Orthodox Church is a union of 14 territorial Churches. It is officially called the Autocephalous Orthodox Church because each is independent and self-governing. "Their principle of unity," historian Donald Attwater has noted, "is purely internal, they have no external or juridical bond corresponding to the Supreme pontificate in the Catholic Church. . . . This unity of faith, morals, and worship is undoubtedly due in some measure to lack of precision in definition and to a willingness to differ; in theory the unity is complete. . . ."

Christianity was embraced by the Emperor Constantine in 312 and under Theodosius became the official religion of the Empire in 380. But whereas "old Rome" was haunted by its long association with paganism and increasingly unstable due to the threat posed by northern tribes, Constantine decided that the future of the empire was in the East—where, not incidentally, Christians were a more vital presence than in the West. In 330, the emperor founded a new "Christian" capital in the Greek fortress city of Byzantium and renamed it Constantinople.

At the council of Constantinople held in 381, it was determined that its bishop "shall have primacy of honor after the Bishop of Rome because Constantinople is the New Rome." For the next thousand years the patriarch of Constantinople led the church in the eastern part of the Empire.

Over time, disagreements emerged between the Western and Eastern Church. It came to a head in the year 1054 when Rome excommunicated the patriarch of Constantinople and vice versa.

After Constantinople was conquered by the Turks in 1453, they made the patriarch the civil head of the various Orthodox patriarchal Churches throughout the Ottoman Empire. However, this arrangement eventually began to dissolve, a process that was accelerated when the Greeks rebelled and established an independent Greek state in 1832.

After the First World War, the domain and oversight of the patriarchate was limited to Turkey, small sections of Greece, Mount Athos, Crete and the Dodecanese Islands in the Sea of Crete. Because it is viewed as the Mother Church, it still maintains its status of "first among equals" and is referred to as the Ecumenical Patriarchate of Constantinople. The patriarch has certain prerogatives, which include the authority to hear appeals over clerical disputes and the power to ordain bishops outside his see.

In the Middle East today, there are an additional three Orthodox patriarchates—those of Alexandria, Antioch and Jerusalem.

The Orthodox Patriarchate of Alexandria

Because most of Egyptian Christians became Copts after the Council of Chalcedon, the membership of the Orthodox patriarchal see of Alexandria declined to a very small number of faithful, most of whom were Greek. The decline continued, particularly after the Arabs conquered Egypt in the seventh century and most of the more than 100 dioceses were destroyed. The number of Copts at the time of the Arab invasion was in the vicinity of 17 million, and Christians who supported the Chalcedon decrees totaled 200,000. By the thirteenth century, the traditional Alexandria liturgy had been supplanted by Greek usages and the Chalcedonian flock had less than a dozen churches.

The patriarch was appointed by the Ecumenical patriarch and was dependent on Constantinople's largesse. The oversight authority of the Ecumenical patriarch continued until 1858. At that time the Pasha of Egypt, Muhammad Ali (1769–1849), demanded that the patriarch reside in Alexandria and in 1847 appointed Hierotheos II to the post.

After the Pasha's death in 1849, the patriarch of Constantinople once again took control of appointments, but in 1899 the Egyptian faithful and clergy took charge and offered the position to Photius, a priest from Palestine.

During his 25-year reign, Photius revived the Orthodox Church. He held synods, built schools and hospitals and Church membership increased due to an influx of Greek and Syrian Christian immigrants. Photius's most important action was the revision of the patriarchate bylaws that codified independence from Constantinople. To ensure its success, Patriarch Meletios asked the Egyptian government to approve the document. The government happily recognized the independence of the Church and promised protection.

After his death in 1925, his elected successor, Patriarch Meletios II (1871–1935) continued to pursue policies of change and reform. He established two new dioceses, reformed the ecclesiastical courts and opened a seminary.

While the number of Orthodox Christians in Egypt grew to 200,000 in the early twentieth century, by the year 2000 it stood at just 2,000. Because of this dramatic decline of the faithful, the jurisdiction of the patriarch of Alexandria was expanded to include all of Africa.

Today the Orthodox patriarch, who is known as "His Beatitude, the Pope and Patriarch of Alexandria and all Africa," is Theodorus II. He was unanimously elected to the position in October 9, 2004. Membership totals some 300,000 and is split evenly between Africans and Greeks.

The Orthodox Patriarchate of Antioch

As noted earlier, Antioch was the center of Christianity in the early years of the Church and it was the first patriarchate of the Church in the East.

The Church in Antioch was hurt by disagreements after the Council of Chalcedon. Most Christians became Nestorians—who would later form the Assyrian Church of the East. The vast majority of those who remained loyal to Chalcedon were Greeks. After Antioch was conquered by the Arabs in the seventh century, the seat of the Greek patriarch was often left vacant or was occupied by a cleric who resided outside the see.

The Crusaders drove the Arabs out of Antioch in the late eleventh century, establishing a patriarchate that fell under the jurisdiction of Rome. The Greek patriarchs continued to remain in exile until the Egyptians conquered Antioch in 1268 and permitted the patriarch to return. In the late fourteenth century, the seat moved to Damascus, a more flourishing city, where the patriarchate has been located to this day.

In 1724, there was a split in the Antioch Orthodox Church, and a large subset of its members sought full communion with Rome. They became known as Melkite Greek Catholics. As a result of this split, there would be two parallel patriarchs of Antioch, one Catholic, the other Orthodox.

By the end of the nineteenth century, the Antiochian Orthodox Christians were mostly Arab. When Patriarch Spiridon retired in 1899, the hierarchy elected a Syrian to replace him. The Church's Holy Synod, which consists of the patriarch and the metropolitans, meets yearly. It collectively elects bishops and chooses the patriarch.

In recent years, the patriarchate has reached out to the Syrian Orthodox Church and to the Melkite Greek Catholic Churches. The Orthodox patriarch and the Syrian Orthodox patriarch in July 1991 signed a pledge of "complete and mutual respect between the two Churches." A theological commission was established to determine how the ancient schism might be bridged.

The present patriarch, John X, known as "His Holiness the Patriarch of the God beloved City of Antioch and All the East," was elected to the post in 2012. John X resides in Damascus and his patriarchate includes churches in Syria, Lebanon, Iraq, Kuwait, Iran, North and South America and Australia. Total Church membership is approximately 750,000.

The Orthodox Patriarchate of Jerusalem
Acknowledging that Jerusalem ranked as one of the holiest cities in Church history, the Fathers at the Council of Chalcedon in 451 determined that it should no longer be a diocesan see and elevated it to the rank of a patriarchate. To achieve this end, a subset of Antioch's territorial sees, some 60 dioceses, were reorganized and placed under the jurisdiction of Jerusalem.

Jerusalem flourished as an important Christian center until the Arabs conquered the city in 637. Over time, a large part of its population embraced Islam and many of the Christian churches and monasteries were destroyed.

When European Crusaders freed the city from Muslim rule in

1099, they set up a Latin kingdom and appointed a Latin patriarch. As a result, the Byzantine patriarch was forced into exile and moved to Constantinople. He and his successor eventually became wards of the Ecumenical patriarch.

The Orthodox patriarchs, all of whom were Greek, did not live in the Jerusalem region until Saladin, the Sultan of Egypt and Syria, re-conquered Jerusalem from the Crusaders in 1187 and forced the Latin patriarch to flee. When the Ottoman Turks became rulers of Jerusalem in 1516, Constantinople secured its grip on the sacred city and all the patriarchs selected to this day have been Greeks.

Disputes between Roman Catholics and Orthodox over control of many of the Christian holy sites in Jerusalem and its surroundings went on for centuries until the Turkish government, in the nineteenth century, ruled that the Orthodox were to have jurisdiction over them. "This arrangement," Father Ronald Roberson has written, "remained unchanged during the British mandate which began in 1917, and under subsequent Jordanian and Israeli Administrations." (To this day, the Orthodox Church has primary oversight of the Church of the Nativity in Bethlehem and the Church of the Holy Sepulchre in Jerusalem.)

In the early twentieth century, the Jerusalem Church underwent a significant internal crisis when Palestinian Church members insisted on a larger role in day-to-day operations of the patriarchate. To resolve the conflict, an agreement was reached—with the help of the British High Commissioner who was in charge of Jerusalem—that granted Palestinians some say in the administration of the Church, and patriarchal and episcopal elections—much of which remains a "dead letter" to this day.

Today, the Holy Synod that governs the patriarchate consists of the patriarch, who presides, and no more than 18 clerics. A candidate for patriarch must be a member of the monastic Brotherhood of the Holy Sepulchre, which was created in the sixteenth century to care for holy sites throughout Jerusalem. The great majority of the Brotherhood's approximately 100 members are Greek, with a few Arabs among them. The selection of the patriarch from this group has ensured that the position remains firmly in the hands of the Greeks. However, the clergy that serve the parishes within the boundaries of the patriarchate are all Arabs.

Since 2005, His Beatitude Theosophilos III has been the patriarch of the Holy City of Jerusalem and all Palestine. He resides in Jerusalem and the number of faithful of the patriarchate is approximately 130,000.

MIDDLE EASTERN CATHOLIC CHURCHES

Melkites

The Melkite Church is a so-called Byzantine or Greek Catholic Church. Originally, after the Council of Chalcedon in 451, those Christians who remained loyal to the council's decrees in Alexandria, Antioch and Jerusalem were labeled as "Melkites." The term is derived from the Syriac word "malko" or "king." Being a "Melkite," in this context, meant one subscribed to the position held by the Byzantine Emperor that Christ possessed both a divine and a human nature. Once there was a complete split between Rome and what is now known as the Orthodox Church, Byzantine Catholics living in the sees of Antioch, Jerusalem and Alexandria became commonly known as Melkites.

Since the excommunications of 1054 between the Churches of Constantinople and Rome, many Antiochian Orthodox had sought to heal the breach. Greek dominance and neglect during the Ottoman period and the presence of Catholic missionaries in the Middle East served to create a pro-Western, pro-union party among the Orthodox in Antioch. Things came to a head in 1729 when Pope Benedict XIII backed the unionist claimant, Cyril, as patriarch of Antioch. In the ensuing strife, Orthodox Antiochians appointed their own patriarch. Eventually, the term "melkite," which once applied to all Chalcedonian Christians, came to designate only those Antiochians who had embraced union with Rome.

After the Melkite Greek Catholic Church expanded into Palestine and Egypt, the Vatican decreed in 1838 that the patriarch's see would also include Alexandria and Jerusalem.

The Melkite patriarch, however, was forced to reside in a monastery in Lebanon for more than a hundred years until the Ottoman authorities gave the patriarchate legal recognition in 1848. Only then was Melkite patriarch able to establish his official residence in Damascus.

The patriarch is elected by the bishops of his ecclesiastical jurisdiction. The election is confirmed by the Vatican after the Pope receives a profession of faith from the patriarch-elect.

Today most Melkites reside in Syria, Lebanon, Jordan and Israel. Due to emigration, the Church has also expanded into the United States, Canada and Australia.

Since 2000, His Beatitude Gregory III has served as Melkite Greek Catholic Patriarch of Antioch and All the East, of Alexandria and Jerusalem. Membership in the Melkite Greek Catholic Church is 1.2 million.

The Maronite Catholic Church

Maronites began as a monastic movement that was evangelical in nature. They were originally Syrians who descended from the Antiochene Rite and have resided for most of their history in Lebanon.

After the Council of Chalcedon, Syriac monks who opposed the monophysite revolt built a monastery around the shrine of the popular fifth-century hermit St. Maron, located between Antioch and Aleppo. However, when the Arabs conquered Syria in the seventh century they destroyed the monastery of the Maronites, as they became known. Leaving the area, the monks settled in the more secure and isolated Lebanese mountains and elected their own leader who was eventually declared the patriarch of Antioch and All the East.

By the time of the Crusaders in the twelfth century, the Maronite flock had grown to 40,000. Maronite Patriarch Jeremias II al-Amshiti attended the Lateran Council held in Rome in 1215. To further enhance the relationship, Pope Gregory XIII chartered the Maronite College in Rome.

The Maronite Church held several synods, but the major synod in 1736, held at Our Lady of the Almond monastery in Saidat al-Luaizeh, was a key to the development of the Church. The papal delegate, Joseph Assemani, a Maronite and a noted scholar, helped develop decrees that the Maronite Church still draws upon to this day —in particular, to move from a monastic church to a diocesan structure.

From the sixteenth century until the end of the First World War, Maronites were subject to the Ottoman Empire which ruled them through appointed local Emirs. Through most of that period the Maronites were left alone, but in the mid-nineteenth century violence broke out between the Maronite peasants and the Druze overlords in the region known as Mount Lebanon. (The Druze are a small secretive sect of monotheists with an eclectic set of Shia doctrines.)

On May 30, 1860, the well-armed Druzes destroyed Maronite villages throughout Southern Lebanon. More than six thousand Maronites were killed and scores of monks martyred. By the time French troops arrived to quell the violence, at least 16,000 Maronites were dead, more than 100,000 lost their homes and 560 churches were destroyed.

With order restored, a European commission convened and imposed a constitution that made Lebanon a self-governing province of the Ottoman Empire with a Christian governor-general. At the end of World War I, the Ottomans were evicted from Lebanon and the Republic of Lebanon, a French protectorate, was established in 1926. The northeastern section of Beirut was designated a Maronite district.

The Lebanese gained their independence during the Second World War, but before evacuating, the French put in place a constitution that protected the Maronites and decreed that the country's president must be one of their number. These arrangements, for the most part, fell apart in the course of the Lebanese civil war (1975–1990), but after the war the same constitution is in place with a Maronite president, a Sunni prime minister and a Shiite speaker of the parliament.

The Maronites have always been the largest Christian community in Lebanon and at its high point comprised some 770 parishes. The seat of the Maronite patriarch has been in Bkerke, outside of Beirut, since the late eighteenth century.

Today there are estimated to be more than three million Maronites, including more than 200,000 in the United States, 80,000 in Canada and 500,000 in Brazil. Patriarch Moran Mor Bechara Boutros al-Rahi is the 77th Maronite patriarch of Antioch, a position he has held since 2011.

The Chaldean Catholic Church

After the Nestorians were brutally attacked in the late fourteenth century by the Mongols, remnants of the Church, located in Mesopotamia (modern-day Iraq and Kuwait), were governed by a family that handed down the office of patriarch from uncle to nephew. The opposition to this patriarchal arrangement was led by John Sulaka, then an abbot of a Nestorian monastery. On the advice of Franciscan missionaries, he traveled to Rome in 1551 and asked to join the Roman Catholic Church. Pope Julius III appointed Sulaka the patriarch of all the Chaldeans—a title that set the new patriarchate apart from that of the Nestorians. Sulaka, who was ordained a bishop by the Pope in St. Peter's Basilica on April 9, 1553, took the name of Simon VIII.

After returning to his homeland, Patriarch Simon implemented reforms that were aggressively opposed by the Nestorians. Captured by the Pasha of Amadya, he was tortured and martyred in 1555.

Chaos ensued and for the next two centuries subsets of the Chaldeans fell, time and again, into schism. Finally, in 1830 the Vatican reached an agreement that returned the Chaldeans to full communion with Rome. Pope Pius VIII named John VIII Hormiz patriarch of Babylon of the Chaldeans. His see was at Mosul, in present-day northern Iraq.

To eliminate territorial battles between the Chaldeans and the Syrian Catholics of Mulabar, the Holy See decreed that episcopal appointments be made by the Pope. Patriarch Joseph

Audo's charge, voiced at the First Vatican Council (1869–1870), that the ruling infringed on the historic rights of succession was dismissed.

In World War I, more than 70,000 Chaldeans, including four bishops and hundreds of priests, were murdered by the retreating Turkish forces and by the Kurds. Scores of churches in four dioceses were destroyed. In 1933, thousands of Chaldeans were murdered by the Iraqi army.

After World War II, the see of the patriarch was moved from Mosul to Baghdad. Most of the Chaldean Church's approximately 500,000 members are Assyrians, most of whom, until recently, have lived in northern Iraq and in parts of Turkey, Syria and Iran. There are 18 Chaldean dioceses in the Middle East, ten of them in Iraq.

In recent years, negotiations between the Chaldeans and the Assyrian Church of the East resulted in the signing of a Christological agreement in 1994. More than 1,000 Assyrian families led by Mar Bawai Soro left their Church in 2008 and joined the Chaldean Catholic Church.

Since February 1, 2013, the Chaldean leader is Patriarch Louis Raphael I Sako. His predecessor, Emmanuel III Delly, was the first patriarch to be raised to the College of Cardinals. The Eparchy of Oceania, whose episcopal jurisdiction includes Australia and New Zealand, was created in 2006 and the Chaldean Catholic Eparchy of Canada was established in 2011. In the United States, Eparch Francis Kalabat was appointed ordinary of the Eparchy of St. Thomas the Apostle of Detroit in 2014; and Mar Sarhad Joseph Jammo has led the Eparchy of Saint Peter the Apostle of San Diego since 2002.

The Armenian Catholic Church

The Armenians, often cited as the first Christian nation, converted to Christianity in 294. St. Gregory the Enlightener baptized Tiridates, the King of Armenia. Fifty years after the Council of Chalcedon, the Armenian Church—in part for political reasons—rejected the Council's Christology and broke with the

Catholic Church. This led to the establishment of the Armenian Apostolic Church, an Orthodox communion.

Armenian Christians were to endure persecution for centuries from the Persians and the Arabs. During the period of the Crusades, a group of Christians escaped Muslim oppression. They established the Kingdom of Little Armenia and rejoined the Roman Church. That union lasted until 1375 when the Tartars conquered the territory.

However, a group of Armenian monks under the protection of the Dominicans formed the Friars of Unity of St. Gregory the Enlightener in the late fourteenth century. They impressed upon the faithful the importance of being in communion with Rome. Thanks to these efforts, four Armenian clerics attended the Council of Florence in 1439. The remnant faithful were granted a decree of reunion, *Exultate Deo.*

While the proclamation had no immediate impact on the Armenian Apostolic Church, the Friars continued their missionary work. Thanks to the success of the Friars, the Catholic Armenian population grew to the point that an ecclesiastical framework became a necessity. Accordingly, in 1742, Pope Benedict XIV created the see of Cilicia, which was to be headquartered in Lebanon and granted spiritual authority over Armenian Catholics in the southern region of the Ottoman Empire. Armenian Catholics in the northern regions of the Empire remained under the jurisdiction of the Latin Vicar Apostolic, who resided in Constantinople.

This ecclesiastical arrangement led to numerous conflicts and the persecution of many Armenian Catholics. Under the Ottoman millet system, the various religious minorities living in the empire were permitted to rule themselves. But the Turks ruled that all ethnic Armenians came under the legal domain of the Orthodox Armenian Apostolic Patriarch in Constantinople. Many Armenian Catholics and Protestants who objected to this imposed oversight were punished. This clash continued until the French government pressured the Ottoman authorities to permit a separate millet for Armenian Catholics.

In 1846, a separate archdiocese with both civil and religious authority was established in Constantinople. "This anomaly," Church historian Father Ronald Roberson has written, "of having an Archbishop with both civil and religious authority in the Ottoman Capital and an exclusively spiritual patriarch in Lebanon was resolved in 1867 when Pope Pius IX united the two sees and moved the patriarchal residence to Constantinople."

The Armenian Catholic Church, along with its Orthodox counterpart, suffered immensely during the World War I Turkish massacres. Seven bishops, more than a 100 priests, 47 nuns, and a 100,000 faithful were murdered and more than 800 Church facilities were destroyed. In all, the total number of Armenians killed by the Turks—the majority of them Armenian Apostolic—has been estimated at between 1 and 1.5 million. After the war, the life of the Armenian Church was hampered by Soviet rule.

To deal with these tragic events, the Vatican held a conference in 1928 to reorganize the Armenian Catholic Church. The see of the patriarch was moved back to Beirut, Lebanon, and Istanbul was made an archdiocese.

In 1989, when the Iron Curtain fell and Armenia became an independent nation, its believers were finally able to openly practice their faith. The Vatican established an Armenian Catholic Ordinariate headquartered in Gyumri, Armenia which combined Armenia, Georgia and Russia as part of a single jurisdiction.

The patriarch of the see of Cilicia, Nerses Bedros XIX Tarmouni, is the spiritual head of the Armenian Catholic patriarchate in Bzommar, Lebanon. There are approximately 700,000 Catholics with about half under the spiritual authority of the Ordinate for Eastern Europe. The Eparchy of Our Lady of Nareg in New York has jurisdiction over the 36,000 Armenian Catholics in the United States and Canada.

The Coptic Catholic Church

By the end of the sixth century most Egyptian Christians had identified with the Coptic Orthodox Church. There remained, however, a small group of Christians loyal to Rome who survived the bitter inter-faith quarrels and persecution by the Arabs and Turkish conquerors.

After the Crusades, efforts were made to unify the two branches of the Coptic Church and the document *Cantate Domino* was signed during the Council of Florence in 1442. The terms of the agreement were never executed, however, because most Egyptian Christians rejected it out of hand.

In 1630, Capuchin missions were formed in Cairo and the Friars took over many of the Catholic Churches, while preaching in Orthodox Coptic monasteries in the hopes of fostering an atmosphere that would lead to reconciliation. Their efforts, however, failed. Further attempts at reconciliation were made in the late seventeenth century by the Friars Minor of the Observance as well as by the Jesuits—but little progress was made.

The situation began to improve in the mid-eighteenth century when a Coptic Orthodox bishop, Anba Athanasius, was received into the Catholic Church. He was named Apostolic Vicar of the struggling Coptic Catholics by Pope Benedict XIV. Because the fledgling community had no churches of its own, the Franciscans turned over ten Latin-rite churches for the exclusive use of the Copts. There was a succession of Apostolic Vicars after Anba returned to the Coptic Orthodox Church.

It was not until the 1890s that the Franciscans made serious inroads and established about a dozen Catholic Coptic parishes. Impressed with the progress, Pope Leo XIII created three Egyptian dioceses in 1895: Alexandria, Hermopolis Major and Thebes. Four years later, the Pope named the Apostolic Administrator, Bishop Cyril Makarios, patriarch of Alexandria and the Copts. Patriarch Cyril II later became involved in inter-Church controversies and resigned in 1908. The office of patriarch remained vacant until 1947.

At the end of the nineteenth century, there were approximately 5,000 Catholics of the Coptic rite; 63,000 in the mid-twentieth century and in the early twenty-first century approximately 190,000.

Since 2013, Ibrahim Isaac Sidrak has served as patriarch of the approximately 200,000 thousand Coptic Catholics. In Egypt there are 100 parishes, a major seminary in Cairo, three minor seminaries, as well as a number of grammar and high schools, hospitals and clinics. In the United States there are parishes in Brooklyn and Los Angeles. Catholic Coptic parishes have also been established in Australia, France and Canada.

The Syrian Catholic Church

Unlike Egypt, which evinced solid support for anti-Chalcedonian sentiment, Syria's Christians were varied in their responses to the ecclesiastical crises of the early Church. Syrian Christian relations with the European Crusaders was less hostile than in Egypt and other parts of the region. It's not surprising, then, that, with the encouragement of Franciscan and Dominican missionaries, some Syrian bishops showed interest in unity with Rome as early as the thirteenth century. At the Council of Florence in 1444, a decree of union, *Multa et Admirabilia*, between Syrian Orthodox bishops and Rome was signed—but it was never implemented.

Sensing an opportunity to expand the Catholic Church in Syria, Pope Gregory XIII in 1583 appointed a legate to the region who succeeded in opening the doors for Jesuits and Capuchins to commence missionary activities in Aleppo in 1626. Forty years later, a growing Catholic community elected Andrew Akhidjan as patriarch. When he died in 1677, fighting broke out between Catholics and the opposing Orthodox rite and the outcome was the election of two patriarchs.

The Catholic patriarch, Peter, was thrown in prison by the Turks in 1701, along with an archbishop and about a dozen priests. Peter died a year later and for the next 80 years the see was vacant, while Syrian Catholics continued to be persecuted by Ottoman authorities.

The situation for Catholics changed for the better when, in 1782, the Metropolitan of the Syrian Orthodox Church Michael Jarweh, announced his submission to Rome. He moved to Lebanon, built Our Lady of Sharfeh monastery and governed the Syrian Catholics from that site until his death in 1801. He was considered the first Catholic Syrian patriarch of Antioch. As historian Father Ronald Roberson has noted, "There has [since] been an unbroken succession of Syrian Catholic Patriarchs." All have been elected by the Syrian Catholic bishops and confirmed by the Vatican.

Patriarch of Antioch since 2009, Ignatius Joseph III Younan—spiritual leader of some 130,000 faithful—resides in Beirut. There are 15 dioceses, with metropolitans in Damascus and Homs. The Diocese of our Lady of Deliverance encompasses the United States and Canada; it is headquartered in Newark, New Jersey.

CHAPTER 2

THE BIRTH OF ISLAM AND THE RISE OF
ISLAMIST TERRORISM IN THE MIDDLE EAST:
AN OVERVIEW

In 610 A.D., a 40-year old merchant from Mecca named Muhammad claimed he had been receiving revelations from the Archangel Gabriel instructing him to found a religion based on "one God." Winning few converts among the polytheistic Quarysh tribes, he moved on to Yathrib, which was later renamed Medina, "the City of the Prophet."

It was in Medina—in present-day Saudi Arabia—that Muhammad promoted "Islam," the word denoting the religion of "submission" to the one God, "Allah; his followers became known as Muslims. The key slogan of this faith was and remains: "There is but one God, Allah, and Muhammad is his prophet."

Before long, Muslims took over the governing of Medina, conquered Mecca—also in Saudi Arabia—in 623 and declared that city to be the capital of the new religious movement.

Muhammad died in 632 but he left a foundation that ensured the religion he founded—which is based solely on prophetic revelations and which, unlike Christianity, does not rely on reason to discern divine intentions or develop theology—would live on. The foundational revelations of Muhammad, all of which he claimed were revealed to him by God through the Archangel Gabriel, were collected later on in a work that contains 114 chapters called the Quran.

This authoritative work, which assumed its definitive written form about 20 years after the death of Muhammad, consists of narratives about figures in both Jewish and Christian Scriptures, dogmatic teachings (*Iman*) and moral instruction *(Din)*. Over time, commentaries were added by recognized authorities who explained and expanded on the traditions of the faith. This secondary body of early Islamic lore is called the Hadith ("account" or "narrative"), a compilation of deeds, sayings, and rulings attributed to Muhammad but not found in the Quran. The Quran outlines the rules of conduct and worship and describes the mission of Islam in the world—a mission involving not only the propagation of a faith but the establishment of a state as well. Historian Karen Armstrong, in her book *Islam*, points out that "a Muslim had to redeem history and that meant that state affairs were not a distraction from spirituality but the stuff of religion itself. . . . Politics . . . was the arena in which Muslims experienced God and which enabled the divine to function effectively in the world. . . . Consequently . . . political assassinations, civil wars, invasions, and the rise and fall of ruling dynasties were not divorced from the interior religious guest but were the essence of the Islamic vision."

At the time of his death, Muhammad did not name his heir to rule the Islamic faithful. He died without sons and without leaving a clear will. His closest male relative was his cousin and son-in-law, the philosopher-warrior Ali ibn Abi Talib, whose followers are called the *Shiat Ali* [followers of Ali], or Shiite. They considered Ali the rightful heir of Muhammad. The Sunnis, however, opted for someone they saw as better equipped for leadership, choosing Muhammad's father-in-law Abu Bakr to be the first caliph. This fundamental schism—between the majority Sunnis who believe that leadership of the Muslim community (or ummah) should be determined on the basis of election and consensus and the Shia minority who believe that Ali and his descendants constitute the sole legitimate line of succession—continues to this very day.

After Abu-Bakr's death in 634, the next caliph, Omar, declared himself *Amir-al-Mu'minin*, Commander of the Faithful. Caliph Omar sent forces to impose the faith on Christian strongholds throughout the Middle East and North Africa. The Byzantine armies that defended these Christian areas were defeated on every front and by 643 the forces of Islam gained control of the major Christian cities of Antioch, Aleppo, Damascus, Emesa (today's Homs), and Jerusalem. In a span of five years, the patriarchates founded in the early years of the Church—Antioch, Alexandria and Jerusalem—had fallen under Muslim rule. Amazingly, within a century, through religious zeal and military conquest, Islam supplanted Christianity throughout the Middle East, northwest Africa and southeastern Europe. It must be noted that a number of Christian rulers and elites in the region—seeking relief from Byzantine military persecution of theological dissent —welcomed the arrival of Muslim forces.

After Omar's assassination in 644 (by a captured Persian soldier), his successor, Othman, continued the Muslim invasions and by 651 his armies had conquered all of Iran and Afghanistan. Othman was also assassinated but this time it was a Muslim soldier who committed the deed. Foreign invasions came to a halt because the split that had begun within the Islamic religion after Muhammad's death took on new dimensions after Ali ibn Abi Talib was declared Caliph by his followers, resulting in a *fitnah*, a civil war between Shia and Sunni Muslims. As noted, Shiites held that Ali was the true Caliph and that all his successors should come through his family line. They believed that the descendents of Ali are the true heirs of the Prophet Muhammad, the Imam, and are infallible. During the conflict Ali was assassinated.

Imams in the Ali line continued to rule precariously until 872; most were poisoned by rivals. When the eleventh Imam died in the ninth century, Shiites believed his heir, the twelfth Imam, went into seclusion and was transformed into a state of "occultation" and would one day return. This expected one, referred to as the *Mahdi*, would be the messiah who would reveal himself to be the leader of all of Islam. During the interregnum, elected ayatollahs would serve as temporary leaders.

Sunnis, on the other hand, continued to reject the position that only direct descendants of Muhammad should rule the Islam world. The Caliph, they argued, should be elected by religious leaders, who possessed the authority to interpret the Quran for the faithful and to preserve and promote the oral tradition.

Over time, radical factions evolved out of each of these two camps. Extremist Shiites are known to look upon martyrdom for the faith as the ultimate sacrifice. Today, Sunnis who belong to the Wahhabi sect (Osama bin Laden, for example) are radical fundamentalists who argue that the Quran must be interpreted literally and that it serves as the sole source of both religious and civil law.

The followers of Ali lost what is known as the "First *Fitnah*" and the victors established the Umayyad Dynasty that was headquartered in Damascus in 661. Ali's camp led by his son Hasan agreed to retire to Medina.

Under the Umayyad Caliphate of Damascus, Roman institutions and the form of central government were maintained to a degree but managed by Muslims, generally Arab chieftains. The Caliphate of Muawiyah I (661 680) successfully led forces into Asia Minor, but was stopped at the gates of Constantinople in 678. A subsequent Umayyad Caliph, Sulayman (715–717), also failed to take Constantinople in 717.

The Umayyad caliphate, which over time had become secularized, began to experience internal dissent which led to its overthrow in 750 and the creation of rival caliphates in Bagdad and Cordova, Spain. In Egypt, a group known as Fatimites set up a caliphate in Cairo, declaring they were the true successors to Muhammad.

Battles throughout this period continued between Muslim armies and the Byzantine Empire. Asian mercenaries, Seljuk Turks who had converted to Islam, routed the Greeks badly in 1071, forcing them to appeal to the Roman Pontiff and the monarchs of the West to bail them out. This appeal was the eventual catalyst for the Crusades described later in this chapter.

When Muhammad founded Islam, he revered Abraham of the Old Testament whom he viewed as his predecessor and precursor. The writings, which later were incorporated in the Quran, were highly influenced by the texts of both the Old Testament and the Gospels. Islam adopted the Jewish and Christian teachings that held there was one God who will judge each person after death and mete out reward or punishment.

While Muhammad rejected the doctrine of the Trinity, along

with the Redemption brought about by Christ's crucifixion, Catholic historian Philip Hughes has pointed out that Muhammad's "doctrine of the end of creation, of judgment, heaven and hell, is derived from Christian sources. . . . Heaven is a place of never ceasing pleasure where every human desire, even the most lowly, finds limitless opportunity for its fullest satisfaction."

Unlike Christ's apostles, who preached to all nations but did not coerce or threaten non-believers, Muhammad told his followers that they had a duty to wage holy wars and to destroy pagan non-believers, referred to as infidels. "Kill all pagans," he declared.

Although the Muslims rapidly conquered Christian territories in the Middle East, they did not force Christians or Jews to embrace Islam. Over time, however, some Christians converted. Nevertheless, despite disabilities and hardships, most remained loyal to the Christian faith of their fathers to the present time.

While the Muslims did not grant equal rights to Christians or Jews, they were for the most part tolerant. "There was," Middle-East scholar Bernard Lewis has written, "a willingness to coexist with people of other religions who, in return for the acceptance of a few restrictions and disabilities, could enjoy the free exercise of their religions and the free conduct of their own affairs."

Nevertheless, Christianity and Judaism are viewed by Muslims as earlier, incomplete divine revelations given by God. While they consider the Old and New Testament as inspired by God and refer to Christians and Jews as "People of the Book," Muslims believe that God's final revelation was given by way of the Archangel Gabriel to Muhammad. In other words, Islam has superseded Judaism and Christianity. In his work "Islam and the West," Bernard Lewis explains the relationship this way:

> For the Muslim, Christianity was an abrogated religion, which its followers absurdly insisted on retaining, instead of accepting God's final word. They could be tolerated if they submitted. If they did not, they were to be fought until they were overcome and either accepted the truth of the Muslim faith or submitted to the authority of the

Muslim state. For Christians, Islam was at best a heresy, more usually a false doctrine, founded by one who was variously depicted, at different states in the evolution of European consciousness, as a heretic, an impostor, and later, in the age of the Enlightenment, an Enthusiast.

Christians, Jews and Muslims also shared similar cultural backgrounds. They spoke the same Arabic language, believed in one God and in many of the same prophecies and revelations. They were also influenced by Roman institutions, particularly its laws and structure of government.

Despite these similarities, Islam, during its centuries of conquest, made it clear that while God had revealed himself to Christians and Jews, these believers were corrupted by error and obstinacy and no longer worthy of carrying out the commands or teaching of the Almighty. The Judeo-Christian order was to be replaced definitely by that of the Muslim caliphate. To make this point, Muslims erected a monument in Jerusalem to overshadow the Jewish temple, and sacred Christian places, such as the Church of the Holy Sepulchre. Inscribed on one of the entrances to the Dome of the Rock in Jerusalem, as it was called, is a phrase that clearly rejects Christianity: "Praise be to God, who beget no son and has no partner. . . He is God, one, eternal. He does not beget, He is not begotten, and He has no peer."

To further emphasize that Muslims were in charge of the formerly Christian-dominated Holy Lands, a gold coin was issued known as the *dinar*, which had on its face the name of the Commander of the Faithful, the current caliph. This coin superseded the Roman *denarius* and sent this message to Rome and to all Christians, to the effect that their faith was corrupted, their time had passed, and that the ruling caliph was now the ruler of God's empire on earth.

Christians and Jews became known as *dhimmis*—that is, protected peoples. They were considered second-class citizens who were required to annually pay Muslim authorities a personal tax, *jizya*, and a land tax, *kharaj*. Their communities were permitted to form so-called millets, which granted Jewish and Christians leaders a circumscribed degree of both political and spiritual self-governing authority; the communities were entitled to protection from Muslim armed forces. Christians were required to wear distinctive clothes and they were not permitted to ride horses. However, a few Christians were granted positions within the governing body of the Caliph. An example was St. John Damascene (676–754)—one of the greatest of the Greek Church Fathers, a monk who defended the doctrines of the Church and wrote an early summary of theology—who served for a time as a chief councilor to the caliph of Damascus.

Coming to the aid of the beleaguered Byzantine monarch who had lost his empire to the Muslims, Pope Urban II made this declaration to an assembly of clerics and laymen at Clermont, France on November 18, 1095:

> An accursed race . . . has violently invaded Christian lands and depopulated them by pillage and fire. . . . They have either destroyed God's Churches or taken them for the rites of their own religion. They have robbed us of the tomb of Jesus Christ, that wonderful moment of our faith. . . . On whom is the duty of avenging these wrongs and recovering the territory, if not upon yourselves? . . . Let internal quarrels cease; soldiers of hell, become soldiers of Christ! Enter on the road to the Holy Sepulchre; wrest that land from the wicked race; subject it instead to yourselves.

The great crusade that commenced in 1095 was to be the first of seven such crusades that spanned 200 years and attempted—but in the end failed—to keep the Middle East, or the Levant, as the Crusaders called it, under Christian rule.

The Crusades were not simply an exercise in imperialist conquest, although they are so regarded, even today, by many in the Muslim world—these military campaigns were a *reconquista*. They were, observed Bernard Lewis, a long-delayed Christian response to the jihad, "an attempt to recover by holy war what had been lost by holy war. . . ."

The Franks, who led the First Crusade, re-conquered Jerusalem in 1099 and once order was restored, Crusader leadership was often tolerant in their dealings with Muslims and the Oriental Christians they inherited. Nevertheless, the Franks reintroduced the teachings and ceremonies of the Roman Church.

In battle, both the Crusader and the Muslim armies could be brutal. Towns and villages were destroyed and looted. The Muslims, however, waged their holy war not against forces they viewed as Christians or "People of the Book," but as an enemy they considered to be little better than barbarians. Eventually, under the forces of Saladin, they recaptured Jerusalem on July 4, 1187, after the battle of Hattin. The city was to remain under Muslim rule until the British took command of it at the end of World War I.

Subsequent Crusades, which continued until 1270, had limited success. By 1291, the citadels of Acre, Antioch, Tyre, Beirut, Haifa and Tripoli had fallen to the new Islamic power in the region, the Mamluks, based in Cairo, who rose in response to the last Crusade under St. Louis of France in 1249. During three centuries of Mamluk rule, much of the Middle East became a depopulated backwater. The threat of bandits and lawlessness reduced Christian pilgrimage to the holy places.

A new and more vigorous Muslim actor entered the scene in 1515 when the Ottoman Sultan Selim conquered Egypt and took control of the Mamluk empire. The Ottoman Turks took their name from Othman, "the chosen one among the tribe of brave and noble people." His heirs became known as Ottoman Turks. They were to lead the charge against Christendom, conquering great portions of the Byzantine Empire until they were stopped at the gates of Vienna by an army led by the King of Poland, John Sobieski, in 1683.

Under the rule of the Muslim Ottoman Empire, Christians not only continued to be second-class citizens but were excluded from any direct roles in government. However, the Ottomans did provide, in Karen Armstrong's judgment, a "framework which enabled the different groups—Christians, Jews, Arabs, Turks, Berbers, merchants, *ulama, tariqahs* and trade guilds—to live together peacefully, each making its own contribution, and following its own beliefs and customs."

In "A History of the Arab People," Albert Hourani described how in the various Christian communities, patriarchs and bishops exercised their authority:

> Under the Abbasid caliphs the Nestorian patriarch in Baghdad, and under the later Egyptian dynasties the Coptic Patriarch in Cairo, held a special position of influence and respect. The heads of the communities were responsible for ensuring that the terms of the *dhimma* or contract of protection between the Muslim ruler and the non-Muslim subjects were honored: peace, obedience and order. They may have played a part in assessing the poll tax, but normally it seems to have been collected by officials of the government. They also had a function inside the community: they supervised the schools and social services, and tried to prevent deviations in doctrine or liturgical practice. They also supervised the courts in which judges administered law in civil cases involving two members of the community, or reconciled disagreements; if they wished, however, Jews and Christians could take their cases to the Muslim *qadi* [judge], and they seem to have done so frequently.

Middle Eastern Christians were also tolerated by Muslim Turks because the ruling classes looked to the Christians to facilitate trade, commerce and access to Western goods, particularly European-manufactured weaponry. Hence, Christians living under the Ottomans had a positive influence by acting as intermediaries between Muslims and Westerners. Syrian Christians, for example, brokered trade between the Syrian coast and Damietta, a port city in Egypt. In Egypt, Christians were employed as managers and financiers for Muslim farmers.

By the thirteenth century, the Middle East was exporting scientific and medical discoveries as well as scholarship in literature and philosophy. The West also imported various foods, drugs and commercial articles, including the game of chess. Middle Eastern Muslims imported and utilized Western inventions including guns, telescopes, eyeglasses, printing and scientific equipment. Westerners also used their trading power to ensure that Middle Eastern Christians were decently treated by their Muslim overseers.

Over time, European influence began to increase in the Middle East. The Western powers did more than trade—they began to invest in the region. As the investments of the various nations began to grow and produce profits, the European nations not only wanted to protect their interests but also maintain a balance of power in the region.

As early as 1798, the French, under the leadership of Napoleon, occupied Egypt for three years. Later, in 1830, the French Republic occupied Algeria. During this same period, the British and Russians gained considerable influence in Iran.

In 1860, after the Druze rebels slaughtered more than 10,000 Christians, the French demanded that Lebanon become an independent state. Twenty years later, the French colonized Tunisia.

Meanwhile, Great Britain gained control of Egypt in 1882 after the Egyptian military and a group of reformers took control of the government. The English then proceeded to occupy the Sudan in 1889. After oil was discovered in Iran in 1901, the British were awarded contracts to produce and distribute the oil.

Throughout the nineteenth century, major cracks appeared in the Ottoman Empire that still controlled most of the Middle East and the Balkans. The Ottomans, after they lost the Russo-Turkish War in 1774, ceded Crimea and recognized the Czar as the protector of Orthodox Christians throughout the Ottoman Empire. The militant fundamentalist Wahhabi sect, with the support of the House of Saud, drove the Ottomans out of the Arabian peninsula between 1803 and 1913. The Serbians revolted against the Ottomans in 1815 and the Greeks fought and won their war of independence in 1821.

Muhammad Ali, the founder of modern Egypt—whose dynasty would rule that country until a military coup in 1952—overran most of Syria in 1831. The French and British, fearing an alliance between the Egyptians and the Russians to dominate the area, intervened to prop up the collapsing Ottoman Empire. The European powers negotiated the Convention of Kutahya, a deal that gave Crete and Hejaz (the western part of what today is Saudi Arabia) to Muhammad Ali in exchange for his withdrawal from Anatolia, a part of modern-day Turkey.

The European powers intervened again in 1840 after Muhammad Ali's forces defeated the Turks at the Battle of Nezib. In return for withdrawing from Syria and parts of Mount Lebanon, he was granted hereditary rule of Egypt. The presence of British Naval forces in the eastern Mediterranean persuaded Muhammad Ali to accept the deal.

The Europeans made further inroads into Egypt in the late nineteenth century. In 1875 the bankrupt nation sold the Suez Canal to the English and ceded control of its finances to the Western powers. To put down a revolt by Egyptian officers and other groups in 1882, the British occupied the entire country.

When the Great War began in August 1914, the Ottomans sided with the Germans and the Austrians. Retaliating, the British declared Egypt a protectorate and, along with their Russian ally, occupied Iran. To further weaken the Turkish hold on the Middle East, the British supported an Arab revolt in 1916. With the effective dissolution of the Ottoman Empire towards the end of the World War I, England and France became the dominant powers in the Middle East. Francois Georges-Picot of France, and England's Mark Sykes, were given the task in 1915–1916 to determine the new regional map for the post-war era. Discarding promises of independence for Arab provinces, they carved up the former Ottoman Empire into European protectorates without regard to ethnic or religious lines.

The secret Sykes-Picot agreement, as it became known, which was approved by the participating parties in May 1916, gave France control over Lebanon, Syria and parts of Galilee. Britain was given control of the territory between the River Jordan and the Mediterranean, Trans-Jordan proper, and southern Iraq. Russia, the third party to the agreement, was to be awarded Istanbul, the Ottoman Armenian vilayets and the Turkish Straits.

The Bolsheviks, who took control of Russia in 1917, published the secret agreement on November 23, 1917 to embarrass the Allies. Both the Arabs and the Zionists, who were promised a "Jewish homeland" by the British in the Balfour Declaration signed just three weeks before the leak of Sykes-Picot, were appalled.

To fix the mess, in November 1918, a new Anglo-French declaration agreed on a new arrangement for the region. The agreement states that Great Britain and France were committed to "assist in the establishment of indigenous Governments and administrations in Syria and Mesopotamia by setting up of national governments and administrations deriving their authority from the free exercise of the initiative and choice of the indigenous populations." In other words, the Allies agreed to permit the liberation of countries that had been under the control of the Ottoman Empire.

Despite this promise, both England and France maintained protectorates in Lebanon, Palestine, Iraq, Syria and Transjordan and generally controlled the economies, particularly in the oil producing regions.

The name Iraq was given to a British-created kingdom that included the former Ottoman provinces of Mosul, Baghdad and Basra in the eastern edges of the Middle East; in the west, the northern part of the region was named Syria and came under the control of the French; Palestine was established in the south, under a British protectorate.

In the post-World War I era a hybrid system was set up; Britain and France were able to interfere in the affairs of the newly-created Middle Eastern states but they did not have full governing power and responsibility. Hence, as Bernard Lewis has pointed out, this lack of control "would neither create nor permit stable and orderly government." Unlike India, where the British had control and promoted a class of administrative locals, Lewis added, the people of the Middle East "got the worst of both worlds, receiving neither the training in administration of the colonial territories nor the practice in responsibility of the old independent states."

Based on European models, the new constitutional monarchies and republics—most of which failed over time—were pressed to grant equal rights to indigenous Christians. This did not sit well with many Muslim elites who were expected to abide by the constitutional guarantees. "First Turkey and then other Muslim countries," Bernard Lewis has written, "enacted legislation or promulgated constitutions declaring the equality of all religious communities before the law. In practice, it did not always work out, and both Western emissaries and native Christians from time to time received sharp reminders that it was not wise to go beyond what public opinion was prepared to accept. There were times and places when the non-Muslim subjects of the Muslim states were worse off after emancipation than before. The old status given to them under Islamic law, with limited but well-established and universally recognized rights, had been abolished. The new status as equal citizens meant less and less in a situation in which citizenship itself was losing all meaning."

The only area where Christians enjoyed a true and unambiguous role in governing was in the Republic of Lebanon that was formed by the French in 1926. Historically, Lebanon had been a region where multi-religious groups had flourished; the local tradition had been greatly influenced by Western traditions as far back as the time of the Crusades. The fact that both Christians and Muslims both spoke Arabic and shared a common culture also made it easier for them to co-exist. This amicable arrangement was to last until a civil war tore the country apart in the last quarter of the twentieth century. The experiment still works today, but is fragile.

The British and French mandates in the region began drawing to a close at the end of World War II and the Western powers gradually withdrew by the 1950s. In the end, the successor states that gained independence did not necessarily seek truly representative forms of government. Most attempts at governing that employed Western democratic principles failed; they were at best illiberal democracies. Republicanism came to stand for non-monarchical autocratic rule. In the post-World War II era, only three countries had had success in forming democratic governments: Israel, Turkey and, up until its civil war, Lebanon.

The Western retreat from the Middle East also opened the doors, according to Bernard Lewis, for a "tremendous upsurge of religious movements, expressing a messianic radicalism." Militant groups that opposed cultural and governing modernization, like the Muslim Brotherhood, began to emerge. These called for new holy wars that would save Islam from the non-believers. For many of these radicals there could only be the one caliphate, one Islamic order, and anyone who stood in the way of their efforts to reestablish it had to be eliminated. These extremist movements, in conjunction with democratic movements and secularists, helped engineer the fall of the Shah in Iran 1979 and the assassination of Egypt's President Anwar Sadat in 1981—and reintroduced into the Middle East revolutionary ideologies, often based on narrow or misguided readings of Islamic sources that now began to employ terrorist tactics.

The word "terrorist" was coined during the French Revolution and first appeared in the Dictionary of the French Academy in 1799. The term was employed to describe the 1793–1794 "Reign of Terror" period when the Committee of Public Safety was led by the Jacobin radical, Maximilien de Robespierre. The Law of Suspects approved by the committee, ordered the arrests and execution of so-called "suspects" who "by their conduct or their relationships, by their remarks or their writing, are shown to be partisans of tyranny and federalism and enemies of liberty."

Thousands of French people from all walks of life were convicted and guillotined. Robespierre, the last victim of the reign of terror, was himself executed in 1794 after the other members of the governing committee turned on him out of fear for their own lives. He proved his own maxim: "Terror is nothing other than justice, prompt, severe, inflexible."

In the nineteenth century, Sergey Nechayev (1847–1882), the founder of the secret Russian revolutionary group the People's Retribution, wrote the "Catechism of a Revolutionary." In that tract, he called for a new class of terrorists who would use advanced techniques to achieve their end: "The revolutionary [terrorist]," Nechayev declared, "knows only one science: the science of destruction. For this reason and only for this reason, he will study mechanics, physics, chemistry . . . their characteristics and circumstances and all the phenomena of the present social order." By taking this approach, he concluded, terrorists "can destroy the entire state at its roots, exterminate all imperial traditions, the whole social order, and all existing classes."

Late in the century, systematic forms of terrorism began to be aimed at government officials and royal houses. In addition to anarchists like Nechayev, radical nationalists in Russia, Ireland and Serbia were all guilty of such acts. Some argue that World War I was sparked by an act of terrorism—the June 28, 1914 assassination in Sarajevo of the Austrian heir to the throne, Archduke Franz Ferdinand and his wife, Sophie, Duchess of Hohenberg, by Gavrilo Princip, a member of the extremist Young Bosnia movement.

The twentieth century also saw the dawn of "indiscriminate terror," that is random acts of murder and destruction. Indiscriminate murder, terrorist expert and renowned historian Walter Laqueur has noted, "dramatizes the demands of the terrorists; it spreads a climate of fear and discredits the government incapable of suppressing it; and if frequently repeated, it disrupts the normal functioning of society."

Fanatics came to believe that their mission was to indiscriminately take innocent human life because not only government leaders were the enemy, but all the peoples of a given society. Killing women, children and the aged, especially indiscriminately, would instill more fear and produce more panic more effectively than merely targeting political and military officials.

Throughout the twentieth century, various international organizations have tried to define terrorism. The League of Nations in 1937 decreed it to be "all criminal acts directed against the state . . . and intended to create a state of terror in the minds of particular persons or the general public." In 1999, the UN stated that terrorism "consisted of criminal acts intended to provoke a state of terror, and were in any circumstances unjustified whatever the considerations—that of a political, philosophical, ideological, racial, ethnic religious, or other nature." After the 9/11 attacks on the United States, the European Union came up with a definition that human rights activists charged was too broad: "Terrorism [is] an organized act of violence or threat of violence that caused terror and fear such as killing, assassination, the taking of hostages in airplanes and ships and the use of bombing aiming at advancing political aims." Possibly the best and most succinct definition was penned in 1990 by the U.S. Department of Defense: Terrorism is "the unlawful use of or threatened use of force or violence against individuals or property to coerce and intimidate governments or societies, often to achieve political, religious, or ideological objectives."

Terrorism has played an important role in the history of the Middle East. In fact, experts agree that the first terrorist group in recorded history to commit acts of systematic murder for political and religious purposes were Shiites known as "the Assassins" or *Nizari*. They first appeared in Iran in 1095 and later spread out to Syria. Theirs was a violent response to two centuries of oppression by Sunni Muslims who had assassinated many Shiite leaders. "Religious in inspiration, political in purpose," Bernard Lewis has written, "their aim was no less than to overthrow the existing Sunni order in Islam."

Their spreading of ruin and terror was not limited to Muslim princes and government officials. From time to time they targeted Christians, particularly leaders of the Crusades. In 1192, for example, this radical group assassinated the King of the Latin Kingdom of Jerusalem, Conrad of Montferrat, and later Count Raymond of Tripoli in Syria.

While "the Assassins" clearly failed to destroy the existing order in the Middle East, they were the first of the messianic movements. As Lewis has written, "the undercurrent of messianic hope and revolutionary violence which had impelled them flowed on, and their ideals and methods found many imitators. For these, the great changes of our time have provided new causes for anger, new dreams of fulfillment, and new tools of attack."

In the twentieth century, what Lewis calls "sacred terrorist" groups have come into being, dedicated to creating an Islamic caliphate and ridding the Middle East of Western ideas and mores, particularly nationalism. All these movements, in Lewis's judgment, have been "driven by the same feeling of revulsion against the West, of frustration at the whole new apparatus of public and private life, inspired by or derived from or mimed after Western originals, and all of them were drawn by the same vision of a restored and resurgent Islam, through which God's law and those who uphold it would prevail over all their enemies."

Middle Eastern Christians have been a frequent target of these Islamic militants because they have generally supported nationalism and democratic reforms. What's more, many of their leaders and clerics were (and are) educated at Western educational institutions. Christians, especially Lebanese Christians, Lewis has pointed out, have "contributed disproportionately to the foundation and development of the newspaper and magazine press in Egypt and in other Arab countries, and Christian names figure prominently among the outstanding novelists, poets and publicists in the earlier states of modern Arabic literature." This level of social and cultural Christian prominence flew in the face of radical Islamist goals as well as traditional second-class status of Christians in Muslim society that had once been the norm.

The Muslim Brotherhood, founded in 1928, is the first militant group to appear in the twentieth century that would, throughout its history, persecute Christians as well as other non-Muslims— along with Muslims who opposed its aims. Its founder, Hasan al-Banna (1906–1949), declared that "The Supreme martyrdom is only conferred on those who slay or are slain in the way of God. As death is inevitable and can happen only once, partaking in jihad is profitable in this world and the next." In the 1930s and 1940s, this group—dedicated to restoring the Caliphate—employed systematic terrorism in the assassination of numerous government leaders.

The Muslim Brotherhood's leading intellectual leader was Sayyid Qutb (1906–1966). The author of more than two dozen books, he served as the editor of the organization's journal. Describing Qutb's views in "Terrorism and Liberalism," Paul Berman wrote that he "wanted Muslims to understand that, if tolerance and open mindedness were accepted as social values, the new habits of mind would crowd out the divine. He wanted Muslims to remember that in Islam, the divine is everything, or it is not divine." Achieving that end would entail making sharia, Islamic law, not the Western-style constitutional norms, the legal code of the state.

Qutb promoted the creation of an elite revolutionary vanguard that would do battle—using violence if necessary—to topple governments that did not adhere to sharia law. In this view, Dr. Patrick Sookhdeo, director of the Institute for the Study of Islam and Christianity, has observed, jihad is a legitimate "method for actively seeking to free all peoples on earth from non-Islamic authority."

A fierce anti-Semite, Qutb held that the battle to be fought must engage both Christians and Zionists. For Qutb, "Judaism and Christianity," Berman has written, "were inferior and had led to lives of misery, and those doctrines could not possibly survive in the face of Islam and its obvious superiority."

As to dying for the cause, Qutb wrote on martyrdom and jihad in "In the Shade of the Quran":

> The Surah tells the Muslims that, in the fight to uphold God's universal Truth, lives will have to be sacrificed. Those who risk their lives and go out to fight, and who are prepared to lay down their lives for the cause of God are honorable people, pure of heart and blessed of soul. But the great surprise is that those among them who are killed in the struggle must not be considered or described as dead. They continue to live, as God Himself clearly states.
>
> To all intents and purposes, those people may very well appear lifeless, but life and death are not judged by superficial physical means alone. Life is chiefly characterized by activity, growth, and persistence, while death is a state of total loss of function, of complete inertia and

lifelessness. But the death of those who are killed for the cause of God gives more impetus to the cause, which continues to thrive on their blood. Their influence on those they leave behind also grows and spreads. Thus, after their death they remain an active force in shaping the life of their community and giving it direction. It is in this sense that such people, having sacrificed their lives for the sake of God, retain their active existence in everyday life. . . .

In 1966, Sayyid Qutb was hanged after being found guilty of participating in a plot to assassinate Egyptian President Gamal Abdel Nasser who had outlawed the Muslim Brotherhood. Viewed by members of the Muslim Brotherhood as a martyr, he has gone down as the leading ideologue of the organization, profoundly influencing a wide range of other radical fundamentalist Islamic groups.

Dormant for several decades, the Muslim Brotherhood experienced a revival in the 1980s, expanding beyond Egypt and leading a 1982 uprising in Hama, Syria. The Assad government eventually brutally put down the revolt, with fighting leaving some 25,000 dead.

In Egypt, the government of President Hosni Mubarak attempted to repress the Brotherhood after 88 of its members were elected to the legislature in 2005. When the revolt against Mubarak began in Egyptian streets in 2011, the Brotherhood endorsed the movement that brought down the government. The roles played by the Brotherhood's Freedom and Justice Party and their anti-Christian acts in the post-Mubarak era are described in the chapter on Egypt.

The Muslim Brotherhood has encouraged the creation of other Islamist terrorist groups, particularly Hamas based in the Gaza Strip. Hamas was founded in 1987 and is dedicated to destroying Israel and establishing an Islamic state in that region.

Another radical Islamist group that has systematically persecuted Christians is Hezbollah. Founded in 1982 during the

Lebanese civil war, Hezbollah, which means "Party of God," is a Shiite movement that has been financed, in part, by the followers of Iran's Ayatollah Khomeini, the founder of the Islamic Republic of Iran. In 1999, Hezbollah was classified by the U.S. State Department as a Foreign Terrorist Organization.

Professor Martin Kramer of Tel Aviv University, in an essay titled, "The Moral Logic of Hezbollah," described the framework of the movement:

> It is a pervasive sense of divinely-sanctioned mission that Hezbollah's leaders invoke when they insist that their movement is something other than a mere political party or militia. Hezbollah's official spokesman maintains that the movement is "not a regimented party, in the common sense," for the idea of an exclusive "party" is foreign to Islam. Hezbollah is a "mission" and a "way of life." Another Hezbollah leader has insisted that Hezbollah "is not an organization," for its members carry no cards and bear no specific responsibilities. It is a "nation" of all who believe in the struggle against injustice, and all who are loyal to Iran's Imam Khomeini. Still another Hezbollah leader maintains that "we are not a party in the traditional sense of the term. Every Muslim is automatically a member of Hezbollah, thus it is impossible to list our membership." And in the mind of Iran's chargé d'affaires in Beirut, Hezbollah is not "restricted to a specified organizational framework. . . . There are two parties, Hezbollah or God's party, and the Devil's party."

Hezbollah has employed what is known as "suicidal terrorism." Terrorists willing to give up their lives for Islam and become human weapons have wreaked havoc on civilians and military forces across Lebanon. Other tactics have included random murders, assassinations, kidnappings and hijackings. In his essay "The Readiness to Kill and Die: Suicidal Terrorism in the Middle East," Ariel Merari wrote about suicide attacks: "In addition to evoking a widespread sense of horror, such terrorism has had significant strategic outcomes. For example, some high casualty suicidal terrorist attacks on American and French targets in Lebanon contributed to the decisions of these countries to withdraw their forces from Lebanon; decisions that may have influenced the future of Lebanon for a significant period of time."

Hezbollah, which has been described as "a state within a state," has expanded its activities in recent years. It was responsible for a bombing in Istanbul that injured eight people in 2011. A year later, the Bulgarian government accused Hezbollah of bombing a bus in Burgas that killed five Israeli citizens. Since the outbreak of the Syrian civil war in 2011, Hezbollah members have been fighting in support of President al-Assad. It has been held responsible for planning and carrying out civilian massacres in various Syrian towns and communities. In May 2013, U.S. Ambassador Eileen Chamberlain Donahue condemned "Hezbollah's direct role in the [Syrian] hostilities, a role which inflames regional tensions, escalates violence inside Syria, and incites instability in Lebanon."

The latest radical Islamic group to emerge in the Middle East that is persecuting Christians—as well as Shia Muslims and those who reject sharia law—is the Islamic State, known in the West variously as ISIS, or the Islamic State of Iraq and the Levant (ISIL). Originally a branch of al-Qaeda in Iraq, ISIS was expelled by the parent group in February 2014 due to disagreements over tactics—not goals.

Catholic political philosopher and theologian Father James Schall, S.J., summarized ISIS's raison d'être this way:

> First, we must understand that the Islamic State conceives itself to be the true Islam. Its apologists maintain that they represent the authentic understanding of Islam's Scripture and tradition. The Islamic people who disagree with them are both cowards and heretics. They too will be dealt with. The aim of the new Caliphate is nothing less than world conquest, so that Islamic law is accepted

by all people as Allah's will. The use of violence to accomplish this end is justified in the Quran and in philosophic voluntarism that explains how Allah can at one time talk of peace and next talk of war without any problem. Reason has no place in this system. The world itself and all events in it are directly caused by Allah's will.

To achieve its goals, ISIS, in June 2014, publicly declared a Caliphate comprising the territories conquered in Syria and Iraq. The group's leader Abu Bakr al-Baghdadi was named Caliph Ibrahim. Writing in the September 15, 2014 issue of *The Weekly Standard*, Thomas Joscelyn, a senior fellow at the Foundation for Defense of Democracies, wrote that ISIS believes "a resurrected caliphate will be capable of defending Muslims from all sorts of imagined conspiracies against the Islamic world."

By August 2014, ISIS controlled areas in Syria and Iraq totaling at least 13,000 square miles. In June of that year alone, it was estimated that 1,400 civilians were killed in ISIS-controlled areas and 2,500 wounded. In Iraq, many of the towns and villages overran were populated by defenseless Christians, Yazidis and Shiites, assuring the jihadist juggernaut territory for the caliphate with little or no opposition.

Having declared that being a Christian and refusing to convert to Islam or pay dhimmi-style taxes and other penalties declared by its leaders is ultimately punishable by death, ISIS military victories have caused tens of thousands of Christians to flee towns, villages and cities where they have resided, in some cases, for more than 2,000 years. In Mosul, for example, the second largest city in Iraq and for centuries a major Christian center, ISIS decreed that Christians who did not convert or at least agree to pay protection taxes would be executed. The jihadists also went door-to-door and marked the homes of Christians with the first letter of *Nassarah*, the ancient Arab pejorative term for Christian. Christian property was simply taken over, some of it by Christians' former Muslim neighbors.

In August 2014, ISIS reportedly killed a number of Christian children, displaying their heads on poles in a Mosul city park. To avoid systemic executions, all of the city's Christians fled. Archbishop Amel Nona of Mosul announced in June 2014: "My diocese no longer exists; ISIS has taken it away from me."

In its reign of terror, ISIS has not only murdered Christians or driven them from their homes; it has also destroyed scores of ancient Christian shrines, churches, monasteries, relics and a host of historic documents and manuscripts.

Many Western leaders, including President Obama, have condemned the atrocities committed by ISIS and other radical Islamic jihadist groups as being un-Islamic. However, there is another viewpoint, as articulated British journalist Douglas Murray, writing in the October 6, 2014 issue of the *National Review*: "Rather than being a 'perversion' of Islam, it is truer to say that the version of Islam espoused by ISIS, while undoubtedly the worst possible interpretation of Islam, and for Muslims and non-Muslims everywhere obviously the most destructive version of Islam, is nevertheless a plausible interpretation of Islam. The extremists do not get where they get to from nowhere. . . . It is not solely because they are monsters that ISIS and similar groups decapitate people. It is also because they believe that, as Muslims, they have been instructed to do so by their religious texts."

An oft-cited example from the Quran of such an exhortation is: "When you meet the unbelievers, smite at their necks."

Reacting to the plight of the Christians in territory controlled by ISIS in the Middle East, the spokesman for the St. Thomas Chaldean Catholic Diocese in the U.S., Auday Arabo, told the *New York Times* (September 16, 2014): "We call this slow motion genocide." His ordinary, Bishop Francis Kalabat added: "We are called the Church of Martyrs. That's our pain and saving grace. Our faith isn't a theory. It's not a set of teachings. It's a person and we are called to be like him. When I look at this evil, I want to be Rambo. But that won't do any good. We carry the cross for a reason."

Part Two:
The Unthinkable in the Twenty-First Century

CHAPTER 3
TURKEY

In the late nineteenth century, the geo-political influence and prestige of the Ottoman Empire was rapidly declining. To maintain his hold on absolute power, the reigning Sultan Abdul Hamid II (1876–1909), employed espionage and acts of barbarism. To dissuade Christians from seeking more rights and freedoms, the Sultan turned to loyal Muslim tribesmen, particularly the Kurds, to attack and massacre them.

In 1894, Christian Armenians were brutally slaughtered by the Kurds and other Muslim tribes. As many as 200,000 Christians perished. What American newspapers at the time called a holocaust, historian Philip Jenkins called "a dress rehearsal for the later genocide" that would occur in World War I.

When the Great War began in August, 1914, the Ottoman Empire was in the hands of a military junta. In 1908, a group known as the Young Turk Committee of Union and Progress had imprisoned Abdul Hamid II, made his ineffectual brother Mehmed V a figurehead; and established a government dominated by military officers.

After a revolt against the Young Turks was put down in 1909, the government falsely blamed the Armenians and retaliated. Turkish forces destroyed the City of Adana in southern Turkey, murdering 15,000.

To maintain the tottering empire, radicals ejected moderate Young Turks from the government and began a program of radical nationalization. Turkish was declared the official language of the empire; Turkish schools were opened in captive countries and military service was made compulsory for all Turkish, Arab and Christian men.

This policy proved to be disastrous and caused Christians, particularly in the Balkans, and Arabs in Asia Minor to resist the Ottoman government. By 1914, as a result of a series of revolts, the Ottoman Empire had shrunk to what today are the countries of Turkey, Syria, Lebanon, Iraq, Saudi Arabia, Jordan, Israel and Palestine.

During the war, the Turks joined forces with Germany and Austria against the British, French and Russians. When declaring war, the Sultan proclaimed a *jihad* against what he labeled the infidel Allies.

After being beaten by the Czar's forces—which included an Armenian division—at the battle of Sarikamish in 1914, the Turkish generals blamed their setbacks on Armenian traitors. In response, the Turkish government approved laws to confiscate the property of Armenian Christians, and one month later the Parliament approved the *Tehcir* legislation that authorized the forced removal of Armenians from their homelands.

These laws, historian G.J. Meyer points out in his work "A World Undone: The Story of the Great War 1914–1918," gave the Young Turks:

> . . . all the justification they needed for actions that in peacetime probably would have been unimaginable. They began in comparatively innocuous fashion, disarming their Armenian soldiers and assigning them to labor battalions. Then they proceeded to work, and starve, those battalions to death. Next, having eliminated the part of the population most capable of defending itself, they sent an army onto the plateau that had long been home to most of Turkey's Armenians. In town after town and city and city, all males over the age of twelve were gathered up and shot or hacked to death en masse. Women were raped and mutilated, and those who were not killed were sold into slavery. Hundreds of thousands

of civilians were marched off to the deserts of Syria and Mesopotamia. Many died of exposure, starvation, or exhaustion along the way, and others were murdered by their Kurdish escorts. The pogrom spread across all of Turkey. In Constantinople thousands of convicted criminals were organized into death squads whose only assignment was to kill every Armenian they could find, giving first priority to those intellectuals, professionals, and religious and political leaders who might have the potential to serve as leaders. The families of Turkish officials took the choicest booty; the death squads and rabble took the rest.

Henry Morgenthau, U.S. Ambassador to the Ottoman Empire during World War I, wrote that the Turkish government knew that of the 1.2 million Armenians driven into the Syrian Desert "the great majority would never reach their destination and that those who did would either die of thirst and starvation, or be murdered by the wild Mohammedan desert tribes. . . . When the Turkish authorities gave the orders for these deportations, they were merely giving the death warrant to a whole race."

The distinguished British statesman and historian Lord James Bryce, who condemned the genocide in the House of Lords in 1915, argued that the Turks hatched a "plan for exterminating Christianity root and branch." Here's how he described the Turkish cleansing of the City of Trebizond, located on the Black Sea coast of northeastern Turkey: "They hunted out all the Christians, gathered them together, and drove a great crowd of them down the streets of Trebizond, past the fortress, to the edge of the sea. There they were all put on board sailing boats, carried out some distance on the Black Sea, and there thrown overboard and drowned. Nearly the whole Armenian population of from 8,000 to 10,000 was destroyed—some in this way, some by slaughter, some by being sent to death elsewhere."

Leslie Davis, U.S. wartime consul to Haput, who personally witnessed Armenian Christians being driven from their homes and the destruction of their communities, wrote: "Everywhere it was a scene of desolation and destruction, the houses were crumbling to pieces and even the Christian churches, which had been erected at great expense and with much sacrifice, had been pulled down. . . . The Mohammedans in their fanaticism seemed determined not only to exterminate the Christian population but to remove all traces of their religion and even to destroy the products of civilization."

The murderous rampage expanded to northern Syria. Untold thousands of Chaldeans and Assyrian Christians were murdered. By the end of the war two-thirds of them were dead.

The slaughter did not stop, however, when the Armistice was signed in 1918. "The final convulsion," historian G. J. Meyer has written, "would not come until 1922, when a new Turkish government took possession of Smyrna [on the Aegean coast of Anatolia], set the city afire, and systematically slaughtered its tens of thousands of Armenian and Greek inhabitants."

It is estimated that between 1914 and 1923, when a new state in Turkey was established, 1.5 million Armenian Christians, out of a total population of 2.5 million, were murdered by Turkish Muslims. Sadly, no government or military officials were ever brought to justice for these crimes. Worse yet, to this day, Turkish officials continue to deny that the genocidal acts ever took place. Loath to alienate Turkey as an economic and military ally, most Western governments, including the U.S., have so far refrained from labeling the murder of Armenian Christians a genocide.

In 1919, in the aftermath of World War I, Mustafa Kemal Atatürk, a leftist Young Turk who had been critical of various war policies, established a nationalist government in Constantinople. By 1923, Atatürk had unified the provinces under his government, seized control of Constantinople, deposed Sultan Mohammed VI, ended the Caliphate and established the Republic of Turkey.

The new government negotiated the Treaty of Lausanne with the Allies. The terms dictated that Turkey give up all claims to Hejaz (Saudi Arabia), Palestine, Trans-Jordania, Mesopotamia (Iraq and Kuwait), and Syria. The new boundaries for the Turkish Republic included Anatolia, Cilicia, Adalia, Smyrna, eastern

Thrace, and Constantinople. By agreeing to demilitarize the Straits and to permit freedom of movement in the waterways additional restrictions imposed by the Versailles Peace Conference that ended World War I were eliminated.

The Turkish government on paper was republican. The 1925 constitution permitted elections of a legislature and voting rights for all citizens. Every four years there were to be elections for the office of President and the Assembly. The reality, however, was that Mustafa Kemal Atatürk had become a dictator. As President, Commander of the Army, and head of the People's Party, he made all important decisions and the Assembly merely endorsed his wishes.

Under Atatürk, Turkey became a secular nation. The legal system based on the Quran was abolished; religious schools were taken over by the state; polygamy was prohibited; and only civil marriages were recognized. In addition, the wearing of a fez or turban was forbidden and women could no longer wear veils. A constitutional amendment approved in 1928 declared that the Turkish Republic was no longer an Islamic state. Religion became a strictly private matter.

Since 1928, the Turkish constitution, at least on paper, has granted freedom of conscience and religious belief and liturgical celebrations may be conducted freely and without government interference. In addition, no one can be criminally charged because of one's faith. The constitution states that Turkey is a "democratic, secular and social state that respects human rights; all individuals are equal in the eyes of the law without distinction as to language, race, color, gender, political opinion, philosophical beliefs, membership of a religion or a sect" and everyone enjoys "total freedom of conscience, creed and religious conviction."

However, Atatürk's definition of a secular state did not mean the state was truly neutral regarding religious matters. Oversight of Christian missionary work, for example, was sterner under Atatürk's government than it had been under the Sultan. In addition, under the Treaty of Lausanne only members of the Jewish faith, the Greek Orthodox Church, and the Armenian Apostolic Church were recognized as protected classes who were granted the same civil, political and cultural rights as the Muslim majority. Those religious minorities not recognized by the state, including the Assyrian, Chaldeans, and Maronite Churches, were barred from purchasing property and building churches; and their religious practices and traditions were subject to numerous restrictions. In addition, the 15 million Shiite Alevis, Turkey's largest religious minority, as well as the other Muslim Shiites, did not enjoy all the rights described in the Constitution. They do not have any representations at the *Diyanet*, as that body only represents Sunni Islam.

Even the recognized minority religions are kept under the watchful eye of the *Diyanet*, a government agency established in 1924 "to execute the works concerning the beliefs, worship, and ethics of Islam, enlighten the public about their religion, and administer the sacred worshiping places."

The *Diyanet,* which is headed by the President of Religious Affairs, oversees all religious activities in Turkey. Religious teachers, clerics and ministers depend on the department for their appointments, training and salaries. The *Diyanet* does not have any Christian or Jewish members.

Atatürk claimed to be agnostic, but he created the *Diyanet* in acknowledgement of the fact that the vast majority of the Turkish people are Sunni Muslims, as well as to give the government a tool with which to maintain control over their religious activities.

In 1935, the protected minority religions became subject to a law that required them to create a detailed list of their possessions. In later years, other regulations issued by the state police forced the closing in 1971 of the Armenian Apostolic Seminary of the Holy Cross in Istanbul. The following year, after Patriarch Bartholomew I of the Greek Orthodox Church—and the leader of all of Orthodoxy—refused to permit his theological institute on the Island of Halki to come under the authority of the *Diyanet,* the institute too was closed by the government. Many Church leaders believe that the Turkish government moved to shut down these centers of Christian formation in order to prevent the training of native clergy that could minister to Turkish Christians.

To further impede the spiritual work of Christian Churches, the state imposed high taxes on non-Muslims. The state also seized numerous Christian orphanages, hospitals and schools that had opened after 1936. To justify its moves, the government claimed that these institutions had not been included on the 1935 official registry list; hence, they were considered state property and were placed under a government-controlled trust. More than 4,000 properties belonging to Greeks, Armenians and Jews were seized in these confiscations, which went on until the 1990s.

In September 1955, the so-called Nika riots, a pogrom directed principally against Greek Orthodox, but also against Armenians and Jews in Istanbul, was organized by elements in the secret service, police, and by nationalist groups. Bogus charges that Atatürk's birthplace had been bombed in Thessalonica (Greece) was the pretext for anti-Greek mayhem that claimed more than a dozen lives and resulted in the destruction of thousands of Christian-owned businesses, hotels, homes, schools, and more than 70 churches. Mass Christian exodus from Istanbul ensued, only to be aggravated by a law passed in 1964 forcing those with Greek citizenship to leave.

In the twenty-first century, the persecution of Christians has continued to intensify. Father Yusuf Akbulut, a Syrian Orthodox priest, was arrested on December 21, 2000 for publicly condemning the murder of 500,000 Syrian Christians in 1915. He was prosecuted under Article 312 of the Turkish penal code which states that it is illegal to "incite religious or ethnic hatred." The *Hurriyet* daily described the priest as "a traitor in our midst."

There were numerous reports in 2001 and 2002 of Christians being arrested on charges of insulting Islam and Muhammad. One Syrian Orthodox man, who had a Swiss passport, was taken to a military camp and later transferred to a civilian prison in Midyat. He was making a documentary on life in Turkey's Tur Abdin region and was caught filming a Christian cemetery.

Protestants—who are not recognized at all by the government—are also being persecuted. In early 2002 local authorities initiated plans to close 40 Protestant churches. In April of that year, a mob interrupted a Protestant service in Istanbul shouting, "No to missionaries" and, "We don't want churches in our neighborhoods."

Ahmet Guvener, a Protestant minister, was arrested in May 2002 on the grounds of "making illegal modifications to the architecture of a completed church." *Compass Direct* reported that he was charged despite the fact that the project in question had been officially approved. Turkish officials justified the arrest by citing "fears of an increase in missionary activities." In June 2002, a 42-year-old church in Iskenderun, The New Testament Church, was closed by the government on the grounds that it had "no legal basis."

Reacting to the incidents, various Christian leaders in August 2002 accused the Turkish government of conducting an "anti-European and anti-Christian press campaign." All Church activities, they charged, were being criminalized as illegal proselytizing. Further bolstering the argument, the Roman Catholic Apostolic Vicar of Istanbul, Bishop Louis Pelatre, announced that the activities of the Catholic charitable organization, Caritas Turkey, had been proscribed.

With Turkey a prospective candidate for European Union membership (its application for full membership has been pending since 1987), many organizations have been reminding the Turkish government that it has to put an end to discrimination against Christians.

The German Society for Threatened Peoples declared in 2002 that it was unacceptable for a prospective EU member to prohibit ancient Christian communities in Turkey from building new churches and to ban the reopening of a Christian college which had been closed back in the 1970s.

Bartholomew I, the ecumenical patriarch of Constantinople, agreed with the German organization. In 2004, he said publicly: "On the issue of religious freedom, Turkey is not yet ready to become a serious candidate for the European Union." Although Christians are permitted to hold Church services, the Patriarch confirmed that they are forbidden to own or operate schools, monasteries, convents, church yards, and church buildings. He also cited the government's forced closing of the Greek Orthodox theological seminary 30 years earlier. What the Patriarch did not touch on specifically were the abuses perpetrated by Turkey in the north of Cyprus, after it had invaded the island in 1974. After the establishment of the Turkish Republic of Northern Cyprus, the local population of some 200,000 Greek Orthodox Christians escaped or were deported south. The Christian community in the territory has dwindled to about 450 faithful, their access to places of worship and religious sites heavily restricted. Since its takeover, Turkey has damaged, vandalized or destroyed hundreds of churches, transforming some into military storage facilities and even stables, casinos and night-clubs. Some five dozen churches have been turned into mosques."

The Patriarch's comments provoked strong reactions. In September 2002, hundreds of nationalists staged a protest outside the Patriarch's headquarters, claiming he worked against Turkish interests. They burned him in effigy and threw stones at the building. In early October, an explosion shattered the windows of the patriarchate.

Meanwhile, the Turkish government continued to ignore complaints about its anti-Christian activities. The Minister for Religious Affairs, Mehmet Aydin, went to the opposite extreme, informing Parliament in March 2005 that Christian missionaries were threatening the entire nation. "The aim of their activities," he said, "is to threaten the cultural, religious, national and historical unity of the Turkish people." He urged that the "missionary propaganda"—which had resulted in the conversion of just 368 Muslims between 2000–2005, in a nation of 73.3 million people—"has a historical background and is conducted in a planned manner with political motives." He urged the government to "enlighten the Turkish people, eradicate the ignorance and defend the moral principles and beliefs of Islam."

The European Union's Ambassador protested that Aydin's remarks were "divisive"; but complaints from the U.S. Ambassador concerning ten attacks on Protestant groups were ignored by the government, and violence against Christians continued.

In August 2005, hundreds of Muslims rioted in the Greek-Orthodox neighborhood of the town of Altinozu. Screaming that "there is no room for the infidels here," they injured five people, including the wife of the community's priest, and damaged ten houses.

In January 2006, five Muslims, entering a Protestant Church in Adana after falsely claiming they were converts, proceeded to beat the pastor unconscious for refusing to embrace Islam. "We don't want Christians in this village," the assailants yelled out; and "renounce Jesus, or we will kill you," they screamed as they threatened to cut the pastor's throat before he passed out.

One month later, Father Andrea Santoro, an Italian Catholic priest, was shot to death while praying in the Church of Our Lady, Trabzon, a city on the Black Sea. The murderer—who shot the priest in the back numerous times, while shouting "Allahu Akbar" or "God is great!"—claimed he acted in response to cartoons deemed offensive to Islam which had been published in a Danish newspaper.

The Catholic Apostolic Vicar of the area, Bishop Luigi Padovese, said "the true motive of the murder of Don Santoro was religious excitation, motivated by the anti-Christian climate. . . . The only news put out regarding the Catholic Church is either defamatory of Christianity or trivial." The prelate also reported that recently the Catholic cemetery in Trabzon had been "flattened by bulldozers"; the gravestones had been defaced and "now there are only headstones left," he said.

Five months later, Father Pierre Brunissen, who had reopened the Church of Our Lady, was stabbed in the street. Bishop Padovese told Aid to the Church in Need that the attack on the 75-year-old priest was driven by false reports in the media that he had tried to bribe Muslims to convert to Christianity.

The bishop charged that the media were leading a campaign to undermine the visit of Pope Benedict XVI to Turkey which was due to take place in November 2006. "The newspapers are trying to aggravate, to show the Christians as enemies of the Turkish people," he said, adding that "many, many people" were opposed to the planned meeting between the Pope and Ecumenical Patriarch Bartholomew I of Istanbul.

The papal visit happened as scheduled, however. The president of the Turkish republic, Ahmet Necdet Sezer, had invited Pope Benedict XVI to visit his nation so that the Pontiff, the official said, "could witness for himself the climate of cultural tolerance" prevailing in the country. The presidential invitation followed an earlier one extended by the Patriarch Bartholomew.

The Pope portrayed his four-day trip to Turkey (November 28–December 1, 2006) as a "mission of dialogue, brotherhood and reconciliation," even as the visit took place against a backdrop of protests by tens of thousands of Muslims in Istanbul. He met with the head of the *Diyanet,* visited a Mosque and stressed that Christians, Jews and Muslims believe in the same God. He also celebrated the feast of St. Andrew alongside Ecumenical Patriarch Bartholomew.

Pope Benedict made it a point to remind the Turks of their obligations to respect the free expression of religion beliefs and worship. In a speech to the diplomatic corps, the Pope said:

> The fact that the majority of the population of this country is Muslim is a significant element in the life of society, which the State cannot fail to take into account, yet the Turkish Constitution recognizes every citizen's right to freedom of worship and freedom of conscience. The civil authorities of every democratic country are duty bound to guarantee the effective freedom of all believers and to permit them to organize freely the life of their religious communities. [. . .] This assumes, of course, that religions do not seek to exercise direct political power, as that is not their province, and it also assumes that they utterly refuse to sanction recourse to violence as a legitimate expression of religion.

The Pope also made it clear in his remarks that he was cognizant that the growing mistrust of Christian minorities reflected the ongoing efforts to re-Islamize Turkey.

The papal message was later reiterated by the Archbishop of Smyrna, Ruggero Franceschini, who said in 2007 that "if they [the Turks] really were secular, they would respect all believers in the schools, whatever their religion. Instead we have had to put up with long years of education that exalt only the importance of Turkey—not its historical importance or that of its scenery, but the importance of its military conquests and Quranic doctrines, a compulsory subject in all schools and often taught by ill-trained people. The teachers endeavor above all, to deny the reality of Christianity, or to belittle its importance, treating the Gospel as an invented story."

Violence against Christians continued even as Turkey's new ambassador to the Vatican told Pope Benedict, upon presenting his credentials on January 19, 2007: "As confirmed by the leaders of my country a few weeks ago, the Turkish Constitution guarantees freedom of worship and of conscience for all its citizens, whatever their origins or personal beliefs may be. Within the framework of secularism, the heart of democracy in Turkey, the Turkish State treats all religious communities according to criteria of equality. In other words, the individual freedoms of our citizens are correctly guaranteed in this sector, with no discrimination based on ethnic or denominational criteria."

On that very day in Istanbul, the Turkish-Armenian journalist Hrant Dink was assassinated outside the offices of his magazine *Agos*. Dink was a prominent proponent of the movement to secure official recognition of the Turkish genocide of the Armenians.

In April 2007, five Muslims broke into the offices of Zivre, a Christian publishing house in the southeastern province of Malatya that distributed Bibles and other Christian literature. The perpetrators cut the throats of three Protestant workers. Several months later, a man was arrested in the city of Izmit after torching the entrance of the local Protestant church. The community's pastor was the brother-in-law of one of the men murdered at the Zivre publishing house.

During the 2007 Christmas season, a 65-year-old Italian Capuchin, Father Adriano Francini, was stabbed outside the Church of St. Anthony in Smyrna. According to newspaper reports, the assailant was a mentally unstable Muslim who claimed he had been driven to the crime after watching the television show *Kultar Vadisi* (Valley of the Wolves), which portrays Christian missionaries as "infiltrators" who bribe poor families to convert to Christianity. Tired of hearing the same old excuses for violence from the authorities, Bishop Franceschini said, "Once again, they will say this was the act of a madman. But it has to be said that during the last year and a half, attacks by these mentally ill people have increased significantly in Turkey."

Bishops speaking out against Turkey's biased justice system and condemning the country's increasing Islamic extremism has clearly aroused public opinion in Turkey. On June 3, 2010, the most outspoken prelate, 63-year-old Bishop Luigi Padovese, Apostolic Vicar of Anatolia and president of Turkey's Catholic bishops' conference, was assassinated by his driver, Murat Altun.

The initial response of police authorities was, again, to stress that the assassin had mental health problems, that the man was suffering from severe depression, and that his motives had been strictly personal. The autopsy, however, revealed that Padovese had been the victim of an Islamic ritual killing. He received numerous stab wounds and was beheaded. Witnesses reported that Altun had shouted: "*Allahu Akbar.* I have killed the great Satan."

Rejecting the authorities' version of the incident, Archbishop Franceschini of Izmir, who was appointed administrator of Padovese's see by the Vatican, said publicly that the murder had been premeditated, the work of "religious fanatics and ultra nationalists." The government dragged its feet on the case, but bowing to international pressure, finally deemed Altun competent to stand trial in June 2011. It wasn't until January 2013 that the man was convicted of murder and sentenced to 15 years.

Still hoping to become a full member of the European Union, the Turkish government expressed its intentions to improve the status of religious minorities after the Council of Europe's Commission for Religious Freedom demanded that Turkey grant legal recognition to those religious minorities that had not been included under the 1923 Treaty of Lausanne.

To improve its international image, the government also announced the restitution of property seized from recognized religious minorities, promising to restore a number of churches and monasteries to their original owners. In July 2011, the Syriac Orthodox were permitted—for the first time since the fall of the Ottoman Empire—to celebrate Liturgy in two of its churches. In October of that year, St. Giragos, an Armenian Apostolic church in Diyarbakir, was able to hold Mass for the first time in 30 years.

However, observers consider these government-decreed concessions as gestures meant to placate the international community—not as signs of real and permanent change. Christians and Jews are still not represented on the *Diyanet*. The authorities continue to interfere in the Greek Orthodox Church's Holy Synod which elects the Patriarch; Roman Catholics, Syriac Orthodox and Protestants have still not been legally recognized and they cannot own or operate their own schools and seminaries—nor can they build new churches.

The Roman Catholic Apostolic Vicar of Istanbul, Bishop Louis Pelatre, expressing his frustration, said: "Our real problem remains our basic property, we have no ownership papers and have never had any. This is not an easy situation. I am not recognized as a bishop, I can open a bank account in my own name but not in the name of my diocese."

The Armenian Christian community continues to be in the most precarious situation, suffering from frequent attacks. Articles of the penal code are still in force that prohibit any formal commemorations of the genocidal acts committed by the Ottoman Empire against Armenian, Assyrian and Greek Christians. Calling attention to these tragedies is deemed an insult to the Turkish state and is punishable by up to two years in prison.

Anti-Armenian fervor is still strong in Turkey. In February 2012, more than 20,000 participated in an anti-Armenian protest on Taksim Square in Istanbul. Professionally-produced signs read: "You are all Armenians, you are all bastards" and, "Today Taksim, Tomorrow Yerevan [the capital of Armenia]." The Turkish Interior Minister was one of the speakers at the demonstration.

The U.S. House of Representatives in December 2011 called on the Turkish government to return Church properties and to end the repression of Christians. The approved resolution stated: "Despite Prime Minister [now President Recep Tayyip] Erdoğan's recent claims of progress on religious freedom, Turkey's Christian communities continue to face severe discrimination." That same month, the Turkish government approved new history textbooks that contained expressions of hatred toward both Armenian and Assyrian Christians.

In September 2014, Pope Francis visited Turkey. Upon his arrival, he thanked President Erdoğan for hosting 1.6 million refugees who had fled Iraq and Syria, many of them Christians. The Pope subsequently said he approved of military force to stop ISIS as "an unjust aggressor" from further advances in Iraq and Syria and to stop the exodus of Christians who have lived in the region for 2,000 years.

In addition to visiting Muslim historic sites, including the famous Blue Mosque where he prayed with the Grand Mufti, the Pope concelebrated a prayer service with Patriarch Bartholomew to mark the feast of St. Andrew at Istanbul's St. George Greek Orthodox Church. In a joint statement, the leaders declared that "the value of human life has been lost" in the Middle East. The Pope also said that the violent acts committed by Islamist extremists are "a profound grave sin against God." Before departing, Francis met with a hundred Christian youth who had fled Iraq. He called on all Christians to unify in the face of Islamic extremism.

Reporting on the papal visit, the *Christian Science Monitor* quoted President Erdoğan to the effect that the emergence of extremist groups like ISIS are a consequence of "the rise of Islamophobia" in the West. "Those who feel defeated, wronged, oppressed and abandoned . . . can become open to being exploited by terrorist organizations," said the president, who is clearly committed to restoring Turkey's Muslim identity and seemingly less and less concerned about this country's acceptability in the eyes of the European Union.

In Turkey, a nation whose population exceeds 73 million—and for the first 14 centuries of Christianity home to a vibrant community of believers—the 150,000 Christians continue to endure outbreaks of intolerance and even violence. Assessing the situation, Nina Shea and her Hudson Institute colleague Paul Marshall, in their book "Persecuted: The Global Assault on Christians," wrote:

> Now a prosperous democracy under the rule of an Islamist party, modern Turkey is home to remnant Christian communities who find themselves at risk of being extinguished altogether. They suffer not so much from violence . . . [although] violence can occur—as from more sophisticated measures. They confront a dense web of legal regulations that thwart the ability of churches to survive and, in some cases, even to meet together for worship. These laws, aimed at promoting an extreme secular nationalism, also encourage a climate of animosity toward Christians, who are seen to defy "Turkishness," despite Christianity's two-thousand-year presence there.

CHAPTER 4
EGYPT

At the end of the twentieth century, the Egyptian people were governed by a constitution that had been enacted in 1971 and amended in 1980. That body of laws guaranteed religious liberty and tolerated all forms of worship that do not violate any legal statutes. It also guaranteed that all citizens are equal before the law and that "they have equal public rights and duties without discrimination due to sex, ethnic origin, language, religion or creed."

However, Article 2 of the Egyptian constitution stated that "Islam is the religion of the state. Islamic jurisprudence sharia law is the *principal source* of legislation." As a result of this clause, every potential change in law must be analyzed and approved by sharia scholars at the Al-Azhar University in Cairo.

The fact that Islamic professors have significant impact on the interpretation and execution of laws does not bode well for Christians and other minority religions. Often, these scholars subscribe to fundamentalist forms of Islam, and this means that in many instances laws and practices perceived to be contrary to sharia are restricted or banned. The radical Muslim Brotherhood—though illegal and suppressed—gained considerable influence during the 30-year reign of President Hosni Mubarak. The organization encouraged Muslim youth to be more traditionally religious, lessening public support for tolerance and inclusiveness vis-à-vis Christians.

Due to this precarious situation, the nation's ten million Christians—more than 90 percent are Orthodox Coptic Christians—are underrepresented in the government, the educational system and in the media. They hold only 1.5 percent of civil service jobs and even in Christian-majority towns and villages mayors cannot be Copts. Paul Marshall, in his 2001 book *Religious Freedom in the World*, pointed out that no Christians have ever been elected to the 545-member People's Assembly and that "the government has given media access to Islamic preachers who have engaged in hate speech against Copts while denying Copts the chance to reply." This, Marshall concluded, contributes to an environment that "encourage[s] terrorist violence." These circumstances dissuade Christians from participating in the country's political sphere. "We feel like foreigners in our own country" is an oft-heard lament.

As for schools, there is no mention of Coptic Christians in history, language or literature courses. Exams are even scheduled to conflict with Christmas.

Through the years Egyptian Muslim converts to Christianity had to endure severe persecution and discrimination in employment. In late 1999, President Mubarak signed a decree ordering Christian groups to obtain permission from local government officials to construct and repair churches and other Christian facilities. For Christians, it was not exactly the best way to end the century; and sadly matters only got worse in the first decade of the new century.

On January 2, 2000, Muslims attacked Copts in the town of El-Kosheh. Twenty Copts and one Muslim were killed and more than a hundred Christian businesses and homes were destroyed. The Coptic Christians killed in this incident were considered martyrs of the Coptic Orthodox Church by Pope Shenouda III. One year later, 57 Muslims and 32 Christians arrested in El-Kosheh were put on trial for murder. Four Muslims were convicted and received light sentences. All the others were released. President Mubarak blamed the incident on "foreign elements" and the judge in the case, Mohamed Afify, placed the blame on three Coptic priests, claiming they did nothing to stop the riots. The local bishop publicly condemned the verdict saying, "all the murderers were acquitted. That means Muslims are encouraged to kill Christians . . . this verdict means that the life of Christians has no value in Egypt."

The same month that verdict came down, Egyptian security forces, using bulldozers protected by armored vehicles, demolished a church building in Shobra El Khaima. The wrecked four-story building, which was bought by the Copts in 1988, was refurbished and was to be used as a daycare and medical facility, and facility to teach religion to children.

The next year, on February 20, 2002, Copts were attacked by Muslim radicals during Sunday Mass in the small village of El-Minya. The locals believed the attack was provoked because they applied for a construction permit to build a church, which must be issued by the government. They and other Christian sects that have applied for permits have reported that it generally takes years to get permission to commence construction. Christians have also reported that when Muslims learn of church-building plans filed with the state, they often build a mosque nearby the proposed site and assault Christians who live in the vicinity.

Hisham Samir Abdel, a 26-year-old convert from Islam to Christianity, was abducted in May 2002 and five months later it was discovered that he was in prison. In correspondence with Coptic Church officials, he confirmed that he was arrested by the police on the charge of reviling Islam.

The kidnapping and arrest of Abdel was not an isolated case. Twenty-two Egyptians who left the Muslim faith and embraced Christianity were arrested in October 2003. They were subsequently released, but shortly thereafter two were re-arrested.

There have also been numerous reports of Christian girls being kidnapped and forcibly converted to Islam. There have been many instances of Muslim militants approaching young Christian girls in shops and telling them that they had won a prize and to claim it they had to sign a document. The unread fine print of the papers signed stated that the girl had converted to Islam. In one case, the police refused to list as missing an 18-year-old Coptic girl, Ingy Helmy Georgy Labibe, who was kidnapped while shopping in her home town of Mahalla el Kubra. The family learned that she was taken to become an Islamic convert when the assailants demanded ransom. Even though the family agreed to pay the money, the kidnappers refused to release her. Miss Labibe's whereabouts are not known to the present time.

On January 5, 2004, Egyptian solders attacked the Patmos Christian Centre. Bulldozers operated by military men destroyed the walls of the centre. The bishop's assistant was killed during the assault and seven others were badly injured. Later that month, four Christians at the University of Cairo were arrested in their lodgings by police in Sharm-el-Sheikh. They were charged with possessing Bibles and recordings of religious music. Coptic Patriarch Pope Shenouda III's condemnation of the arrests from his pulpit was ignored by the authorities.

During the 2004 Christmas season, hundreds of Christians held a sit-in at the Cairo Coptic Cathedral to protest the abduction of a priest's wife who was subsequently forced to convert to Islam. At one point during the protest, Egyptian police arrested 34 protestors, falsely claiming they were stoning the police and passers-by. Another group of Coptic men and women were imprisoned and subjected to sexual abuse until they agreed to convert to Islam.

In October 2005, more than 5,000 Muslims in Alexandria stoned St. George's Church and stabbed a nun to protest a movie that portrays a Christian convert to Islam who is ordered to burn churches and kill priests. The riot spread to various parts of the city. The Church was torched, while a Coptic hospital, pharmacy and Christian-owned stores were ransacked. The rioters then clashed with the police; three people were killed, 20 police officers were injured and six cars were overturned and set on fire.

Violence continued in Alexandria. Fourteen Christians were stabbed, one was murdered and dozens were injured in early 2006. When the Egyptian government was accused of failing to investigate these crimes, Parliament agreed to form a fact-finding committee that would determine the cause of the attacks and report back with its findings in 30 days. The deadline passed and no report was filed. Coptic Metropolitan Wissa told his faithful, "even if a committee does meet and even if they come out with a report, that report will not see the light of day."

On Maundy Thursday, April 14, 2006, in Alexandria, two

Muslims attacked the Church of St. George, the Church of All Saints and the Church of the Blessed Virgin. One Christian was murdered, numerous others were wounded. The noted French journalist Marie Gabrielle LeBlanc, an expert on the Coptic Church, after investigating the incidents, observed: "While the discrimination that makes the Christians in Egypt into second-class citizens is continuous, the violent persecution tends to surface sporadically and in an erratic manner. It has, however, increased significantly over the last five years, in parallel with the Islamization of the police." In the latter part of the first decade of the twenty-first century, anti-Christian discrimination and violence against Christians continued to rise.

In government-run schools, Christians cannot receive top grades from teachers or be ranked at the top of their class. Teachers who are Copts are prohibited from teaching Arabic even if it is the educator's mother tongue. The only exception is in lower grammar school grades where reading is taught without using the Quran. A 2007 United Nations report called "Equality at Work: Tackling the Challenge" condemned these policies. "One of the most resilient forms of discrimination," the U.N. pointed out, "is that of targeting Copts in Egypt, who are denied equal access to education and equal opportunities in recruitment and promotion."

As for Christian university students, they too endure discrimination in state schools. While they are not forced to study the Quran, in Arab language and grammar courses they must read passages from the Quran because it is considered the basis of the language. Christian religious instruction and Bible study are forbidden, and history texts contain no references to Christianity. Textbooks describe the era of the Pharaohs, skip over the first five centuries of Christianity and then go on to describe the Islamic conquest as liberation from Roman oppression.

Christians have also continued to be the targets of physical violence. In Bamha, a small village south of Cairo, a group of Muslims in May 2007 looted and burned to the ground Coptic-owned shops and houses. The reason for the violence: the "infidels" were executing government-approved church expansion plans.

In June of that year, Muslims in Zawyet Abdel-Qader, a town west of Alexandria, attacked two Coptic churches and looted Christian stores, injuring seven Christians. Four days later, in the same area, the Church of Our Lady was attacked and ransacked.

Members of the Organization of Near East Christians were arrested, charged and found guilty of "attacking Islam" and "denominational sedition," because they had instructed a young Muslim couple who desired to convert to Christianity. The converts, Muhammed and Zeinab Negazy, who fled and went into hiding, were condemned by the rector of Al-Azhar University and a *fatwa* was issued that accused them of apostasy and pronounced on them the death sentence. Zeinab's father told Egyptian media: "I want the judges to make her divorce him and I want her sent back to me alive or dead."

When 25 Cairo Christians visited a priest living at a Coptic facility in the village of Ezbet Bouchra-East in June 2009, Muslims attacked and destroyed the homes and harvests of Christian residents. The Muslims claimed they initiated the riot because the visitors were going to participate in a religious celebration.

At the end of a Coptic midnight Christmas Mass on January 7, 2010, at St. George Church in Nag-Hammadi, three Muslims jumped out of a car and began shooting worshippers as they walked out of the church. A dozen were wounded and seven were killed, including a policeman. The murderers justified the attack as an act of vengeance for the alleged rape of a 12-year-old Muslim by a Copt in November 2009. Muslims also set fire to Christian homes in the community, destroyed 80 percent of Christian businesses and abducted seven Christian women. The police did not intervene until after the crimes were committed and government authorities urged the Christians not to file complaints or to seek damages from their attackers. No compensation was ever received.

Pope Shenouda III, outraged by the lawless attacks in Nag-Hammadi, called on the Egyptian courts to increase their efforts to bring murderers to justice. He pointed out that during the previous

30 years more than 1,800 Christians had been murdered and more than 200 acts of vandalism had been committed against Christian property, with few if any convictions.

Four hundred Copts who attended a religious service at a site of a proposed nursing home in Mersa Matruh were attacked in March 2010 by 3,000 Muslim fanatics—Bedouins and Salafists. Twenty-five Copts, including women and children, were wounded. One Christian, while walking to the prayer service, was stopped by the mob and threatened with violence unless he converted to Islam. When he refused, he was stabbed in the leg. There were credible allegations that the local imam instigated the mob attack. At Friday prayers, he is said to have called on Muslims to fight against the "enemies" of Islam, adding: "we do not tolerate Christian presence in our area."

After a series of suspicious fires in church buildings and the burning to the ground of the Coptic Church in the village of Hagazah, Coptic Catholic Bishop Johannes Zakaria appealed to his flock to pray for peace. The bishop told the Christians in Hagazah that the local police dismissed charges of arson, saying the various fires had been caused by short circuits. The bishop was also denied permission to say Mass the next Sunday for 600 Coptic Catholics in one of the remaining Catholic facilities.

On New Year's Day 2011, in Alexandria's Sidi Bechr district, a car bomb exploded outside the Coptic Church of Two Saints while 1,000 people were attending Mass. More than 20 Mass-goers were killed and more than 70 were wounded. The violence was sparked by false accusations that the Coptic Patriarch was holding two women who converted to Islam against their will.

Looking back on the first decade of the century, Kyrillos William, the Coptic Catholic Bishop of Assiut, conceded that in recent years the spirit of Islamic fundamentalism had become increasingly fierce. "There are people who simply cannot accept that there are Christians in Egypt. . . . They do not allow people to take a different approach to them and they are very active. . . . The sheer size of the Christian presence in Egypt is deeply abhorrent to many sections of Egyptian society."

The bishop also pointed out that in mosques, Christian Churches and their members are often criticized. "On Fridays," he said, "imams always speak against the other religions. It is very painful. They look at Christian teachings and say what we believe is not true. They criticize the moral life of Christians."

Frustrated that the ever-increasing Islamization of Egypt was forcing many of his flock to emigrate, Bishop Williams observed: "Many Christians want to leave for the West—Australia and the U.S.A. They want to find security. Emigration is a big, big problem for us—a problem for the Church across the Middle East." Little did the bishop know at the time of his interview that the problem of emigration was to explode during the so-called Arab Spring that commenced in 2011.

In mid-January 2011, protesters took to the streets in Cairo demanding the resignation of the autocratic long-time ruler of the country, President Hosni Mubarak, who had been in office since the assassination of President Anwar Sadat in 1981. The protests quickly turned into a popular revolt against the government, and on February 11, 2011, Mubarak stepped down. The Supreme Council of the Armed Forces took on the role of a transitional government.

The leader of the Coptic Catholics, Cardinal Antonios Naguib, Patriarch of Alexandria, welcomed the interim military regime's stated aim of dismantling the Mubarak's autocratic government. "Moving towards a civil democratic government," he said, "rather than a religious or a military one, has been our hope for a long time—it has been a dream." As for the role the Muslim Brotherhood might play in the new government, the patriarch warned, ". . . if they want to transform Egypt into a religious country with sharia law, then I think that not only the Christians but more than half the population will not accept that."

Parliamentary elections for the Upper and Lower Houses of Parliament that were held at various times between November 28, 2011 and February 22, 2012, gave a large majority to the radical Islamic parties. The Muslim Brotherhood—formerly banned by Mubarak—and the even more extreme Salafites received a combined total of 65 percent of the votes cast and together garnered 369 out of 508 seats in Parliament's Lower House and 150 out of 176 seats in the Senate. The secular parties polled about 20 percent and the Christians came up dead last, winning just four seats in the Lower House and none in the Senate.

Christians were shocked by the Salafites' strong showing in the elections and confessed it did not bode well for them. The spokesman for the Roman Catholic Church in Egypt, Father Antoine Greiche, offered a pessimistic assessment, "[Salafites] speak about forbidding tourism . . . and forcing women to be totally covered up. They look at Christians and even moderate Muslims as *kuffars* [repulsive and ignorant non-Muslims] and say they want to implement the sharia Islamic law rigorously." He added that "the Salafists' attitude toward Christians is to say that they can get their passport to go to the U.S.A., France, U.K. or somewhere else in the West."

The high hopes of Christians that the success of the populist uprising would enhance national unity and bring about true democratic reforms were quickly dashed. The temporary Military Council consulted the Salafites before making any decisions and after the parliamentary elections a coalition government was formed that was clearly illiberal and bent on imposing Islamic rule on everyone.

Before the elections, violence against Christians reached levels not seen during the Mubarak years. A week after taking control of the government in February 2011, Egyptian soldiers attacked three Coptic monasteries. Monks were wounded and property was destroyed. Coptic priest Father Daoud Boutros was found dead February 23 in his residence in the village of Shotb, having been stabbed 22 times and beheaded. He was accused of proselytism on a website.

Thirteen Christians were murdered and 120 wounded on March 9, 2011 in Cairo during anti-Christian rallies involving 15,000 armed Islamists. Homes, businesses and equipment owned by the Copts were set on fire. Police forces that arrived at the scene of the violence did next to nothing to protect the Christians and there were reports that some of them even fired their weapons at the Copts.

That same month, Mitri, a 45-year-old Christian school administrator in Qena, in Upper Egypt, was accused by local Islamists of breaking sharia law. They cut off his ear, cut his arms and face and burned down his apartment. When the police arrived, the Islamists were reported to have told them: "We have applied the law of Allah, now come and apply your civil law." At first Mitri demanded compensation for the loss of his home, but during a reconciliation meeting he was persuaded to drop all charges. Asked to explain his actions on a Coptic TV show, he said: "I was threatened and they threatened to kidnap the female children in our family."

The worst act of violence in the first months of the post-Mubarak-era took place on May 7, 2011 when Salafites attacked and burned three Coptic churches, looted Christian businesses, and destroyed 14 Christian homes in the Cairo suburb of Imbaba. Fifteen Christians were killed and 260 were wounded. The attack began when a Christian woman, married to a Muslim, took refuge in one of the churches that was subsequently attacked and destroyed. Angry over the lack of police protection, the local Coptic Catholic leader, Bishop Antonios Aziz Mina, said: "The [police] will not stand up against the people who do this sort of thing. They want to stay neutral. The police appear very slowly. They are frightened. They have not been strong enough."

When a Christian man in June 2011 tried to defend his wife from being sexually harassed at a bus station, he was badly beaten by Islamists. The Muslim mob then descended on a nearby Christian village and looted and burned to the ground three Christian supermarkets, various other businesses and six Christian homes, including the one owned by the man who protected his wife at the depot. Witnesses reported that the mob, which grew to more than 1,000 people, surrounded Christian homes shouting "Allahu Akbar" ["God is the greatest"] as they began to torch the houses. Once again, the police were missing in action. A local priest said in a televised interview that "the army commander and the military police were contacted but arrived three hours later and did not take action while the properties were looted and torched."

To shed light on these acts of violence and to demand greater protection, in October 2011, the Coptic Church organized peaceful demonstrations outside the headquarters of the Egyptian national television station, on Maspero Square in Cairo. The protest was disrupted by mobs armed with swords, sticks, stones and rifles chanting Muslim religious slogans. Thirty Christians were killed and more than 300 were injured. Father Greiche told journalists: "We are accusing [state security] who used . . . a rabble force of street fighters to attack the demonstrators. They did not have to use force. It was a peaceful demonstration." The Supreme Council of Armed Forces dismissed the complaints by the Church, claiming the demonstration and rioters were "foreign elements."

These events explain why Coptic Bishop Stephanos of Beba and Elfashn has said that "Christians are currently experiencing their worst time in recent centuries" and why the Egyptian Union of Human Rights Organizations was able to report in late 2011 that six months after the fall of Mubarak's government, more than 100,000 Christians had fled Egypt. After Muslim Brotherhood senior official Mohamed Morsi was elected president of Egypt in 2012, Christians did not fare any better.

One of President Morsi's first acts was to draft a constitution that deferred to Islamic sharia law. Coptic Church members of the panel charged with writing the constitution resigned their positions when they realized the majority of the delegates were determined to create an Islamic state that would be intolerant of Christians and other minorities.

Upon seeing the proposed document, new Coptic Patriarch Tawadros II publicly criticized it, demanding that a constitution "that hints at imposing a religious state must be absolutely rejected." Shortly before the December 2012 referendum on the proposed constitution, 50,000 Muslims marched in the city of Assiut, chanting that Egypt will be "Islamic despite the Christians." During the Constitutional Referendum voting period—December 12–17, 2012—many Christians were unable to reach polling places because they were pelted with stones and forced to return home. After the approved Constitution took effect in December 2012, Coptic Catholic Bishop Kyrillos Williams concluded that it "paved the way for an Islamic caliphate." His fellow Catholic bishops put out a statement pointing out that the "pre-eminence of sharia in diverse aspects of law and government effectively took away key human rights of non-Muslims, women and children."

More than 50 people in January 2013 were killed by violent protestors marking the second anniversary of the fall of President Mubarak. Commenting on the deaths, Father Greiche accused President Morsi of gross incompetence. "The people," he said, "are dissatisfied with the Islamist regime. Divisions are increasing. The bloody protests in the Suez region and in Cairo show how the country is falling apart."

Attacks on a Christian funeral service in St. Mark's Cathedral in Cairo that killed two people and injured 90 prompted Coptic Catholic Bishop Kyrillos Samaan to say: "Nobody could have imagined that anybody would attack such an important symbol for all Egyptians as St. Mark's Cathedral in Cairo. It is shocking." Father Greiche condemned the police who had arrived two hours late and then protected the attackers. He also asked: "But what has the President done to protect the Christians?"

After huge protests throughout Egypt against the government in June 2013, President Morsi was removed from office by the military on July 3. An interim government was installed and an Egyptian judge, Adly Mansour, was sworn in as acting president. "The ousting of President Morsi," Father Greiche declared, "is a joyous day for Christians."

Although the military cracked down on the Muslim Brotherhood and Salafist radicals, they continued to terrorize the Christian population. In July 2013, Salafist Muslims attacked Al Dabaya village after a Christian was accused of killing a Muslim; four Christians were killed. The accused, who went into hiding, was later beaten to death by the Salafists. The people who helped him were stabbed and beaten and their homes were looted and torched.

One month later, the Muslim Brotherhood, having accused

Christians of ousting President Morsi, destroyed 80 Christian buildings, including the oldest church in Egypt, the Virgin Mary Church in Delga, built in the fifth century. Defending his flock, Catholic Bishop Kyrillos William maintained that Christians were not alone in bringing down Morsi. "There were 35 million who went on to the streets against Morsi," he said. "Christians are being punished. We have been scapegoated."

In January 2014, the month a new constitution was approved with 98.1 percent of votes cast, 45 Christian facilities were burned to the ground.

Under the new government, life has continued to be difficult for Egyptian Christians, even though the new constitution respects freedom of religion. "Every day we leave our house not knowing what will happen," said one Egyptian Catholic who lived in Helwan, a city south of Cairo. Since the revolution, that Catholic and his family have noticed a decline in civility due to a surge in Muslim radicalism. "The parts of the Quran they are teaching the kids to memorize tend to be the ones that lead people to hate the other," said the wife. "They don't choose the ones emphasizing prayer, or the verses which say that the other may be different but that he has his own religion and you have yours."

This family pointed out that "there are two types of persecution: Physical, when you are threatened with death, and mental, which is worse. . . . If you are killed, it's over. But if you are subject to mistreatment it may drive you to kill yourself. We are made to feel inferior. This is the persecution that is present in Egypt."

Mistreatment of Egyptian Christian women has been particularly severe. Many have had to endure kidnapping, forced conversion, female circumcision and social discrimination. A Coptic lawyer and human rights activist said in March 2014 that "before 2011 [the various types of persecution] affected perhaps six or seven girls in the whole of Egypt. But now the numbers have grown into the thousands."

The Coptic Catholic Church has been offering safe havens to women who escape their tormentors. There is a residence in Minya for girls who have been kidnapped and they can stay for at least six months or longer if necessary. The priest who runs the home said: "Here the girls are looked after and can speak about everything that has happened to them. We try to equip them to find their place in society again."

Ongoing discrimination, violence and harassment since the Arab Spring began may help explain why in May 2014, it was reported that over 200,000 Christians have left Egypt since 2011.

The rise of ISIS in Syria and Iraq is also a serious concern for Egyptian Christians. Father Greiche said in an October 2014 interview that the Christian community in Egypt does feel threatened by Islamic extremists from abroad: "We feel under threat, if obviously not in the same way as the Christians in Iraq and Syria. We are afraid of jihadists based in neighboring Libya who are sending weaponry into Egypt. There are also jihadists on the Sinai Peninsula."

Greiche went on to point out that when ISIS started to drive Christians out of Mosul, Iraq in the summer of 2013, the Sunni Al-Azhar University remained silent about ISIS atrocities. "Unfortunately," he said, "the curriculum of the university and that of the schools managed by Al-Azhar feature many aspects that are pretty much in line with ISIS transgressions." Nonetheless, 2015 began on a hopeful note when President Abdel Fattah al-Sisi, the formerly military chief, attended the January 7, 2015, Christmas Eve liturgy, joining Coptic Pope Tawadros II at Cairo's St. Mark's Cathedral. al-Sisi is the first president in the history of Egypt to attend Christmas services.

That historic event came just days after he called on Muslim leaders for a "religious revolution" within Islam. In a speech delivered on the day Muslims celebrate the birthday of Muhammad—which coincided with New Year's Day—the President told Egypt's imams: "the entire world is waiting for your word . . . because the Islamic world is being torn, it is being destroyed, it is being lost."

Clearly condemning the violence and extremism of ISIS and other groups, he proclaimed that "it's inconceivable that the thinking that we hold most sacred should cause the entire Islamic world to be a source of anxiety, danger, killing and destruction for the rest of the world."

Will the Egyptian leader stand up for religious freedom across the board, and grant Egyptian Christians basic rights—such as the unhampered liberty to build churches and protection from Muslim hostility? Observers believe al-Sisi is more concerned with keeping Islamic extremism at bay than with a substantial reform of Islam that would separate mosque and state and give religious minorities genuine breathing room. While the President's words and gesture were momentous, his long term response to the beheading of 21 "people of the cross"—Coptic Christians—by a Libyan contingent of ISIS, will be a significant indication of whether he is truly committed.

CHAPTER 5
LEBANON

From the sixteenth century until the end of World War I, Lebanon was a part of the Ottoman Empire. The League of Nations recognized the Republic of Lebanon in 1926, putting it under a French mandate.

In the middle of World War II (in March 1943), with France's blessing, a national covenant established a Parliament to be dominated by Christians. A Maronite Christian would be president of the Constitutional Republic; a Sunni Muslim would serve as Prime Minister; and a Shia Muslim would hold the office of Speaker of the Chamber of Deputies. But in a country whose religious groups were accustomed to having autonomous powers over their own peoples in their respective regions, a genuine power-sharing arrangement proved not sustainable in the long run.

The precarious situation led to revolts against the government; a short-lived civil war in 1958 that was put down by U.S. forces sent into Lebanon by President Eisenhower; and a protracted civil war began in April 1975 after Muslim forces attempted to assassinate Pierre Gemayel, the leader of the Maronite Christians.

For 15 years war ensued that included incursions by Syrian troops, members of the Palestinian Liberation Organization, and Israeli troops. The U.S. also entered the fray in 1982, but withdrew its peacekeeping forces after Muslim extremist suicide bombers attacked the U.S. embassy and killed 63 people, and when on October 23, 1983 a truck bomb killed 241 American Marines and 58 French troops at a military compound outside Beirut.

The civil war effectively came to an end in October 1990 when the Christian military government was overthrown. The long conflict took a major toll on the Lebanese population. More than 125,000 civilians were killed; 13,000 were kidnapped and 200,000 were wounded. Of the dead, more than 80 percent were Catholic. Also, 213,000 Christians fled the country, while 450,000 people became displaced. Approximately 440 Christian churches and facilities were destroyed.

Throughout that period Hezbollah grew in power and became a virtual state within the state of Lebanon. Its paramilitary arm is considered stronger than the Lebanese army; since 2008, Hezbollah has been part of the government, enjoying effective veto power because, along with its allies, it controls 11 of the 30 cabinet posts.

Since the turn of the twenty-first century, a variety of coalitions and so-called unity governments have sought to abide by Article 9 of the Lebanese Constitution, which guarantees respect for all religions—granting all faiths autonomy with regard to such issues as marriage and inheritance—and states that the president of the Republic must be a Maronite Catholic. However, these unique provisions have not stopped radical groups like Hezbollah from gravely hampering the freedom of Christians. Many of the Christian sites and institutions have been desecrated or destroyed.

In the first year of the second millennium, in February 2001, Hezbollah desecrated burial sites in the town of Aytaroun. Dozens of bodies of Christian men were dug up because they had collaborated with the Israelis during their 1982–2000 occupation of southern Lebanon. When a group of women tried to intervene and stop the desecrations they were threatened and told that they would be punished if they told the authorities of the incident. Hezbollah told other protesters that these dead men were "traitors who did not deserve to be buried in Lebanese soil."

Lebanese Maronite Patriarch Nasrallah Sfeir was threatened that same winter by Lebanese Muslim sheikhs. They insisted he cease his public objections to Syrian troops' continued occupation of parts of Lebanon. The Patriarch and his fellow bishops refused to back down and, at their annual meeting later in the year, demanded the complete withdrawal of the Syrian Army from

Lebanon. There were also reports that Hezbollah violence against Lebanese Catholics increased throughout the country after Pope John Paul met on March 2, 2001 with Emile Lahoud, the president of Lebanon.

In July 2001, Hezbollah members, during the middle of the night, banged on the doors of a convent in Alma el Shaab, demanding access. When the nuns who operated the De la Sainté School refused to comply, the intruders informed them: "We are representatives of Hezbollah, all doors must be opened for us without protest. Those who want to prevent this must be destroyed immediately. We are the masters and rulers of this country."

Hezbollah ordered the sisters to force all their female students over the age of nine to wear the Islamic veil, the *hijab*. They threatened to destroy the school and convent and to murder the nuns if they failed to comply.

In August of 2001, the Lebanese Army arrested more than 200 of the supporters of the exiled Christian leader Michel Aoun, as well as two Christian journalists. Pope John Paul II demanded their release, calling on the government and armed forces to act responsibly. "The values of democracy and national sovereignty," the Pontiff argued, "must not be sacrificed to the political interests of the moment." His words fell on deaf ears.

Two months later in the town of Saida, bombs exploded during a ten-day period in front of a Maronite cathedral and another local Christian church. No one was killed but there was damage to the places of worship.

At the end of 2001, it was reported that Christians in Muslim-dominated southern Lebanon had been leaving in droves. The total number of Christians living in the region was estimated to be 27,000, down from 90,000 in 1975. Also, it was estimated that the total Christian population of Lebanon, which historically had stood at 50 percent, was down to 30 percent.

In 2002, the Lebanese government continued to chip away at the freedom of Christians. It shut down a Christian TV station on the questionable charge that the programming was "jeopardizing relations with Syria."

During the night of November 20, 2002, an American missionary in southern Lebanon was murdered. The victim, a 31-year-old American nurse named Benny Witherall, was shot three times. The killer was never found and the authorities suggested the murderer was anti-American, not anti-Christian.

After political cartoons ridiculing the Prophet Muhammad appeared in the Danish press in early 2006, a mob that grew to 20,000 burnt down the Danish Consulate in Beirut on February 5. They also attacked the Christian neighborhood in the Achrafieh district. Numerous stores, buildings and churches were damaged.

The Maronite Patriarch, Cardinal Sfeir, condemned "fanaticism, fundamentalism and violence." Concerning the continued assaults on Christians, Maronite Archbishop Bechara Rai of Jbeil—the eventual successor of Cardinal Sfeir—expressed "profound sadness" about statements made by Hezbollah's secretary general Hassan Nasrallah, saying he "continues to assert [Hezbollah's] right to carry arms, while Christians continue to suffer the tragic consequences of the conflict between Israel and the Party of God [as Hezbollah is known]."

In early January 2007, two Christian websites—belonging to the International Catholic Union for the Press (UCIP) and the Middle East Council of Churches—were hacked. All the content of the websites was deleted and replaced with Muslim material.

The media reported that the attackers belonged to unidentified "non-Christian extremist movements." Father Anthony Khadra, the director of UCIP in Lebanon, bluntly stated that the hacking was "an attack on the shared values of co-existence between Christianity and Islam." In his judgment, radical Muslim groups opposed any public initiatives that promote dialogue between Christianity and Islam.

Maronite Archbishop Bechara Rai, in July 2007, condemned "Islamization schemes" being implemented in Lebanon. He deplored the government's decision of June 2007 that cancelled Good Friday as a national holiday, accusing the government of acting as though it was a "theocratic Islamic state." Citing the "Charter of Children's Rights in Islam," issued by the government in May 2007, the prelate charged that "with this decree, the government is ignoring the presence of the Christians and infringing Article 9 of the Constitution, the co-existence pact and the particular and specific character of Lebanon, transforming it into an Islamic state and society."

Another serious problem in 2007 was the plight of Iraqi Christian refugees, most of them Chaldean Iraqis who had sought refuge in Lebanon from the fighting in their country. The Lebanese government, which refused to grant them temporary legal status, left the refugees with only two alternatives: prison or returning to Iraq.

A December 2007 report by the Human Rights Watch entitled "Rotting here or dying there," put a spotlight on the crisis. "Iraqi refugees in Lebanon live in constant fear of being sent to prison," the report stated. "Those who are arrested can only avoid being imprisoned indefinitely if they agree to return to their homeland." Hence, they could choose prison or going home, where they would most likely be killed.

Chaldean Bishop Michel Kassarji of Beirut summed up the refugee situation this way: "The vicissitudes of Chaldean Iraqis in Lebanon are paradoxical. They travel to Lebanon because they know there is a strong Christian minority here and that the head of state is a Christian. They soon discover how things really stand. Crossing the border illegally costs between 200 and 300 U.S. dollars per person, but once they have entered they constantly risk arrest for having entered the country illegally. If caught they spend between three to five months in prison waiting for a trial (though I have met Iraqis who have spent a whole year in jail) then after sentencing they are deported. The director of national security contacts the Iraqi embassy and organizes their repatriation. I often receive phone calls, from Lebanon and from Iraq, from relatives of people who have been arrested, asking me to intercede. I always go to the prisons, even if they are far from Beirut and near the border where they crossed. I have also sent an open letter to the head of state pleading the case for these people trying to reach safety, but so far without result."

On December 18, 2007, 31 people linked to al Qaeda were

charged with planning an attack on Christian neighborhoods and on a church in Zahle, the capital and largest city of the Beqaa Governorate. With a population of 200,000 Christians, Zahle is the largest predominately Christian city in the Middle East. Eighteen of the accused, who included Lebanese, Syrian and Saudi nationals, had been previously arrested in the area but were set free.

Threats and violence against Christian settlements continued. In June 2010, a bomb detonated in the Christian section of Zahle killed one person and injured others. The explosion took place a few hours before Maronite Patriarch Cardinal Sfeir was scheduled to consecrate a new local church. According to various sources, the cardinal was the intended target.

That same month, Islamist leaflets threatening Christians were distributed throughout the coastal town of Sidon. The messages warned Christians that if they wished to save their lives they had to leave the area within one week. If not, they would "bear the consequences." Soldiers were ordered to guard the neighborhood as the deadline approached and two suspects were arrested.

In late August of 2012, a failed assassination attempt targeting the new Patriarch of the Maronite Church—an attack was to have taken place at the home of a Member of Parliament the Patriarch was to visit—did not keep Pope Benedict XVI from the country in September of that year. "The Christians in Lebanon are looking forward to the Holy Father's visit with great joy," said Cardinal Boutros Rai at the time.

During his visit, the Pope released an apostolic letter that reflected on the results of the Special Assembly for the Middle East of the Bishops' Synod held in 2010. The Lebanese hierarchy counted on the papal visit to have a strong impact on public opinion, hoping that the Apostolic letter would stimulate ecumenical dialogue, encourage vocations and the formation of the laity, and would develop a vision for Lebanon that would halt the exodus of Christians.

The great hopes sparked by the Pope's trip were short-lived. A month after the papal visit, on October 19, in Beirut, and on October 21 in Damascus, radical Muslims attacked Christian communities, killing eight and ten people, respectively, and injuring more than 100 others. Bishop Maroun Nasser, who was appointed Apostolic Visitor to all Maronites in Europe immediately after the Pope returned to Rome from his Lebanon trip, feared that the attacks would "unleash a new wave of refugees." The bishop said that the situation in Damascus was already dire, adding that "now many, including those in Beirut, will believe they can no longer live in safety, even in the Christian quarters."

The Chaldean Catholic Archbishop of Kirkuk, Iraq, Louis Sako—today the Patriarch of the Chaldean Church—praised the papal visit for promoting "a culture of peace." "The Pope's smile," he added, "was a message in itself."

Things, however, would get worse. The Syrian civil war that began in 2011 caused countless Christians and Muslims, fearing for their lives, to flee to Lebanon. Today, both Christian and Muslim Lebanese are afraid that Islamic State, also known as ISIS, will mount an invasion of Lebanon from its strongholds in Syria. The Daily Beast, in November 2014, interviewed Rifaat Nasrallah, a commander of a Christian militia that is charged with preventing Islamic militants from coming over the border. "If it weren't for us, it would be another Mosul for the Christians in Lebanon," Nasrallah said. "We will never stand to not hear our church bells ring. That will never happen here." The fighter was referring to the fall of the largest Christian city in Iraq, which was captured by Islamic State in June 2014.

The crisis is making for strange bedfellows. To protect the Lebanese border towns from ISIS incursions or outright invasion, Nasrallah has been allied with Hezbollah, an ally of Syrian President Bashar al-Assad. They have collaborated on patrolling the borders and Christian fighters have received training and supplies from Hezbollah. "We are sharing a common enemy now—ISIS is trying to kill us both," one of Nasrallah's deputies explained.

Nasrallah made it clear that he has no intention of leaving Lebanon and is critical of those who have emigrated to other countries. "We are not guests in the Middle East," he said. "We are the owners of this region . . . [and] we have the will to fight."

Syrian-born Archbishop John Darwish, the head of the Melkite Archdiocese of Furzol, Zahle and Bekaa in Lebanon, reported in December 2013 that 2,000 Syrian Christian refugee families resided in his diocese. "While the Syrian Christians are fortunate enough to live in homes, sometimes with multiple families in a single home or set of rooms," the bishop stated, "by contrast, there are at least ten thousand Syrian Muslim families living in refugee camps." Since then, the number of refugees has grown tenfold.

The bishop's primary concern is to secure for the Christian refugees the basics of daily life: food, educational opportunities for their children, medical care. "We help the poorer Christian families," he said, "to pay their rent; we also try to find work for the young men and adults." The bishop also created a chaplaincy to minister to the refugees. He pointed out that "many of them are in bad shape, emotionally and materially . . . Jihadist rebels came to them at night and forced them to leave immediately; they are traumatized because they were unable to mourn and pray for their dead."

Syrian refugees have continued to flee into Lebanon. In 2014, the U.N. estimated that there were more than 1.1 million registered refugees in Lebanon and another 500,000 unregistered Syrians. Shockingly, more than 25 percent of Lebanon's current population are people who have fled Syria.

Historically, Lebanon has been recognized as the nation in the Middle East with the most religious freedom because, as per the French legacy, its government has been structured to accommodate representation of the country's different faiths. However, many Christian leaders fear that latent persecution and the Islamization of Lebanese society pose a growing threat to those freedoms. In addition, there is growing support for political groups demanding a fully secular state which, if implemented, would mean the "deconfessionalization" of the government. In practice, this would allow the majority Muslims to take over almost the entire government and subsequently impose their will on the minority Christian population.

Assessing the obstacles Christians face in Lebanon, Archbishop

Georges Bacouni of Tyre, Lebanon, recently told Vatican officials: "Christians are facing major challenges and various problems due to the many changes that affect not only Lebanon, but the entire Middle East. Particularly from the point of view of Catholics, we are faced with a decline in the number of believers, [this is a] time of crisis that creates negative consequences on the process of integration for Christians . . . in a land in which their presence is diminishing over time. What is even more surprising, compared to the last century, is the reduction of the Christian presence within the political institutions, in social sectors, in education, as well as within the ranks of the military." He went on to say that the Christian minority is finding it increasingly difficult to remain fully integrated in society as they find themselves "situated in a hotbed of unrest, something that produces a climate of widespread fear among the local population."

The declining numbers of Lebanese Christians tells the story. In 1926, 84 percent of the new nation was Christian and today Christians represent only about 30 percent of the population. If this trend continues, analyst Benny Auni observed in December 2014, "Lebanon may one day, not too long from now, go the way of the rest of the region, where Christians are an endangered species."

CHAPTER 6
SYRIA

The area that encompasses the present-day nation of Syria was the cradle of Christianity, the roots of its ancient patriarchal sees going back to St. Peter. In fact, the term "Christian" was first coined in Antioch. The oldest standing church in Christendom is the Church of St. Simeon Stylites in Aleppo.

The region fell to Muslim invaders in 640 and became part of the Umayyad dynasty and then was ruled by the Abbasids. After a few centuries of rule by the Crusaders, Syria suffered centuries of poverty, suffering further neglect after 1516, when it became a province of the Ottoman Empire. During the 1,100-year rule of the Ottoman Empire, Syria's population declined by 25 percent, while scores of small towns and villages were abandoned and reclaimed by the desert.

The Ottoman Empire, which was in decline in the late nineteenth century, sealed its fate when it joined the German-Austrian-Hungary alliance in World War I. The rulers did not, however, give up their long-held territories peacefully. Instead, they spread terror and ruin and committed gross atrocities, particularly against Christians. The Islamic Turks, in the area which is today Syria and Iraq, slaughtered at least 200,000 Christians. That figure represented approximately 75 percent of Chaldean Catholics, Syrian Catholics, Syrian Jacobites, as well as Protestants in the region. Also, between 1914 and 1922, more than 1.7 million Greek and 1.8 million Armenian Christians were murdered by the Turks.

The 1916 Sykes-Picot Agreement outlined the boundaries of modern Syria that would be created by the Allies after the war ended in November 1918. The northern zone of what was known as the Arab Levant came under French mandate and included Syria and Lebanon.

At the outset of World War II, Syria was controlled by the German puppet Vichy government until July 1941, when the Free French and British forces conquered the country. Succumbing to pressure from the British and Syrian nationalists after the war, the French gave up all claims to Syria and a parliamentary republic was created in 1946.

During the next decade there was constant unrest in the country. Twenty different cabinets were appointed and four different constitutions were drafted. In 1958, an agreement was signed that joined Egypt and Syria into the United Arab Republic. This agreement was also short-lived. Syria seceded from the union in September 1961 and the Syrian Arab Republic was established in 1963. For the next 48 years, the nation was subject to emergency laws and most constitutional protections remained suspended.

In 1970, the military overthrew the government and Hafez al-Assad took over as president of Syria. Assad, a member of a Shiite minority, the Alawites, was fiercely opposed to Islamic radicalism; like his Baathist counterpart in Iraq, Saddam Hussein, he could be sympathetic to the concerns of religious minorities, including Christians—provided they would not threaten his rule in any way. After he died in 2000, his son Bashar al-Assad was installed as president.

At the turn of the century, about ten percent of Syria's population of 18 million were Christians. Those numbers increased after the American incursion of Iraq in 2003. Acts of violence by Islamic groups caused about 150,000 Iraqi Christians to flee to Syria.

Prior to the Arab Spring, Christians were generally left undisturbed in Syria. While the 1973 constitution states that the head of the government must be Muslim and that Islamic law must be the source of legislation, Islam is not the official state religion. The constitution recognizes the right of other religions to practice their forms of worship. Nevertheless, the Bath Party, officially secular and socialist, keeps a tight rein on all religions, which all must be registered with the government.

Unlike the situation in most other Muslim countries, Christians had been free to build churches and other religious facilities and could organize public religious activities. Christmas and Easter were deemed official holidays and Christian religious ceremonies were broadcast on television.

There were some government restrictions. The Christian press had been censored and Christian schools were nationalized in 1967. The government security forces also monitored the content of sermons in both churches and mosques. As *One* magazine pointed out in August 2014, while Christians were not legally prohibited from seeking converts, the government had made it clear that it frowns upon the practice and from time to time would prosecute Christian missionaries for "posing a threat to the relations among religious groups." In addition, state law does not recognize the conversion of a Muslim to Christianity.

While Christians and Muslims did live in harmony for stretches of time, there were clashes. When Pope John Paul was due to visit Syria in April 2001, the Syrian Grand Mufti, Sheikh Ahmad Kuftaro, and the leadership of the Syrian Muslims made it clear that they did not want to pray with the Pope. The Sheikh said: "Reports that a Christian/Muslim prayer is to be said in the Umayyad Mosque are completely false. No decision has been taken in this matter by the Grand Mufti. Co-existence between Christians and Muslims does not require common prayer."

During his visit, the Pope spent most of his time meeting with the leaders and faithful of the Melkite Church and the Orthodox Church. The head of the Syrian Catholic Church, Archbishop Joseph Mounayer, used the occasion to remind the public and the international media that 150,000 thousand Christians were murdered by the Turks in 1915.

As early as 2006, groups that opposed the Assad government began to organize under an umbrella group called the National Salvation Front. A key constituent was the Muslim Brotherhood.

Five years later, in March 2011, after a series of peaceful protests were suppressed by the Syrian Army, an uprising against the Assad government commenced. The fighting turned into a full-fledged civil war, which would eventually give rise to the Islamic State of Iran and Levant (ISIL), also known as the Islamic State of Iraq and Syria (ISIS), an extremist Sunni jihadist group. Army defectors formed the Free Syrian Army and an interim government was created by the Syrian National Coalition—it did not include any Christian representatives.

Caught in the middle of the uprising were the Christians. Jihadist rebels persecuted Christians because of their religion and because they were perceived as being sympathetic to the Assad regime, which had granted them significant freedoms and provided a measure of safety and stability.

In the early days of the Syrian crisis, the Chaldean Catholic Bishop of Aleppo, Antoine Audo S.J., called on the Syrian government to quell the rebel forces, which he believed were seeking "destabilization and Islamization." He warned that "the fanatics speak about freedom and democracy for Syria, but that is not their goal. They want to divide the Arab countries, control them, seize oil and sell arms. . . . We do not want to become like Iraq. We do not want insecurity and Islamization and have the threat of Islamists coming to power." Defending the Assad regime, he concluded: "Syria [which has 1.5 million Christians] has a secular orientation. There is freedom. We have a lot of positive things in our country."

In January 2012, reliable sources, which insisted on remaining anonymous, gave a report to Aid to the Church in Need that stated Christians were being murdered and kidnapped all over Syria during the 2011 Christmas season. Shortly thereafter, Bishop Antoine Audo of Aleppo spoke out that ethnic cleansing by Islamic militants had driven 100,000 of Christians from their homes in Homs, the city that is home to Syria's second-largest Christian community. Pointing out that Christians were frightened, he said: "[They] don't know what their future will hold. They are afraid they will not get their homes back." Thousands of Christian homes as well as all the churches in Homs were destroyed by bombs and arson. Tens of thousands fled to the mountains 30 miles outside of the city. In December 2013, it was revealed that 3,000 Christians in Homs had died.

Seventeen miles from Homs, the 2,000 Christian families in the town of Qusayr fled their homes after they received an ultimatum from the head of opposition forces, Abdel Salam Harba.

In the summer of 2012, Christians in Aleppo were terrified of being targeted and driven away. Some of the fiercest fighting was taking place in Aleppo, including house-to-house searches, car bomb explosions and the execution of pro-Assad officials, Bishop Audo told the British House of Lords in October of that year: "Aleppo, the city I love so much and where I have been bishop this past 20 years, is now devastated—much of it in ruins." Describing the mass exodus of Christians from the city, he said: "If we Christians . . . [are] reduced to a token few it would be disastrous because until now, ours has been one of the last remaining strong Christian centers in the whole of the Middle East."

Also, in October 2012, a Greek-Orthodox priest in Damascus, Father Fadi Haddad, was found dead, his throat cut, his eyes gouged out and his body mutilated. He had tried to secure the release of a kidnapped Christian doctor.

Two bishops from Aleppo, Greek-Orthodox Archbishop Boulos Yazigi and Syrian Orthodox Archbishop Yohanna Ibrahim, who were negotiating the release of two kidnapped priests, were abducted on April 22, 2013, on the Syrian-Turkish border four miles west of Aleppo. Their driver, Deacon Fatha Kabboud, was murdered by the kidnappers. The two prelates are still missing. A Jesuit priest, Father Paolo Dall'Oglio, was abducted in the Homs Diocese in July 2013 after re-opening the monastery of Mar Musa.

Muslim religious leaders in Douma, the Damascus suburb, issued a *fatwa* in September 2013 permitting Sunni Muslims to seize the homes and property owned by Christians. And as a result of Christian communities being ravaged by Muslim extremists, the Melkite Patriarch Gregorios III reported in October 2013 that out of a pre-war population of 1.75 million Christians, more than 450,000 of them had fled the country or were internally displaced. In the city of Aleppo, which had possessed the largest Christian population in Syria, more than 65 percent of them had been forced to leave.

One radical group, the al-Nusra Front, which was initially financed by ISIS but since 2013 has split with them, attacked the Christian shrine village of Maaloula on September 7, 2013. They destroyed the crosses on the monastery of St. Serge and threatened the nuns at the convent of St. Thekla. They forced their way into Christian homes screaming, "We're here to get you, worshippers of the cross."

When the invaders demanded in one household that three Melkites convert to Islam, they proceeded to murder them, after one had said: "I am a Christian and if you want to kill me because I am a Christian, than do so."

The al-Nusra Front in December 2013 kidnapped 12 Orthodox nuns from the convent of St. Thekla. They were taken to Yabroud. On hearing of the kidnapping the Syrian Orthodox Metropolitan of the area demanded the immediate release of the sisters, saying: "We've now reached the point where even nuns are being abducted. What have they done wrong? The abductors want to demonstrate they know no mercy." The Metropolitan made it clear that "the nuns had been completely apolitical and had dedicated themselves exclusively to prayer and charity works." They were subsequently released in March 2014.

In October 2013, the al-Nusra front captured the Christian town of Sadad, about 200 miles north of Damascus. More than 45 Christians were murdered, while 2,500 families fled after their homes, shops and churches had been destroyed. The rebel forces also used members of 1,500 families as human shields to protect themselves from attacking government forces. One priest who was helping the remaining Christians in Sadad said: "The number of Christians killed because they are targeted for their faith is growing. Sadad is a very clear case. They were slaughtered like animals." Melkite Greek Catholic Patriarch Gregorios III described the atrocities as "bestial."

A study released in January 2014 revealed that as many as 600,000 Syrian Christians, a third of the nation's total, have fled their homes and are displaced within Syrian borders or have been living as refugees in neighboring countries. Open Doors International also reported that Syria headed "the list of the countries in which the most Christians were killed for their faith." Approximately 1,213 were murdered in 2013, followed by Nigeria (612), Pakistan (88), and Egypt (83).

In 2013, ISIS took control of territory in northern and central Syria, and in border towns along the Turkish border ISIS has imposed sharia in the occupied towns.

To put fear into the hearts of Christians, ISIS and other extremists have committed scores of atrocious acts. The Catholic World Report, in a story "The Suffering of Christians in Syria" (October 31, 2014), cited a nun who has worked in the country for years: "There are slaughterhouses, many slaughterhouses, in Syria where Christians are taken to be tortured and slaughtered. People who are not political, who do not choose or take sides in the conflict, are taken from their families, kidnapped, forced to deny their faith and then—whether they have or not—are killed, often by beheading. This is not about siding with the government, not about siding with President Assad, but about sheer persecution of a peaceful but vulnerable minority. Yet the world says so little, and often nothing at all."

Nina Shea, head of the Center for Religious Freedom at the Hudson Institute—who has served as a commissioner on the U.S. Commission on International Religious Freedom since 1999 and is a noted expert on anti-Christian discrimination—wrote on National Review Online February 28, 2014, that ISIS jihadists were forcing Syrian Christians to become Dhimmis under seventh-century rules in the northern provincial capital of Raqqa, which was the home of 3,000 Christians before invasion.

According to Shea, under the Dhimmis arrangement:

> . . . in exchange for their lives and the ability to worship as Christians, they must abide by purported seventh-century rules of the Caliph Umar. According to the Raqqa ultimatum, these include bans on renovating and rebuilding churches and monasteries, many of which need repair because they've been shelled and blown up over the past

three years, and bans against the public display of crosses and Christian symbols and the ringing of bells. They are forbidden from reading scripture indoors loud enough for Muslims outside to hear, and the practice of their faith must be confined within the walls of their remaining churches, not exercised publicly (at, for example, funeral or wedding processions). They are prohibited from saying anything offensive about Muslims or Islam. The women must be enshrouded, and alcohol is banned.

Those remaining Christians in Raqqa were told if they did not convert to Islam or pay for protection they would be considered combatants and put to "the sword." The ISIS policy, "Submit to Islam, or face the sword," drew a response from the U.S. State Department. On March 3, 2014, a statement titled "Christians Under Threat In Syria" read:

The United States deplores continued threats against Christians and other minorities in Syria, who are increasingly targeted by extremists. Last week in Raqqa, the Islamic State of Iraq and the Levant (ISIL) announced it will force Syrian Christians to either convert to Islam, remain Christian and pay a tax, or face death. These outrageous conditions violate universal human rights. ISIL has demonstrated time and again its disregard for Syrian lives, and it continues to commit atrocities against the Syrian people. Although ISIL claims it is fighting the regime, its oppression of and senseless violence against Syrians, including the moderate Syrian opposition, demonstrates that it is fighting for nothing except the imposition of its own brand of tyranny.

While the Assad regime attempts to paint itself as a protector of Syria's minorities, it has brutally cracked down on dissent from all segments of society. The regime has arrested Christian worshippers, human rights advocates, and peaceful dissidents like Akram al-Bunni and

President of the Assyrian Democratic Organization, Gabriel Moushe Gourieh; raided and confiscated church property; shelled Christian communities like Yabrud; and bombed dozens of churches, some simply for being located in opposition-held areas.

The Syrian people have a long history of tolerance and co-existence, but both the regime and ISIL are fueling sectarian strife to justify their brutality. We strongly condemn these abuses and urge all parties to protect and respect the rights of all Syrians, regardless of ethnicity, gender or religion.

In the spring of 2014, it was estimated that since the beginning of the Syrian civil war, 9 million inhabitants have fled their homes, with 6.5 million on the run within Syrian borders and 2.5 million having left the country.

Many uprooted Christians still prefer to stay in their country—despite the suffering, the growing death toll of their co-religionists, and the fact that in areas controlled by ISIS and other jihadist rebel groups, a rigorous version of Islamic law has been applied and all publicly visible Christian symbols have been removed and Christians have to pay special taxes. "We Christians are living in fear, the future is uncertain, but we want to stay in our homeland," the Melkite Greek-Catholic Archbishop of Homs, Hama and Yabroud, Jean-Abdo Arbach, told Aid to the Church in Need. He reported that about 20,000 Christians still live in Homs and that tens of thousands of displaced faithful have settled about 28 miles west of Homs, in the area known as the "Valley of the Christians." Most have arrived with only the clothes on their back and rely on the supply of food, medicine and blankets from international charities.

Shortly before Easter 2014, the Dutch Jesuit priest Father Frans van der Lugt was murdered in his monastery in Homs. The 76-year-old priest who had ministered to Syrian Christians for more than half a century was a target of extremists because he had been trying to broker a peace agreement between rebels and the government. "Since his death, the truce efforts have broken down," *The*

Wall Street Journal reported on April 21, 2014. "[T]he Syrian army and allied militias have been mounting a sweeping offensive to oust rebels from the old quarter of Homs and the adjacent district of Waer. Rebels have hit back with suicide car bombs and mortar and rocket attacks on neighborhoods under regime control." The Syrian Observatory for Human Rights has stated that about 50 civilians had been killed in the renewed fighting in Homs.

Archbishop Jean-Abdo Arbach of Homs, whose archdiocese was created in the fourth century, described the suffering his flock has endured: "From my visits to the houses of the families and from the reports of my priests, it is clear that everyone has been hurt by the tragic events. . . . To date, our archdiocese has counted 96 martyrs. . . . More than 1,800 families . . . have left their houses to seek safety elsewhere in Syria or have fled to Lebanon."

In addition, dozens of churches, many that date back to the Church's very beginning, have been destroyed. "Last February [2014]," the archbishop said, "an armed gang broke into the Church of Our Lady of Yabroud, a fourth-century church. They destroyed the fittings in the church, smashed the crucifix, threw the icons on the floor and tore the pages out of the Gospel. Then the gang burned the altar."

Despite all the suffering, the archbishop insisted that the spiritual life of his flock endures: "The crisis has triggered a major return to faith and prayer among those who have not left their villages. Though having to deal with fear and the constant threat of bombs, families are remaining loyal to their religious convictions."

In the Syrian city of Aleppo, which has suffered the worst violence in the civil war, an Argentinean nun, Sister Maria, of the Institute of the Incarnate Word, has been working with Christians trying to rebuild their lives. Describing her role in Aleppo, she said: "Our task . . . is very special. We are constantly confronted with people's suffering. The war is having a profoundly deleterious effect on human dignity. People are losing their loved ones, their freedom and their rights due to the violence. On top of this there is poverty and a lack of the most basic things, such as electricity and water."

Aleppo, the largest city in Syria, had a pre-war population of 2.1 million, of which 250,000 thousand were Christians. The Christian community consisted of Greek, Syrian and Armenian Orthodox, as well as Catholic Armenians, Chaldeans, Roman Catholics, Maronites and Melkites. Thousands of Christian families have been displaced, and the population of the war-torn city has declined to one million residents. The remaining Christian population, most of whom are Armenian, totals 100,000.

A Roman Catholic priest, who lost an eye during one assault on Aleppo and has a prosthetic cheek and iron rod in his arm, told the *U.K. Daily Mail* in late November 2014: "We will decorate the Christmas trees in church and in homes but not outside out of respect for the martyrs, because a lot of blood has been spilt." Insisting that many of his city's Christians will never give up, he said: "We will still be here 100 years from now because this is our land."

At the National Apostolate of Maronites convention held in Pittsburgh in July 2014, the Maronite bishop of Latakia, Syria, Msgr. Elias Sleman, told the assembly what's at stake in war-torn Syria:

> Remaining in the land is critical, and a very important matter that concerns all Christians, otherwise our land will be emptied from its original inhabitants. Even the Valley of Christians in Syria "Wadi al-Nasara," with all neighboring villages and towns may soon be empty. This constitutes a real threat to the Qadisha Valley as well, and the Holy Land of Palestine, and the Holy Places in the Christian Orient, and our people might face the same fate that faced our people and Churches in Iraq, Egypt and other places. . . .
>
> Let us be united and help in protecting the land of the Middle East and work for the stability of its people in their land, for our land is our identity. In that land our parents and ancestors lived and they witnessed to their Faith, and they handed it on to their successors, and defended it, and shed their blood for its sake. O children

of the Saints and Martyrs, keep on carrying the torch of Faith and perseverance and the attachment to the land. Let us remain attached to that precious heritage and prove ourselves witnesses and people of the Resurrection and children of our ancestors.

I ask you to contribute, to help your brothers and sisters in their land. Emptying the East from its Christians is an environmental catastrophe. Stabilizing Christians in their mother land is so very important, for it secures temperance and moderation in a world threatened by extremism and fanaticism. The process of emptying the East from its Christians begins with the migration of Christians from Palestine, Iraq, Egypt and Syria. The land of the East is in danger, and so is Lebanon. O dear Eastern people, Christians and non-Christians, please wake up and act today before it may be too late, for every day spent without doing nothing is leading our region towards the abyss.

CHAPTER 7
IRAQ

Iraq is an artificially formed state created by the French and the British in the aftermath of World War I. The boundaries, which were drawn without regard to ethnic or religious sensibilities, were based primarily on the United Kingdom's oil interests. The borders were blessed by the League of Nations in 1920 and the new nation was placed under the control of Great Britain.

The British permitted a king to ascend the throne in 1921 and the Kingdom of Iraq was subsequently granted independence in 1932. The monarchy lasted until 1958 when it was overthrown and the Republic of Iraq was established. That national government was controlled by the Baath Party from 1968 until the U.S. deposed President Saddam Hussein in 2003. The Baath Party, whose platform was secular and socialist, guaranteed in its constitution religious liberties of minorities. However, Saddam Hussein, who came to power in 1979, had increasingly during his reign declared himself the defender of the true faith of Islam, and persecuted religious minorities.

At the turn of the twenty-first-century, Iraq had a population of 22.4 million. Approximately 59 percent were Shiite Muslims, 36 percent were Sunni Muslims and a little more than 3 percent (672,000) were Christians, most of whom were members of Churches in union with Rome, particularly the Chaldean Church. A majority of Iraq Christians are Assyrians who claim to be the original inhabitants of the region. The Assyrians were the people of Nineveh—present-day Mosul—the city of the biblical Jonah. The Christian population has declined significantly since 1987 when the Iraqi census put their total at 1.4 million.

Although Christians and Muslims had co-existed for most of the region's history, many Christians, feeling threatened in the wake of the 1991 Gulf War because they were perceived as being sympathetic to the West, began to leave the country. Because the Hussein government falsely blamed the post-war U.N. Embargo on them, life for Christians, which had never been very easy, was getting progressively worse.

While the U.N., after the Gulf War, attempted to prevent the Iraqi regime from oppressing its citizens and declared as a safe haven the area north of the 36th parallel in Iraq, it did not prevent Assyrian Christians in that area from being persecuted. Parliamentary elections that were held in this autonomous safe haven were plagued with irregularities and fraud and caused a period of violence and anarchy. Assyrian Christians were persecuted by the Kurds, becoming victims of murder, kidnappings, forced conversions and the suppression of their language and culture.

A secret document released in August 2004 revealed that Hussein-sponsored militia working alongside Kurds had been guilty of ethnic cleansing, the gassing and Islamization of Assyrian Christians in Northern Iraq. It appears at least 290 Christian villages were destroyed during this campaign of terror.

In 2002, the final year of Hussein's brutal reign, there were growing reports of violence in Baghdad. On August 15, 2002, for example, armed men raided the Convent of the Sacred Heart of Jesus Monastery. A 70-year-old nun was repeatedly beaten and subsequently died of her injuries.

The U.S.-led invasion of Iraq commenced on March 20, 2003. Hussein's government quickly fell and the U.S. installed a Coalition Provisional Authority to govern. In the aftermath of the war, many Christians remained skeptical even though they were told by the interim government that they would be free to practice their religion. Many feared that when the American-led coalition forces left there would be outbreaks of aggression against them, similar to that which occurred after the Gulf War.

Writing for the Christian Broadcasting Network in January 2004, journalist George Thomas, in an article titled "Radical Muslims Spark Fear in Iraqi Christians," summed up the situation this way: "The capture of Saddam Hussein has lifted a cloud that has been hanging over everyone in Iraq. But for some groups in Iraq, including Christians, life is becoming harder. The concern exists that the political and constitutional future of Iraq could threaten the survival of the Christians there. The past several months have been dangerous for Christians in Iraq. A key Christian judge was killed in Mosul, bombs were found at two Christian schools, and many Christian students and families received notes to convert to Islam, or else."

There were other acts of violence committed in late 2003. In November, a leading Christian lawyer, Ismail Youssef, was murdered. Several days later cluster bombs were found at a Christian school. And in December, a Christian from Basra was kidnapped by Muslims. After his family paid a ransom of 10 million dinars (some $10,000) the man was released.

During Christmas celebrations in Baghdad, a bomb went off in a church. Fortunately, no worshippers were killed. One week after that incident, another bomb exploded in St. George's monastery in Mosul.

Christians did not fare much better in 2004. In January, more than 200 Iraqi scholars and politicians appealed to Coalition Authorities to stop attacks by Shiite Muslims on Christians. In their statement, the group said that "appalling crimes, predominately against Christian women, have been committed," and that Muslim groups have been terrorizing "our Christian brothers and pressuring them to become Muslims." On February 21, Assyrian Christians were murdered in Fallujah. On March 15, five missionaries were shot and killed in Mosul.

At the time Father Bashar Warda—today the Chaldean archbishop of Erbil, in Kurdistan—a professor of the College of Philosophy and Theology in Baghdad, complained that many Christians given jobs by the occupying forces were being systematically murdered. He also pointed out that the Christian community was "suffering two to three kidnappings a week; those with more education in particular are the targets of the kidnappers, including the families of hundreds of engineers and doctors."

By June 2004, Christians began leaving the country in great numbers, not only because of the terror but because of Article 7 of the proposed Iraqi constitution, which stated that Islam is the official state religion, and the fact that Christians had not received a single spot on the nation's executive council.

A Christian restaurant owner in Mosul was murdered in July because he had served food to Americans. The murderers, members of an Islamic Wahhabi group, had sent a letter to the victim that said: "You are a Christian. Why do you sell food to Americans? Are you an agent for the Americans?" The terrorists also attacked the man's Muslim business partner, chopping off his hands and gouging out his eyes.

On August 1, 2004, Muslim fundamentalists connected to al Qaeda launched suicide attacks on eight churches in Baghdad and two in Mosul. More than a dozen were killed and more than 200 were injured. The Committee of Planning and Follow-Up that took responsibility for the crimes declared online "the attacks were a response to the American war of crusade and evangelism." It continued: "You wanted a crusade; so here are the consequences. We have warned you. The Mujahedeen brothers have struck painful blows against the lairs of the crusaders, the laws of evil, of corruption, immorality and Christianization, by detonating car bombs."

Bishop Andraos Abouna, the spokesperson for the Chaldean Catholic hierarchy, described the attacks as "striking Christianity in Iraq in the heart. . . . The future is very sad. More and more Christians are thinking of emigrating because the situation is getting worse and worse." The prelate added: "The country cannot be without Christianity. Iraq is our home and we have been here since the very beginning. Abraham was from 'Ur of the Chaldees.' And yet now people are so afraid they want to leave."

And many Christians did leave the country. The Iraqi Minister for Displacement and Migration disclosed that, in the two weeks after the churches were bombed, 40,000 Christians emigrated from Iraq.

Christians continued to suffer kidnappings, bombings, murders and written threats during the balance of 2004. Car bombs exploded minutes apart at two churches in Baghdad on November 8, killing eight people and injuring dozens of others. Bombs on the eve of Ramadan went off in three other churches. Muslims shot Rev. Tarmida Saleein Ghada several times in the legs at the Mandaean place of prayer at the Deeala River.

In the city of Mosul, two churches in the northeastern sector were destroyed on December 9. The Muslim radicals drove the congregations into the streets, and after wrecking the sanctuaries set them ablaze. At the same time, the Chaldean Archbishop of Mosul, Faraj Rahho, was forced out of his residence and watched masked men burn it down.

Shortly before the 2005 elections, the Syrian Catholic Archbishop of Mosul, Basile Georges Casmoussa, was kidnapped at gunpoint after leaving the home of parishioners. The archbishop was released the next day and observers believe the incident took place close to election day to intimidate Christian voters. The kidnapping of the Secretary General of the Christian Democratic Party in January 2005 is believed to have served the same purpose.

As election day drew near, there were numerous reports of campaigns of intimidation against Christian political parties; activists were warned not to wear crosses or to display images of the cross on campaign literature.

When the ballots were totaled after Iraqis cast their votes on January 30, 2005, only six Christians were elected to the 275-member National Assembly. The Shiite Alliance garnered 48 percent of the vote and the Kurds came in second, with 26 percent. The results caused Christians to fear that the country was on the road to becoming an Islamic state.

As violence between Iraq's Shiites and Sunnis increased, Christians often found themselves caught in the middle. They were viewed by both sides of the warring Muslims as supporters of the American occupiers. In March 2005, the Islamist Brigades for the elimination of Christian Agents and Spies commenced a witch-hunt against Christians whom they believed collaborated with U.S.

forces, vowing to pursue them "right into their homes and churches."

As violence against Christians increased and as a new constitution was being drafted that gave Christians little reassurance, the then-Chaldean Patriarch of Baghdad, Emmanuel III Delly, during a visit to France in May 2005, warned that "religious liberty does not exist in Muslim countries, with the exception of Lebanon. . . . In Iraq, there is . . . no religious liberty—nor is there any political or cultural liberty." When the draft of the constitution was released, Christian leaders criticized in particular the clause that read: "No law can be passed that contradicts the undisputed rules of Islam." Patriarch Emmanuel III Delly publicly declared that the constitution "opens the doors" to discrimination against Christians.

On October 15, 2005, the Iraqi electorate overwhelmingly approved the new constitution that Christians had no role in drafting. In the referendum the yes votes totaled almost 80 percent. The clause that "no law that contradicts the established provisions of Islam may be established" remained included. The document also contained two clauses that were designed to quell outcries from political and religious minorities:

* The state defends democracy and basic freedoms as well as the full religious rights of all believers. (Article 2.1B, C and 2.2)
* The state guarantees administrative, political, cultural and educational rights for all different Iraqi ethnic groups, including the Turkmen, Chaldeans and Assyrians.(Article 121)

A new round of general elections were held on December 15, 2005 and once again the Shiite Alliance came in first with 41.2 percent of the vote and the Kurd alliance with 21.7 percent. Although Christians organized their own political parties, they had little impact on the outcome. Only three Christians were elected to Parliament; down from six in the previous election.

Despite the so-called constitutional guarantees, violence against Christians was once again on the rise. On January 29, 2006, bomb attacks hit six churches in Iraq during services. Four people were killed, including a 13-year-old altar boy, Fadi Raad Elias. Patriarch

Emmanuel III Delly barely escaped with his life when a bomb went off in his Baghdad cathedral. That same day dozens of Christian university students were attacked by Muslims and accused of being non-believers and U.S. agents.

Archbishop Louis Sako of Kirkuk—the present Chaldean Patriarch—officiating at the requiem mass of the slain altar server, said that in Iraq Christians were "becoming once again a Church of martyrs." Bishop Andreas Abouna of Baghdad described the situation in these words: "The Christians feel desperate and so many are leaving. In their hearts they do not want to leave their country but because of the situation, they prefer to be outside Iraq."

The kidnapping of Christians was rampant during the balance of 2006. In April an Anglican priest reported the kidnapping and murder of four colleagues who were members of the Alpha Evangelization program. Father Raad Kasaam was forcibly taken from a taxi on July 15, was beaten, and then burned with cigarettes before being released. A Chaldean seminary professor was abducted from his automobile on August 5. He was also badly beaten; he was released after three weeks in captivity. Four weeks later, the secretary of Patriarch Delly, Father Bassel Yeldo, was kidnapped and held for 24 hours.

After Pope Benedict XVI gave his lecture on Islam at the University of Regensburg, Germany September 12, 2006—in which the Pontiff cited some very strong historical criticism of Islam—a Mosul Syriac Orthodox parish priest, Father Ameir Iskander, was kidnapped by Muslims. The extremists demanded $350,000 and apologies from Church leaders for Pope Benedict's statements. On October 11, Father Iskander's beheaded body was found. Another Syriac Orthodox priest was abducted by "The Lions of Islam" October 9. They wanted 280,000 Euros and 30 proclamations to be placed in churches throughout Mosul apologizing for the "Pope's offensive words against Islam." The priest's beheaded body was found October 13. The same day Father Joseph Petros was found murdered in Baghdad. Throughout November and December numerous priests were abducted and later released; a Protestant pastor in Mosul, Mundher Aldayr, was assassinated on November 26.

What was becoming evident in early 2007 was that Shiite and Sunni forces throughout Iraq had become determined to eradicate Christians. Both sides were conducting door-to-door searches for Christians, demanding that they convert to Islam, or be evicted or pay huge fines based on the Islaic *Jizya* taxation of up to $100,000.

A bomb exploded in a Christian village near Mosul April 23, 2007 killing 20 Assyrian Christians. In May the bodies of seven Christians were found next to their burnt-out automobile on a road leading to Bakouba. That same month 24 dead Christians who had been tortured before being murdered were found in Baghdad.

Iraq's entire Christian population was shocked upon learning that a 34-year-old Chaldean seminary professor, Father Ragheed Ganni, and three sub-deacons were assassinated after Sunday Mass on June 3, 2007 in Mosul. The priest, who also served as the pastor of two parishes in Mosul, had dismissed threatening letters forbidding him to celebrate Mass or to speak in public.

Scores of churches, convents and monasteries were looted; priests, nuns and Christian students were kidnapped and thousands of Christian families were driven from their homes. CDs were dropped in mailboxes at Christian homes that contained images of executions, along with demands that the family convert or leave the country—or suffer death like those on the CD.

Iraqi journalist Sahar El Haieri was assassinated in late 2007 for daring to write an article about the plight of Christians that read: "If a strong government does not guarantee their safety, one must fear that Christians will disappear completely from this part of the world."

Bishop Antoine Audo agreed with the slain journalist. At a London event sponsored by the Aid to the Church in Need in October 2007, he said: "This may be the end of Christianity in Iraq. It would be sad and dangerous for the Church, for Iraq and even for Muslims themselves, because it would mean the end of an old experience of living together. If Christians and Muslims are not able to exist in the Middle East it will spell danger for the West in the future."

On Christmas Eve 2008, bombs went off at six churches in

Mosul and Baghdad and car bombs targeted two churches in Kirkuk. Fortunately, only a few were injured.

In 2009 threats and assassinations continued, the major headline event being the kidnapping of Archbishop Paulos Faraj Rahho of Mosul outside his Cathedral February 28. The Muslim attackers grabbed the archbishop after he had completed saying the Stations of the Cross. The kidnappers demanded a ransom of $3 million.

Two weeks later word was received that the archbishop was dead. His body was found in a shallow grave near the center of Mosul. On the day of Archbishop Rahho's funeral Mass, Archbishop Sako said of him: "[He] was a man who gave his life for his Church and for his people. Things for us have been getting worse and worse. Holy week for us has come early and today is our Good Friday—we are living out Christ's passion spiritually and at all levels."

Unrelenting intimidation and violence against Christians was forcing huge numbers of the faithful to flee their homes. The U.N. reported in 2010 that since the fall of Saddam Hussein's government approximately 40 percent of the 1.6 million refugees that left Iraq were Christians. According to the Iraqi bishops, the number of Christians—the great majority of them Chaldeans—declined between 2003 and 2010 from 600,000 to less than 200,000. They expected Christian emigration to continue unabated.

During the same period, more than 2,000 Christians were murdered because of their faith. Reacting to these ever-growing numbers and the continued violence, the Roman Catholic Archbishop Jean Sleiman of Baghdad said: "Let us break the wall of silence that surrounds the killing of Christians in Iraq. Christians are killed in Mosul while the state does nothing. The forces of order serving in the places of the attacks and killings don't see, don't hear, don't speak!"

The most horrific act committed in 2010 was by a group with ties to al Qaeda, known as the Islamic State of Iraq, the forerunner of ISIS. These extremists attacked Baghdad's Our Lady of Deliverance Syrian Catholic Cathedral during Sunday Mass October 31. The terrorists entered the church carrying automatic weapons and demanded the release of al Qaeda prisoners, including the widow of the former leader of the Islamic State of Iraq. The gunmen taunted the Christian captives. The siege came to a head when U.S. and Iraqi forces surrounded the cathedral. In the end, 58 people were dead and 70 were wounded. Two young priests were killed and another was seriously wounded.

The Islamic State struck again one week later in a Baghdad Christian neighborhood. Three were murdered and 26 were injured. Pope Benedict sent word to the Christians in Baghdad that he was "praying for the victims of this absurd violence, which is even more ferocious as it struck defenseless people, gathered in the house of God, a house of love and reconciliation."

The year ended with two people being killed and more than a dozen wounded by bombs exploding in Baghdad Christian neighborhoods during the Christmas season. Commenting on the violence, Archbishop Sako declared: "For us Christians of Iraq, martyrdom is the charism of our Church in its 2,000-year history. We are aware that bearing witness to Christ can mean martyrdom."

In 2011 and 2012 Christians in Iraq continued to suffer. Churches and homes were bombed and more priests and Christian laity were kidnapped. Christian-owned businesses were looted and burnt to the ground. There was continued anti-Christian discrimination in workplaces as well as forced religious conversions.

On Easter Sunday 2011, two bombs exploded outside two churches in Baghdad's Karrada district. In August, in Kirkuk, St. Ephrem's Syrian Orthodox Church and the Holy Family Church were bombed. Thirteen were injured. Another bomb at an Evangelical church failed to explode.

Reacting to the violence, Archbishop Louis Sako said: "We are very shocked. To attack a holy place such as a church makes the crime serious and to attack it during a holy season, Ramadan, makes it even worse. To attack and to put people's lives at risk in this way is always a sin." The archbishop insisted, however, that "despite what has happened we will never give up. We will continue our mission. We will never stop witnessing to Christ."

After weekly prayers on the first Friday in December 2011, over 500 people in Zakho, Kurdistan left their mosque and set fire to Christian-owned shops while shouting "Allahu Akbar"—"God is Great." In another town, Dohuk, a mob of about 3,000 attacked and destroyed Christian properties.

Speaking to the Catholic News Agency, *Asia News*, on December 21, 2011, Archbishop Sako announced that "Midnight Christmas Mass has been cancelled in Baghdad, Mosul and Kirkuk as a consequence of the never-ending assassinations of Christians and the attack against Our Lady of Perpetual Help Cathedral on October 31, which killed 57 people."

A study released in 2012 revealed that between 2004 and 2011, 71 churches were bombed or attacked—63 of them in Mosul and Baghdad. Christian leaders also reported that 600 Christians had been murdered, approximately 60 percent of them in Baghdad, during the same period. Of the dead, 17 were priests. Those murdered in 2012 included children, one being a seven-month-old baby. One teenager was murdered for being a "Christian sinner"; another was crucified in Mosul. And 52 people died in March 2012 when St. Matthew's Syrian Orthodox Church in Baghdad was bombed by Muslim radicals.

Pressure on Christians to leave the country for good continued. One Islamist group, Ansar al-Islam, posted this threat on its website: "The secretary general of the Islamic Brigade has decided to give the Christian Crusader infidels of Baghdad and the other provinces a final warning to leave Iraq immediately and permanently and join Benedict XVI and his followers who have trampled on the greatest symbols of humanity and Islam. . . . There will be no place for Christian infidels from now on. . . . Those who remain will have their throats slit."

In 2014, Iraqi Christians witnessed the jihadist advance of ISIS that threatened their very existence. On June 9, the army of ISIS seized Mosul's airport and the next day it took control of the city, Iraq's second largest. On June 11, it conquered Tikrit, 95 miles north of Baghdad. The International Organization for Migration reported that during ISIS's siege of the city, more than 500,000 people fled to escape the violence.

CHRISTIAN PERSECUTIONS IN THE MIDDLE EAST

The Christians who lived in the provincial capital of Mosul on the Nineveh Plain—in ancient times the City of Nineveh—have ancestors whose roots go back to the very beginning of Christianity. The region had been the traditional home of Assyrian Christians and gave birth to the monastic movement. But in June 2014, all the Christians fled Mosul. The city's Archbishop Amel Nona announced June 11 that the last Christians had left the city. In ten years the number of local Christians had declined from 35,000 to just several thousand.

Describing reports of attacks on churches and monasteries, Archbishop Nona said: "We received threats . . . [and] now all the faithful have fled the city. I wonder if they will ever return here. . . . My diocese no longer exists; ISIS has taken it away from me."

Open Doors, a religious freedom advocacy group, agreed with the archbishop. "This could be the last migration of Christians from Mosul," its representative said referring to the 1,000 Christians who left on June 10, 2014. "The Islamist terrorists want to make Iraq a 'Muslim only' nation and as a result they want all Christians out," Open Doors President Dr. David Curry said.

Pascale Ward, a former Minister of Immigration and Refugees in Iraq, in a June 23, 2014 interview with Medium.com, gave this assessment about the future prospects for Assyrians and other Christians in Iraq:

> The future of the Christians of Iraq as well as Syria and the whole Middle East is in great danger. They face extinction in their original countries because they are easily targeted by fanatics using Islamic rules of sharia interpreted and imposed through the brutal policies of ISIS. Western countries are at a loss when faced with the massive number of immigration requests to join families together from the old country.
>
> As long as an international conscience is not forthcoming and goodwill initiatives are not planned to hear the voices of victims and provide them with protection and compensation for the persecution they have been

subject to for dozens of years, they will continue to flee from their countries. This is a destructive fact not only regarding the Christian presence in Iraq and Syria but for Iraqi and Syrian societies as a whole.

Iraqi Christians are not nomads whose way of life is to pack their tent on their camel and move to another place without leaving an impact. When the Christians of Iraq leave they will close schools, hospitals, colleges. Their flight will put an end to the diversity that represents the beauty and richness Iraqi Society has enjoyed for thousands of years.

The leadership of ISIS announced June 29, 2014 the creation of a Caliphate—an Islamic state in Iraq and Syria. Three weeks later, on July 24, to show their contempt for Christians and Jews, they blew up Jonah's tomb, one of the holiest sites in Mosul.

The most fearless and outspoken Christian cleric throughout this crisis has been Archbishop Louis Sako, whose appointment as Patriarch of Baghdad of the Chaldeans was confirmed by Pope Benedict February 2, 2013.

Commenting on the rise of political Islam, he said in September 2012 that it "is a matter of worry." He pointed out that "we Christians are a minority and there is no prospect of us gaining equal citizenship in the concrete reality of day-to-day life and there is no vision of a better future. . . . Everyone is speaking of democracy and freedom, but the reality on the ground is different. The sectarianism is gaining ground and the majority is not taking care of minority groups."

At his installation as patriarch March 6, 2013, he told members of his flock: "Do not withdraw or emigrate [under] pressure. This is your country and your land. If emigration continues God forbid, there will be no more Christians in the Middle East. [The Church] will be no more than a distant memory."

After ISIS captured Qaragosh, another important majority Christian town near Mosul on August 7, 2014, Sako made a plea to the international community to provide humanitarian aid. "The

Christians," he declared in an open letter, "horrified and panicked, fled their village and houses [with] nothing but the clothes on their back. They are facing a human catastrophe and risk a real genocide. . . . We appeal with sadness and pain to the consciences of all, and all people of good will and the United Nations and the European Union, to save these innocent persons from death. We hope it is not too late."

Two weeks later, disappointed by the lack of response from the West, Sako, in a statement titled "To the Conscience of the World," wrote:

> It has become obvious that Iraqi Christians along with other minorities have received a fatal blow at the core of their lives and their existence whether through displacing more than a hundred thousand Christians by force, or looting their possessions, money, and documents, or occupying their houses *for just being Christian*! I visited the camps of the displaced persons in the provinces of Erbil and Dohok and what I saw and what I heard is beyond any imagination! . . .
>
> The international community, principally the United States and European Union due to their moral and historic responsibility towards Iraq, cannot be indifferent. While acknowledging all that is being done to solve this crisis, it seems that the decisions and actions undertaken until now have made no real change in the course of events and the fate of these affected people is still at stake, as if these people are not part of the human race!
>
> Religious fundamentalism is still growing in its power and force, creating tragedies, and making us wonder when the Islamic religious scholars and the Muslim intellectuals will critically examine this dangerous phenomenon and eradicate it by educating a true religious consciousness and spreading a genuine culture of accepting the other as brother and as an equal citizen with full rights.

What has happened is terrible and horrific, therefore, we need an urgent and effective international support from all the people of good will to save the Christians and Yazidis, genuine components of the Iraqi society from extinction, knowing that silence and passivity will encourage ISIS fundamentalists to commit more tragedies! *The question is who will be next?*

Throughout 2014, many of the refugees sought shelter in Kurdistan. This autonomous zone in the north of Iraq has served for many years as a place of refuge for Christians. It is in that area that Iraqi bishops are hoping many of their faithful can find new homes. This migration of Christians to northern Iraq, however, has presented new challenges for Iraq's various churches. Local church facilities are bursting at the seams trying to accommodate and provide religious, medical and other services to the newcomers.

In the fall of 2014, more than one-third of all Christians in Iraq were living as refugees in their own country. In Erbil, the capital of Kurdish Iraq, for example, there are more than 100,000 Chaldean Christians who have fled their homes in Mosul and surrounding areas.

The bishops are reporting that morale among the people in the refugee camps is low. Aid to the Church in Need official Karin Fenbert, who visited the area and met with leading clergy in October 2014, reported that "the Christians feel betrayed: betrayed by their central government in Baghdad; betrayed by their former Muslim neighbors; and betrayed also by the international community. They feel that they are being perceived merely as collateral damage in geopolitical power plays."

As winter approached, charitable groups like Aid to the Church in Need are attempting to provide adequate shelter for thousands of people. The goal is to get them out of tents pitched on Church properties and into weatherproof residential modules. Schools are also being built and other facilities are being erected to improve sanitary conditions.

Meanwhile, horrors continued. During the 2014 Christmas season, Anglican Canon Andrew White, who is known as the "Vicar of Baghdad," revealed that four Christian children under the age of 15 were beheaded by ISIS for refusing to denounce Jesus and convert to Islam. "ISIS turned up and said to the children, 'You say the words that you will follow Muhammad,'" White said. "The children . . . said, 'No, we love Jesus, we have always loved Jesus.' They chopped all their heads off."

"How do you respond to that?," White asked. "You just cry."

The New York Times, in an article published December 25, 2014, titled "Traditions of Christmas Found Only In Memory," described the plight of Christian refugees who escaped Qaragosh and settled in Baghdad, living in schools and other facilities. Reporter Tim Arango wrote that "to get by, they have relied on the kindness of the nearby church and of local Muslims, too."

One parent said that the children "don't really understand what is happening in their villages. . . . It's very hard. We are always crying. We miss Qaragosh and want to go home." As for the parents themselves, "added to their grief is the burden of memories of what Christmases used to be like. . . . The neighbors, the kisses, the happiness."

Yet, in spite of all the misery and hardship, the refugees still had hope which was expressed in a sign posted to a tree that the *Times* reporter spotted. It read: "Fill Iraqis hearts with love and peace, and deliver my country from this situation, and make Iraq a country where everyone feels that he is accepted and loved, so that the entire people will feel they are one family."

Assessing the refugee situation, Father Andrezej Halemba— who heads the Middle East desk for Aid to the Church in Need— visited the displaced Christians of Iraq in late 2014. He reported that the greatest challenge "is the mentality of the people." He fears that "they may be turning their backs on Iraq and the Middle East forever." When asked if the Christians in Kurdish Iraq still have hope, he said:

> It is a very difficult situation. Without question, we are talking about genocide here. Genocide is not only when the people are killed, but also when the soul of a people

is destroyed. And that is what is happening in Iraq now. It is the most tragic thing that I have ever experienced.

I have seen people who have been deeply wounded in their soul. In the various crises in this world I have often seen people who have lost everything. But in Iraq there are Christians who have had to leave everything and take flight three or four times. They can see no light at the end of the tunnel.

They are all very traumatized. Normally in such situations it is the women who pull everything together. But in Kurdistan I have seen women who are staring into nothingness and have closed in on themselves. Their tears have run dry. It is something that I have never seen anywhere else.

The men, by contrast, tend to aggressiveness. This has to do with the fact that they are no longer able to fulfil [sic] their previous role as the breadwinner and protector of their family. Now they have to beg for everything and they have no perspective.

If Iraqi Christians are ever to believe again in a future in their ancient and beautiful country, Father Halemba added, "the international community must work towards ensuring that the government in Baghdad is strengthened and incorporates all the religious and ethnic groups in the country. Only in this way can ISIS be ultimately defeated."

CHAPTER 8
IRAN

Since the Shah of Iran, Mohammad Reza Pahlavi, was overthrown in 1979, the people of Iran have been governed by Shiite religious leaders. "The Islamic revolution," as the Hudson Institute's Paul Marshall has written, "produced a regime controlled by Islamic jurists and clerics committed to the spirit and ethics of Islam as the basis of all political, social and economic activities."

Iran's political system is highly restrictive. The nation's penal code is based on sharia law and members of the judiciary are chosen based on their religious qualifications. All prospective candidates for office must be approved by the Council of Guardians, limiting participation in elections to supporters of the absolute power of the supreme religious leader, the Ayatollah.

Iran is a nation in which Shia Islam and the state are one and the same. This status is confirmed in Article 4 of Iran's Constitution: "All civil, penal, financial, economic, administrative, cultural, military, political, and other laws and regulations must be based on Islamic criteria. This principle applies absolutely and generally to all articles of the Constitution as well as to all other laws and regulations, and the *fuquha'* [experts in Islam] of the Guardian Council are judges in this matter."

The three minorities that are recognized in Article 13 of the constitution—Christians, Jews and Zoroastrians—are considered *Dhimmi*, that is, second-class citizens who are denied many rights. In "Persecuted: The Global Assault on Christians," Nina Shea and her co-authors point out that in Iran there is systematic discrimination and repression of religious minorities. "All religious groups suffer: Bahais, Christians, Mandaeans, Jews, Zoroastrians, Sunnis, and dissenting Shia Muslims. Many minorities are dwindling; the ancient Assyrians and Mandaeans have almost disappeared. Although Iran is a signatory to U.N. human rights conventions, senior Iranian leaders denounce them as Western aberrations."

Christians and other minorities are prohibited from propagating their faith and those that are found guilty of doing so can be condemned to death. All public expressions of their faiths are also banned. Furthermore, conversion from Islam to Christianity is illegal. Publications of religious materials are forbidden and publishers of the Bible and other non-Islamic faith literature have been shut down by government order.

Religious minorities are also banned from major posts in the government and military, and are forbidden from serving on the judiciary and as principals of schools. In the 290-member Iranian Parliament, there can be only three Christians, one Jewish member and one Zoroastrian.

Catholics of every rite are permitted to worship and celebrate Mass at their churches, but public worship in any form is strictly forbidden. Catholics, like all Christians, tend to go along with the government-imposed modesty rules and dress codes to avoid being fined or arrested by the "modesty patrols" that travel throughout neighborhoods in search of violators.

During Church services, Iranian police are always present. Although the public perception is that the guards are protecting Christians from violence, the actual purpose is to prevent any Muslims from participating in the services.

Protestants are recognized as Christians, but because they are not viewed as being part of the Churches of the apostolic tradition their exact status in Iran is unclear. "House churches" that have been organized as underground communities have become targets of the government. A number of their leaders have been assassinated or sentenced to death.

The Iranian regime claims that religious minorities have rights, but that has not stopped Ayatollah Ahmad Jannati, who serves as chairman of the Council of Guardians, from publicly insisting that non-Muslims are "animals who roam the earth and engage in corruption." Some Iranian laws appear to treat them as less than human. "The penalty for killing women, Christians, Jews or Zoroastrians," Nina Shea has reported, "is less than that for killing a Muslim. Murdering people of other unrecognized religions, such as Bahais, has no legal ramifications. Killing them, or killing those who leave Islam, carries no punishment. But for even consensual sexual relations between a non-Muslim man and a Muslim woman, the non-Muslim faces death."

At the turn of the twenty-first century, there were approximately 200,000 Christians residing in Iran, a tiny fraction out of a total population of 66 million. The largest groups, about 170,000, are Greek and Assyrian Orthodox. About 20,000 are Roman Catholic, Chaldean or Armenian Catholic, while Protestants total some 10,000.

Reports of persecutions of Christians in Iran prompted Pope John Paul II, in a meeting at the Vatican with the Iranian Minister of Foreign Affairs Kamal Kharrazi, to insist that human rights, particularly the right of religious freedom for minority groups, must be guaranteed in every country.

The Pope's reminder did not have any impact. In May 2004, a Protestant minister, Khosroo Yusefi, and his wife Nasrin and their two children were arrested in northern Iran for converting Muslims to Christianity. Five weeks later it was reported that word went out from the government that a recent Iranian convert to Christianity, who had fled to Turkey, should be killed.

The Chaldean Archbishop of Teheran, the Most Reverent Ramzi Garmou, told Oasis International Review in early 2005 that the number of Christians living in Iran was dropping "due to a birth rate that is lower among Christians, but above all due to emigration which has accelerated since the Islamic revolution and the war against Iraq." He added: "Obviously, there are also human, cultural, socio-economic and historical aspects at the root of such a phenomenon. But the fact that the Christians belong to minorities that are distinguished not only by their religious faith but also by their language and culture has made them doubly strangers in the eyes of the people."

This fear of being a stranger grew in August 2005 when Mahmoud Ahmadinejad was elected president. Ahmadinejad was best known for insisting that the Jewish Holocaust was a myth and his call for Israel "to be wiped off the map."

Under his rule, domestic censorship increased and his revolutionary ideas were imposed on all segments of government, including the fire department and traffic police. In addition to beefing up modesty patrols, he cracked down on dissident trade unions, journalists, and intellectuals as well as on the use of the internet and satellite TV.

Under Ahmadinejad, Iran's secret police took on a more active role in persecution of Muslim converts to Christianity. On May 2, 2006, 51-year old Ali Kaboli was arrested for converting to Christianity 33 years earlier. One Iranian familiar with the situation said: "Everybody knew that his house was under [police surveillance] for many years. They even pushed him to leave the country about three years ago, but he told them he preferred to stay inside the country, even if it meant living in an Iranian jail."

At 7 a.m. on September 26, 2006, the secret police entered the home in northeastern Iran of an Iranian Christian, Fereshteh, and her husband Amir. The couple was arrested, their computers and Christian books were removed from their residence and they were incarcerated in a secret prison operated by the Revolutionary Guards, the country's elite military corps.

Thanks to worldwide media coverage of the incident, the couple was released on bail on October 6. *Middle East Concern* reported that the "authorities linked the arrest to the Christian activities of the couple." They had managed a church in their home which was visited by many pilgrims. Also, Fereshteh's father had been arrested when she was six years old on charges of apostasy. Although he was sentenced to death he was released thanks to international pressure. However, he was abducted and murdered a few weeks after his release in 1984.

Iran's secret police launched raids in January 2007 on Christians in four communities. Fifteen members of the Free Evangelical movement were arrested on charges of evangelization and acts against national security. Several weeks later all the suspects were released except the Evangelical leader, Behrouz Sadegh-Khanjani. He remained in detention charged with not paying damages related to an accident with an uninsured rental car.

In May 2008, 12 Christian converts were arrested and held in undisclosed locations. During their detention, they were pressured to renounce their faith. They were released when they agreed to cease missionary activities.

The crackdown continued in 2009. In January of that year, three Church of the Assemblies of God members were arrested in Teheran for holding Bible studies in their homes. A month later they were released on bail.

Two converts to Christianity were arrested in March on charges of "acting against the security of the state" because they had distributed Bibles. A judge told them five months later that unless they renounced what he labeled their apostasy they would be sentenced to jail. They were released in November 2009 and acquitted of charges in May 2010, thanks to international pressure. Nonetheless, the pair felt compelled to flee the country.

That same month, an Islamic court found three Christian converts guilty of "cooperating with anti-government movements." They received an eight-month suspended sentence and five years' probation for being involved with a Christian TV station. The judge instructed the three Christians that they were forbidden to contact one another after their release and warned he would have them tried for apostasy if they disobeyed his orders.

The clampdown on demonstrations after the widely-believed fraudulent re-election of President Ahmadinejad in June of 2009 affected Christians who were being accused of pro-Western sympathies. The U.S. Commission on International Religious Freedom reported that, since the election, "religious freedom conditions have digressed to a point not seen since the early days of the Islamic Revolution of 1979." At least 300 Christians were arrested and detained between June 2010 and February 2012; most experts believe the numbers are much higher. While in jail, these Christians have suffered in solitary confinement and have been deprived of sleep and medical care.

Government harassment and indiscriminate arrests explain why the number of Christians in Iran is dwindling. A report posted on the Foreign Policy website in November 2010 claimed that the number of Assyrian Christians in Iran had dropped from 100,000 in 1979 to just 15,000. This decline occurred during a period when the nation's population increased from 38 million to 72 million.

Throughout 2009 and 2010, people holding services in "house churches" were constantly harassed or arrested, particularly during the Christmas season. In December 2009, at least 14 Christians were thrown in jail for several weeks and denied legal counsel. Their alleged crime was celebrating Christmas in a home. In December 2010, the police arrested 70 Christians for attending Christmas services in "house churches."

In 2011, Christian pastors received jail sentences for "crimes against national security" and "propaganda against the regime." More than 6,000 pocket Bibles were seized while being transported to a northwestern province in Iran. A government spokesman accused the Christians carrying the Bibles of trying to deceive Iranians. "They have begun a huge campaign," he said, "by spending huge sums on false propaganda for deceiving the public. . . . The important point in this issue that should be considered by intelligence, judicial and religious agencies is that all religions are strengthening their power to confront Islam, otherwise what does this huge number of Bibles mean?"

Such anti-Christian propaganda has been sanctioned and promoted by the government via state media. According to the Barnabas Fund, slanderous stories about Christians have appeared in government media. One such article, published on the website Youth Online, alleged that women missionaries "were going into stores, using shopping as a pretext to enter into conversation with staff, and then suggesting sexual liaisons and insulting Islam."

One significant case of a persecuted Christian that received a considerable amount of international attention was that of Protestant Pastor Youcef Nadarkhani. Arrested in 2009 for questioning the "unconstitutional" Muslim monopoly on the religious education of young people, he was initially accused of challenging Iranian law and later charged with apostasy and proselytizing Muslims. Nadarkhani, who converted to Christianity at age 19, declared he was not a Muslim prior to his conversion even though his parents were Muslim. He insisted that he had no religious persuasion as he was growing up.

Despite his claims, an Iranian court ruled in 2010 that he had abandoned his Islamic faith and was guilty of apostasy from Islam and sentenced to death by hanging, a penalty that was excluded from the new penal code approved in September 2008. The Court of Appeals upheld the death sentence in September 2010, but the Supreme Court referred the case to the lower court for further investigation in June 2011.

After the lower court reaffirmed the death sentence on September 30, 2011, international protests, which had persisted throughout the trial, reached new heights. Responding to the pressure, the Iranian representative to the U.N. Commission for Human Rights in Geneva, Mohammad Javad Larijani, publicly insisted that the Nadarkhani death sentence would not be carried out. "In the past 33 years," he said, "since the Islamic revolution, no one has been put to death or persecuted for having changed religion or abandoning Islam."

When Pastor Nadarkhani was pressed once again in early 2012 to renounce his Christian faith and convert to Islam to secure his release, he refused. Coming to his defense, Tiffany Barrans, an international director at the American Center for Law and Justice, stated: "The latest attempt to pressure Pastor Youcef to acknowledge Muhammad as a messenger of God violates both the Iranian Constitution and various principles of international law, which Iran is obliged to uphold."

Protests continued from government leaders around the world, including President Obama. In a statement released on September 30, 2011, he said: "The United States condemns the conviction of Pastor Youcef Nadarkhani. Pastor Nadarkhani has done nothing more than maintain his devout faith, which is universal for all people. That the Iranian authorities would try to force him to renounce that faith violates the religious values they claim to defend, crosses all bounds of decency, and breaches Iran's own international obligations."

Succumbing to pressure, the pastor's case was referred to Iran's Supreme Leader Ayatollah Khamenei. He altered the charges to crimes against national security. He was acquitted of apostasy but found guilty of proselytizing in September 2012. He was set free on the grounds that the time he had already served in jail was sufficient. On Christmas Day 2012, Nadarkhani was locked up again, but he was released in early January 2013.

All the international attention and pressure generated by the Nadarkhani case did not stop Christian persecution in Iran. Only weeks after the release of Nadarkhani, another pastor, Saeed Abedini, who was arrested and placed in Evin prison, was sentenced to eight years in prison January 27, 2013 for damaging national security by promoting his religious beliefs. Officials at the prison told him after his conviction was announced: "Deny your faith in Jesus Christ and return to Islam or else you will not be released from prison. We will make sure you are kept here even after your eight-year sentence is finished."

Many Christians were hopeful that the attitude of the government would change under the leadership of Hassan Rouhani, who, upon his election as the seventh president of Iran in 2013, said he was committed to "upholding justice across the country and civil rights." He even added: "What I wish for is for moderation to return to the country. This is my only wish. Extremism pains me greatly. We have seen many blows as a result of extremism."

Despite his calls for moderation, most Iranian observers have questioned his sincerity. They cite his hard-line religious background and the pre-eminence of the Supreme Leader Khamenei when it comes to making public-policy decisions. Also, there are fears that the government will crack down on the growing numbers of Christians who have fled war-torn Middle Eastern countries and have sought refuge in Iran. There are estimates that Iran is now home to more than 300,000 Christian refugees.

Finally, Aid to the Church in Need reported in its 2014 profile of Iran that "state oppression of Christians and other minorities in Iran has intensified markedly, especially arrests, torture, false imprisonments and executions, with a corresponding increase in raids on churches and confiscation of Bibles."

CHAPTER 9
SAUDI ARABIA

Founded in 1932, the Kingdom of Saudi Arabia, carved out of the formerly Ottoman-ruled kingdoms of Hejaz and Nejd, includes within its boundaries Islam's holiest cities, Mecca and Medina. The first king was Abd al-Aziz and his heirs rule the nation to this day. The king's word in any matter is final and criticism of the regime is strictly forbidden. There are no political parties or elections and the media is controlled by the government.

The nation and Islam are fully integrated, with the Quran serving as the constitution and sharia law as the basis of the legal system. As a result, Peter Marshall reported in his 2000 book "Religious Freedom in the World," "persons convicted of rape, murder, armed robbery, adultery, apostasy, and drug trafficking face death by beheading."

Because Mecca, the birthplace of Islam's founder Muhammad, is within its borders, the regime believes it is the custodian of Islamic values. In addition, the Saudi monarchy has long embraced Wahhabism, a very conservative, even "puritanical' form of Sunni Islam dedicated to purifying Islam of any innovations that deviate from seventh-century practice. This Islamic school of thought, founded by Muhammad ibn Abd al-Wahhab in the eighteenth century, holds a strict, literalist view of sharia law and, in its earliest phases, its champions destroyed Islamic shrines and tombs in the region that it considered inauthentic or idolatrous expressions of the faith, something ISIS has also begun to do. Wahhabism, a Sunni movement, was and remains strongly opposed to Shia practices. Given its literalist bent, Saudi Arabia has shown remarkable intolerance for Christians and Jews, the "People of the book."

Public practice of non-Muslim religions has for most of Saudi Arabia's history been strictly forbidden, as is the wearing of religious symbols.

In a 1994 report titled "When Islam is not tolerant," researcher Lucia Avallone documented "that all forms of worship other than Sunni Islam are forbidden. Many people have been arrested simply for having expressed their religious faith." The *Mutawwa'in*, a ruthless religious police force, monitors the activities of non-Muslim and Shiite Muslims and have been known to make mass arrests of Christians, subjecting them to torture. Often, prisoners will not be released until they agree in writing to renounce their faith.

In the early years of the regime there were very few Christians residing in Saudi Arabia. However, that changed when the oil industry began to expand at a rapid pace. Needing labor, the House of Saud encouraged foreigners in search of employment to emigrate to the Arabian Peninsula (though with the strict understanding that they could only stay as long as they were employed).

By the end of the twentieth century there were six million foreigners working in Saudi Arabia, approximately one third of the total population. It was estimated that 600,000 of them are Christians, with Filipinos accounting for two-thirds of this total.

This growing Christian population is forbidden to celebrate Christmas but is expected to observe Ramadan, an annual month of fasting. And it has been reported that hundreds have been arrested by the religious police for holding or taking part in prayer meetings in private homes.

One of the most notorious examples of persecution was the case of Filipino Donnie Lama. This Catholic was arrested in October 1995 and was not released until March 1997, when an expulsion order was issued. Lama was arrested for having attended a private Mass 13 years earlier. He was released from prison thanks to international pressure. But during his incarceration, Lama was tortured and received 70 lashes.

Other Filipinos were arrested in 1998 for distributing Bibles to co-religionists. Amnesty International reported that the 12 Christians tortured in prison for possessing Bibles were finally released and expelled from Saudi Arabia.

In this century, the Christian population, which has grown to about 900,000 and is mostly Catholic, has continued to be harassed and persecuted despite claims that the anti-Christian laws are less severe for foreign workers.

In 2001, the Saudi government launched a series of attacks on Christians, particularly in the City of Jeddah. International Christian Concern in 2001 published an article by Steven Snyder entitled "Saudi Arabia Continues Sweep of Christians"; he wrote that "during the past three weeks, six Christians in Saudi Arabia have been visited by the Ministry of the Interior. The names of these Christians were obtained by torturing other Christians." By year's end it was estimated that more than 100 Christians had been incarcerated. The common belief among watchdog organizations is that the police would pressure their Christian captives to name any Saudis that have shown an interest in the Christian faith.

In 2002, the arrests continued. One of the detainees, Baharu Mangistu, told International Christian Concern: "On January 28, 2002, by order of the Bremen Deportation Prison Commander Major Bender Sultan Shabani and with no hearing, trial or process of law, we were illegally subjected to severe punishment and physical abuse. Being suspended with chains, the three of us were flogged 80 times with a flexible metal cable, and also severely kicked and beaten with anything that came into their hands. This was witnessed by over 1,000 deportees."

Later in the year, at the start of Ramadan, Christians were warned not to eat, drink or smoke in public. The Ministry of Interior told the non-Muslim population that violators arrested by the police would be subject to "deterrent measures," including loss of employment and deportation.

Brian O'Connor, an Indian Catholic, was arrested by religious police on March 25, 2004 on the charge of evangelizing in Riyadh. International Christian Concern reported that he was imprisoned and tortured in a mosque and later transferred to a police station.

The Indian bishops' conference sent a letter protesting the arrest but it was ignored by the government. Four months later O'Connor was found guilty of selling alcohol and evangelizing. He was sentenced to ten months in prison and 300 lashes. The sentencing was suspended for time served in jail.

Released on November 2, 2004, O'Connor was put on a plane to Bombay. Concerning his time in prison, he told *Asia News*: "I was miserable and, at times, frightened, not knowing what new false charges would be levied against me, all my personal belongings confiscated, my room ransacked. I was imprisoned in a cell with 17 other inmates; people convicted on charges ranging from murder to drug peddling and other such heinous crimes. Initially, whenever I tried to pray, I faced stiff resistance and antagonism from my fellow cell mates."

During the same period, al Qaeda began operations in the country. In May, Reuters detailed a shooting rampage in Khobar. Before murdering innocent passers-by, the Islamic militants asked potential victims: "Are you Muslim or Christian? We don't want to kill Muslims." The al Qaeda operatives went on to kill 22 people, wound 25 and to hold 240 as hostages for 25 hours. What turned this tragedy into a theatre of the absurd was the reaction of Muslim survivors. One told Reuters: "The four gunmen had been polite and calm. They gave me a lecture on Islam and said they were defending their country and ridding it of infidels. The gunmen were so polite. I cannot comprehend this politeness they showed me because I am a Muslim." Strikingly, Reuters headlined its story: "Cool gunmen hunted down Christians."

A textbook for children was issued in 2004 that denigrated Christians and Jews, stating: "All religions other than Islam, are false." The publisher was a Sheikh who is a proponent of slavery and argues that "elections are un-Islamic." There was also a report that a Muslim chemistry teacher was arrested for allegedly referring to the Bible in one of his classes and for making positive statements about Jews. The educator was convicted of "deriding Islam" and sentenced to 14 months in prison; he received 750 lashes.

U.S. Secretary of State Condoleezza Rice, in 2005, urged the

Saudis to recognize the rights of religious minorities or face economic sanctions. The State Department, in their 7th Annual Report on Religious Liberty in the World, which is presented to Congress every year, said that the Saudis were "suffocating religious minorities."

The Center for Human Rights in Saudi Arabia, reported at year's end that despite pressure from the United States and other countries, "the Saudi government has still neither proposed nor applied any provision [of religious freedom]."

Indeed, 2005 was not a good year for Christians in Saudi Arabia. In April, 40 Pakistani Christians were arrested by the religious police charged with attending a service at a private home in Riyadh. The police seized books of alleged Christian propaganda as well as crosses. According to *Al Jazeera*, the police raided the home that had been holding weekly prayer meetings for some time because a Pakistani Muslim, living in the neighborhood, had admitted to authorities of "being influenced by Christian thought."

The next month the religious police arrested the five leaders of a Christian group of Ethiopians and Eritreans. The five, who spent their time in jail in restraints, were released in May. In another incident during May, eight Indian Christians were arrested for meeting to study the Bible. They were freed from jail about a month later after agreeing not to have any more study or prayer sessions.

Father George Joshua, an Indian priest who was sent to Saudi Arabia to help with Easter Masses for Indian Catholics working in the country, was thrown in jail April 5, 2006 for saying Mass in a private room for a group of foreign Catholics. The police, the priest said, "spoke to me and listed all the places I had been until then, all my activities, the group prayers I organized in private homes. . . . Then they forced me to put back on my vestments and made me stand in front of the table we had used as an altar and in front of the crucifix. They took many photographs as evidence that I was a Christian priest performing illegal religious activities."

Father Joshua was released four days later and was immediately deported back to India. But the priest refused to give up. Back home he founded the Christ Army for Saudi Arabia, whose members are dedicated to praying and fasting for the cause of religious freedom.

Throughout 2006 and 2007 there were continued raids on foreign Christian workers practicing their faith in Saudi Arabia. A typical case was that of a Filipino Christian arrested in October 2006 in Jeddah. At first he was accused of possessing drugs. The charge was later changed to proselytism. The Filipino was held in jail for eight months and was given 60 lashes before being deported to the Philippines.

Saudi King Abdullah, who inherited the throne in 2005, was viewed by the West as a modernizer and not an ultra-conservative Sunni. Hence, there were hopes he would trim the powers of the religious police and permit immigrant Christian workers to practice their faith in private. This perception led to an historic meeting between Pope Benedict XVI and King Abdullah in the Vatican November 6, 2007. According to *Al-Jazeera*, the two leaders discussed the "situation experienced by the Christian minority of Saudi Arabia, the need for greater interreligious cooperation and prospects for peace in the Middle East."

The Apostolic Vicar of Southern Arabia, Monsignor Paul Hinder, said about the meeting: "I believe [it] was also an excellent opportunity for discussing the religious rights of Christians in Saudi Arabia. This subject is not explicitly mentioned in the press release but there was mention of 'the positive and industrious presence of Christians.' I believe that within this framework the Pope was also able to discuss freedom of worship in Saudi Arabia."

It was also reported that during the meeting the Pope inquired about plans to build the first church in Saudi Arabia. He pointed out that, by Easter 2008, Qatar would have a church, making Saudi Arabia the only country in the Arab Peninsula without an official public place for the practice of Christian religion. The King replied that he would consider building a church.

It was later learned, however, that the King decided against it. Five months after the Vatican meeting, Saudi Arabian scholar Anwar Ashiqi dismissed any plans of granting permission for the building of a church. *Der Spiegel* reported him saying that "it would be possible to launch official negotiations to construct a church in Saudi Arabia only after the Pope and all the Christian churches recognize the prophet Muhammad."

There had been numerous statements published by the Saudi government during the reign of the late King Abdullah declaring that non-Muslim workers would be permitted to worship in private, but there is little evidence that the decrees have been implemented. This situation is unlikely to change significantly under the reign of King Salman, King Abdullah's brother and successor.

In January 2009, Eritrean Pastor Yemane Gebriel, the leader of an underground church with 300 members for ten years, was forced to leave the country for an unknown destination. Days later, Hamoud Bin Saleh was imprisoned for describing on *The Christian for Saudis* blog his conversion story. Released in March, he was put under a travel ban and was forbidden to publish his writing.

After returning home to the Philippines in December 2009, Norma Caldera described her short stint as a maid for a Saudi family to *Asia News*. She said she was constantly harassed because of her faith, denied a bed and was forced to sleep on the kitchen floor or in a tent outside the house. "When I told my employers that I was Catholic, the first thing they did was lower my salary. . . . Every day I got up early to pray and every time my colleagues and employers saw me they began to insult and mock me because of my Christian faith. I lived through this experience praying and having faith in God. I was willing to make this sacrifice to be able to pay for my two daughters' education."

Forced to go home five months before her contract with the Saudi family ended, Norma also said that she was banned during her stay from attending Mass and was forced to fast during Ramadan.

Twelve Filipino Catholics, arrested October 1, 2009, for attending a Mass celebrated by a French priest, were finally released into the custody of their employers in October 2010. The Philippine Embassy in Saudi Arabia negotiated their deportation.

The Saudi religious police in January 2011 began the new year by arresting two Indian members of a Pentecostal group called

"Rejoice in the Church of the Lord." It happened during a raid on a private home prayer meeting in Batha. During their time in jail, the Christians were pressured daily to convert to Islam, while they were forced to live in terrible conditions. In order to sleep in their tiny cell, one had to stand to allow the other to lie down. When finally released July 12, 2011, they were deported back to India.

There were numerous other reports of Christians being arrested for attending religious services and Bible study groups. Many were held in jail for months without trial. In one case the police not only locked up Christians who organized a Bible study group in July 2011 at a home in Riyadh, but confiscated Bibles, guitars, musical instruments and books. One who witnessed the raid told *Worthy News* that the religious police "broke furniture . . . and painted what I believe were Quranic verses on the walls."

The Human Rights Watch announced in January 2012 that 29 Christian women and six men were arrested and beaten after attending an Advent prayer meeting. *Asia News* reported that the women were forced to strip and undergo "body cavity" searches, while the men were insulted, beaten and called "unbelievers." The police charged their Christian prisoners with "unlawfully mingling" with unmarried people of the opposite sex.

The Grand Mufti of Saudi Arabia, in his capacity as the head of the Saudi Supreme Council of Islamic Scholars, issued a *fatwa* in March 2012 that answered a question raised by the Society for the Revival of Islamic Heritage "concerning the construction of Christian churches in Kuwait." The *fatwa* quoted the prophet Muhammad in proclaiming that Islam is the only religion that can exist in the Arabia peninsula. Calling for an end to all construction, he went on to say that permission for the building of Christian churches in the region would effectively acknowledge that Christian beliefs are true.

The 2013 U.S. State Department's International Religious Freedom Report concluded that during the previous 18 months the problem of acute persecution of Christians had not receded. While the report noted that some language concerning religious intolerance was removed from textbooks, the material still contained content justifying the social exclusion and even the killing of Christians and other religious minorities.

The situation in Saudi Arabia did not improve in 2013. In May, two men were found guilty of persuading a Muslim woman to convert to Christianity and helping her flee Saudi Arabia. The woman, who has remained anonymous, worked with the men at an insurance company. She fell in love with a Lebanese co-worker and converted; when it became public, she fled the country, eventually receiving asylum in Sweden. She later defended her decision on YouTube in July 2012. The boyfriend, who remained behind, received 300 lashes and was sentenced to six years in prison. The other co-worker was ordered to spend two years in jail and was lashed 200 times.

Saudi Arabia continues to have one of the worst records concerning religious freedom. Despite claims of relaxing laws and regulations prohibiting non-Muslim forms of worship, the religious police have continued to raid homes where Christians gather and severe penalties have been imposed on those who have been found guilty of proselytism. Also, clerics and other Christian leaders continue to travel incognito to minister to their flocks, and non-Muslims are prohibited from burying their dead in Saudi Arabia.

Finally, Saudi Arabia during the last 20 years has spent approximately $85 billion to promote Wahhabism throughout the world. Numerous observers have linked the Saudis' spread of Wahhabism to the persecution of Christians. In Bosnia-Herzegovina, for example, Saudi-funded Wahhabism has been identified as the root cause of increasing problems for Christians in the country. Former U.S. Ambassador Curtin Winsor, who served as Ronald Reagan's Special Emissary to the Middle East, has said: "It is the overwhelming wealth of Saudi Arabia that enables the Wahhabi sect to proselytize on a global scale, not the intrinsic appeal of its teachings."

CHAPTER 10
SUDAN/SOUTH SUDAN

In the final decades of the twentieth century, Sudan's single-party authoritarian sharia-based government waged war on the country's 6.6 million Christians and 18 million racial minorities living primarily in the nation's southern provinces. "Two million people," Paul Marshall of the Hudson Institute has written, "may have been killed in fighting and famine in southern Sudan [between 1995–2000] and five million have been made internal and external refugees."

After investigating the carnage, the United Nations Commission on Human Rights determined in 1996 that the principal victims of Khartoum's human rights violations have been members of racial and religious minorities living in southern Sudan. "In Sudan," U.N. spokesman Gaspar Biro said, "the whole range of human rights that are universally recognized have been violated. There have been summary executions, arbitrary arrests, detentions without trial, systematic torture, slavery and slave trade, violation of the rights of children and women, religious persecutions and forced conversion to Islam."

The U.S. Commission on International Religious Freedom concurred with the U.N.'s findings and accused the government of being "genocidal." Branding Sudan a terrorist state in 1993, the U.S. government placed economic sanctions on the country.

At the turn of the twenty-first century, the savage war waged against Christians and other minorities by the Muslims in the 16 provinces of northern Sudan and the ten provinces in the south continued. The Islamic government was funding and supplying weapons to the extremist Popular Defense Force and various Muslim tribes that were—at least prior to South Sudan gaining independence in 2011—spreading ruin and terror in southern Sudan.

"Every year, thousands of people die in the war," a priest in south Sudan told Aid to the Church in Need in 2000. "Some are killed in battle but there are also victims among innocent civilians who get caught in the crossfire. Many die of hunger and thirst because of the war. No journalists visit here to report on what goes on."

Bishop Cesare Mazzolari of Rumbek concurred with his priest. In a 2001 statement, the bishop accused the international community of "ignoring this tragedy." "These people are at death's door," he wrote. "In the evening, you can walk through any village, and you will not see a single fire in a hut . . . they do not cook because there is no food to cook, not even for their children."

One of Mazzolari's fellow bishops, Joseph Gasi, spoke more bluntly: "We are surprised and angry and concerned," he said. "Why does the international community not take any notice? It seems as if we are not part of the human race."

Almost every day in this new century there have been reports of Islamic persecutions, bombs dropped on Christian villages, summary executions, and attacks by radical groups on displaced and vulnerable Christians—just because of their faith.

Christian women, in particular, are treated severely for alleged breaches of sharia law. They are stoned when accused of adultery; jailed for possessing alcohol; denied jobs and whipped for failing to cover their legs and heads in public. All Christians are threatened with physical punishment or are fired from their jobs if they are caught attending Sunday Mass. They are forced to study Islam and are dismissed from civil service jobs if the government discovers that they are members of a Christian faith.

Many Christians in the north live in shanty-towns; their homes and churches and cemeteries are routinely demolished. Missionaries who are devoted to helping the displaced people in camps are often jailed and interrogated; next, if they are lucky, they are deported.

In February 2001, the Sudanese army marched into the villages of Chelkou and Mabior in South Sudan and took at least 103 women and children as slaves. It was estimated by local leaders in the area that perhaps as many as 100,000 Christians were being held in slavery in North Sudan. Muslim masters subject their slaves to violence, sexual abuse, unpaid work and forced conversion.

During the Lenten season in 2001, scores of Christians were arrested for protesting the government's decision to ban Easter services from Khartoum. In April of that year, 47 men were given 20 lashes and sentenced to 20 days imprisonment. Two women and two children received 15 lashes before being released.

That same week, an aircraft carrying Bishop Macram Max Gassis of El Obeid was attacked shortly after takeoff. The bishop and his entourage, who were traveling to Bahr al-Ghazal to celebrate Easter, survived the assault. On the ground one policeman died and two people were seriously injured.

During Holy Week that year, the Sudanese government bombed two civilian targets where Catholic bishops were present. The government then proceeded to drop 16 bombs on targets around the city of Narus, in Eastern Equatoria, on Holy Saturday. The bombs destroyed a marketplace and a Church-run school. Commenting on the attempts on his life, Bishop Gassis said: "The regime has regularly attempted to block my access to Catholics in these marginalized areas, and when it fails to prevent that, it seeks to disrupt our religious celebrations through the constant threat of aerial bombardment."

Bombers appeared in August 2001 over Christian villages and refugee camps in southern Sudan's Torit Diocese while people were attending Sunday Mass. A teenager and four men were injured.

During the month of October, the Sudanese Army attacked six Christian villages near the town of Nyamlell. At least 93 civilians were killed and 85 women and children were taken into slavery. One of the kidnapped women was Juliana Muiruri, a member of the staff of Church Ecumenical Action for Sudan.

Aerial bombing raids continued in 2002 and the Catholic Diocese of Torit appeared to be a particular target. Pointing out that this century the number of Catholics in his diocese had declined from 620,000 to 450,000, Auxiliary Bishop Akio Johnson Mutek said: "They are telling the world that they are not going to bomb. But we know that whenever they say that, bombs will fall the next day."

The ordinary of the Torit Diocese in southern Sudan, Bishop Paride Tabin, pointed out that "many people have already lost their lives in the Torit Diocese, some 9,000 families have been broken up. . . . And in May [2002] alone they murdered almost 500 people."

To punish him for speaking out, the government in June 2002 dropped bombs on the residence of Bishop Mutek in the village of Ikotos. The Catholic youth center and schools were also destroyed in the attack.

In the wake of the successful anti-government campaigns waged by the Sudan People's Liberation Army (and Movement) in central and southern Sudan, people in Darfur, although mostly Muslim, began to rebel against government policies of marginalization and land expropriation in 2003. The Khartoum government responded by launching an ethnic-cleansing campaign in that region.

Within a few months, tens of thousands of civilians were deliberately murdered, most of the victims dying at the hands of a militia supported by the government army known as *Janjaweed* (Armed Men on Horses). They killed, tortured or arbitrarily arrested civilians; burned villages to the ground and looted or destroyed crops and livestock and poisoned water wells. More than 100,000 people, fearing for their lives, took refuge in neighboring Chad.

Typically, the *Janjaweed* would surround a Darfur village around dawn and then attack and kill residents before they could flee or protect themselves. Many victims died while still in their homes. The militia was often backed up by elements of the regular Sudanese army.

Ground attacks were often preceded by Sudanese Air Force bombing raids. According to Amnesty International, most

CHRISTIAN PERSECUTIONS IN THE MIDDLE EAST

bombings "appeared to have disregarded the requirements to distinguish between civilian persons and objects, and military objectives or the principle of proportionality. Both are cornerstones of international humanitarian law regulating armed conflicts. In some instances, the bombings would appear to have deliberately targeted civilians and civilian objects."

Most attacks featured Russian-made Antonov aircraft that dropped boxes filled with metal shrapnel. Other attacks were conducted by low-flying helicopter gunships shelling villages and civilians.

There have been reports of thousands of women—including girls as young as two—being raped by the *Janjaweed*. The exact number of women violated will never be known. Amnesty International was told by locals, "Women will not tell you easily if such things happened to them. In our culture it is a shame, and women will hide this in their hearts so that the men do not hear about it."

While these mass murders and other crimes against humanity were taking place, the Sudanese government refused to condemn them. Its silence was viewed as condoning and encouraging the atrocities.

One witness to the suffering in Darfur told Amnesty International in 2004: "The conflict is now between the government and the civilians. But people are simple, they have nothing, they are killed without having arms. The problem is that the people are told to go away. There are too many people killed for no reason."

The Catholic bishops of Sudan condemned the abuses in Darfur, defending the dignity of the people and calling for respect to their human rights. "As shepherds and pastors," they declared, "we cannot ignore the annihilation of an entire ethnic group whatever their creed, gender or clan."

One missionary who worked in western Sudan, Father Mather Hauman, told news service Fides in July 2004 that in Darfur "there are obvious ethnic aspects, something akin to apartheid that exists between the Arab population in the north and the more African population in the south. Culture and religion play a significant role, too. They are being used and abused in this war as the Arabs try to Arabize the whole country though a concerted effort to Islamize the entire population. . . . What is happening [in Darfur], bombardments, violence against civilians, etc., is what has been happening for 20 years in the south of the country."

The Sudanese government signed the Darfur peace agreement on May 5, 2006. The document, which runs 115 pages, includes power-sharing agreements, demilitarization of the *Janjaweed,* and the promise of referendum on the future status of the province.

But large-scale violence in Darfur continued; in February 2008, humanitarian organizations working in the province estimated that—since the conflict had begun in 2003—more than 450,000 people had been killed and 3.2 million people had been displaced.

The International Criminal Court in July 2008 charged Sudan's President Omar al-Bashir with three counts of genocide for ordering the attacks in Darfur. On hearing of the indictments, al-Bashir dismissed the charges saying, "whoever has visited Darfur, met officials and discovered their ethnicities and tribes . . . will know all of these things are lies."

Violence and the targeting of innocent civilians in Darfur continue to this day.

In early 2005, a Comprehensive Peace Agreement (CPA) was signed between the Khartoum government of Sudan and the Sudanese People's Liberation Army in the south. There were widespread hopes that the CPA would end a 25-year conflict between the Islamist north and the Christian south—a civil war that claimed that claimed 2.5 million lives and left four million people homeless.

To carry out the CPA, the Parliament unanimously approved a new constitution that acknowledged that Sudan has "considerable communities" of Christians. Article I of the document stated: "Sudan is a welcoming country where races and cultures merge and [where] religions are reconciled." The constitution also granted a six-year period of autonomy for south Sudan to be followed by a referendum that, if voters approved, would grant South Sudan independence.

Church leaders had grave doubts. Many believed that the government in Khartoum was still determined to enforce sharia law beyond the borders of the north and to impose Islam on the south. Skeptics argued that the government sued for peace in the south so it could concentrate its resources on the conflict in Darfur.

In the north, meanwhile, the suppression of minority religions continued. Church leaders revealed that a new problem they faced was the expropriation of Church land and property, under the pretext of "enhancement and upgrading." Church schools, prayer centers and other facilities were demolished for the sake of town planning. Also, many Christians were denied access to health care and employment.

In April 2005, the Vicar General of the Khartoum Catholic Diocese was arrested and handcuffed by police and put in the Wad Medani prison. He was accused of paying for a car with a forged check. He was later released and charges were dropped because the alleged witnesses to his crime failed to appear in court. On May 23, he was arrested again and taken to the same prison. He was released hours later. Auxiliary Bishop Daniel Adwok condemned the arrest, claiming the original charge was "nothing more than a pretext." The real reason for the arrest, the prelate charged, was the "government's desire to seize more land that belonged to the diocese."

Commenting on the government's anti-Christian policies, the archbishop of Khartoum, Cardinal Gabriel Zubeir Wako, in 2005 told Aid to the Church in Need: "The masquerade of peace in Sudan produces poverty and injustice, which continue to threaten the population." He reported that his students were being "brainwashed" in government schools; that police and armed forces were putting the country under lock and key; and that the government was using public resources to "Islamize" the South. He also expressed his disappointment in the policies of Western governments, accusing them of failing to heed the warnings of the Church. "If I tell you that the Christians are persecuted and that our life is difficult, how long will it take you to listen to me?" he asked. "How many realize that I put my life in danger by talking to you?"

On New Years Day 2007, Khartoum police used tear gas to attack an Episcopalian church in which 800 people were attending a prayer service. The fact that Sudan's Vice President Abel Alier Kwai was attending the service did not stop the raid. Six people were injured and no punitive actions were taken against the police.

That same month, Khartoum auxiliary Bishop Daniel Adwok publicly accused the government of "playing games" with the people. He argued that Khartoum was not committed to the Comprehensive Peace Agreement signed in 2005, and that the government was reneging on its promise to help hundreds of thousands of displaced people return to their homelands in the South.

In early March 2007, a man blew himself up at an open-air Baptist religious event in Khorfulus, in the upper Nile region. Six children were killed and five were wounded. Four weeks later, four members of the Bahry Evangelical Church in Khartoum were assassinated after holding a catechetical class in the Nuba Mountains. Locals believed the crimes were committed by Islamic fundamentalists.

Pointing to these and other acts of violence, Bishop Adwok in May 2007 once again questioned the government's commitment to religious freedom. "The government," he said, "is ringing the same bell of Islamizing Sudan while at the same time talking about the importance of the Comprehensive Peace Agreement." He also accused the government of using the Darfur crisis as a smokescreen for the spread of Islam into the Christian south.

Five young children were killed in September when a terrorist detonated a grenade after walking into a church in Khorfulus. And in November, a teacher from the United Kingdom, Gillian Gibbons, was arrested for allowing a seven-year-old child in her class to name a teddy bear Muhammad. After a conviction and a 15-day jail sentence, Islamic authorities demanded the sentence be changed to 40 lashes and six months in prison. Surrendering to international pressure, President al-Bashir pardoned Gibbons and ordered her to be deported to Britain.

Displaced people who escaped the war in the south continued to be treated inhumanely. International Christian Concern revealed in May 2008 that in the oil-rich region of Abyei, which is technically part of the south but controlled by the north, a Catholic compound was attacked. The government troops burned down 90 percent of the housing in the region and 80,000 people were forced to flee to the bush.

The most outrageous act of violence against Christians took place in Ezo-Nzara area which is located along the southern most border of Sudan. In August 2008, rebel soldiers broke into Our Lady Queen of Peace Catholic Church during a prayer vigil. The intruders desecrated the Church and kidnapped 17 young adults. One was found dead, tied to a tree and mutilated. The next day three returned to their village but thirteen remained missing. Within hours after the attack on the Church, the same rebels ambushed six people in the nearby town of Nazpa. The captives died after being nailed to pieces of wood. The people who discovered the bodies said it resembled a grotesque crucifixion scene.

Appalled by the reports, Catholic Bishop Edward Hiiboro Kussala called on all Christians in the region to support a three-day prayer march. More than 20,000 joined and marched for miles wearing sack-cloth and ashes, praying for the dead and protesting the government's failure to increase security in the area.

In October 2010, the archbishop of Khartoum, Cardinal Gabriel Zubeir Wako, barely escaped an assassination attack while saying Mass in a city playground. Armed with a dagger, Hamdan Mohamed Abdurrahman rushed toward the cardinal—fortunately he was tackled to the ground by the prelate's Master of Ceremonies. The assassin had apparently entered the park before security arrived and hid until the service began.

As the 2011 referendum vote on southern succession approached, many hoped that the battle between Muslim north Sudan and the Christian south would finally draw to a close. But it did not. Christians in the south continued to suffer from government-approved atrocities. The former rebels, the Sudanese People's Liberation Movement (SPLM), which shared interim governing power with Khartoum, proved to be corrupt and incompetent; the war-torn economy of the South continued to decline. Many

Christians who had escaped to the North chose not to return. There were additional fears that the 2009 national elections—the first in 20 years—that re-elected President Omar al-Baskir, would give him the confidence to cancel the referendum on the South's independence.

Bishop Eduardo Hiiboro Kussala of Tombura-Yambio publicly expressed concern about a return to war due to disagreements over the boundaries between north and south Sudan. Northern Muslims, he said, had warned Christian "cockroaches"—as they called them—of acts of violence and persecution if they did not vote for national unity. "If the referendum goes well," the bishop warned, "it will bring peace to a country which has suffered almost five decades of brutal civil war. If, however, the referendum does not deliver a credible result, then Sudan will descend into violence and instability which will affect the whole region."

The referendum was held January 9–15, 2011. More than 98 percent of the voters endorsed independence and south Sudan formally became a separate nation July 9, 2011.

The new Republic of South Sudan, which consists of ten states and is the home of nine million people, faced numerous challenges. Its infrastructure—roads, schools, hospitals, water supplies—was in a shambles. In addition, hundreds of thousands of refugees that had fled were returning to their former towns and villages that had been devastated during the 22-year civil war (1983–2005).

A transitional constitution approved on July 7 by the South Sudan legislative Assembly established the separation of Church and state and declared that all religions would be treated equally. The constitution guaranteed freedom of worship and assembly; the right to build and own places of worship; the freedom to create charitable institutions; the liberty to distribute religious literature; the right to solicit public and private donations; and the freedom to communicate on religious matters with individuals and communities, nationally and internationally.

So far, religious freedom in South Sudan has been respected. In its 2012 report on religious freedom, the U.S. State Department confirmed that the South Sudan government "generally respects religious freedom" and stated that "there were no reports of societal abuses or discrimination based on religious affiliation, belief or practice."

However, South Sudan is in the grips of a bloody conflict that broke out on December 15, 2013 between South Sudan government forces and rebels led by former deputy president Riek Machar. The U.N. has reported that, since the rebellion began, more than 860,000 thousand have fled their homes.

Bishop Roko Taban Mousa of the Diocese of Malakal has warned that many communities in South Sudan are at risk of starvation. In his own diocese, he pointed out, at least 30,000 homes are destroyed, while communities are subjected to mass lootings by rebel forces.

The bishop of the South Sudanese Diocese of Tombura-Yambio, Edwardo Hiiboro Kussala, has raised his voice against the fresh violence and atrocities. "They abduct children, burn houses down and kill people," he said. Bishop Roko Taban, Apostolic Administrator of Malakal, South Sudan, reported in 2014 that most of his diocese had been "completely destroyed" by rebels and that most of Malakal City's 250,000 people are in desperate need. "Nobody [is] in Malakal. They ran for their lives. It was not possible for anybody to stay. The diocese is completely empty. We have lost everything as a diocese. . . . All documents are gone. There is absolutely nothing left."

In November 2014, the International Crisis Group released a report that estimated that between 50,000 and 100,000 people have been killed since the internal conflict began and that one million people have been displaced.

In the meantime, in the north, Christians continued to suffer. Just after South Sudan gained independence, President Omar al-Bashir of Sudan stated that the Republic's new constitution, then being drafted, would state that "the official religion will be Islam and Islamic law the main source" of legislation. There were reports from Fides news agency that converts to Christianity were being hunted down and that, between 2011–2012, 170 people had imprisoned or indicted for apostasy. In 2012, human rights observers also condemned the Khartoum government's policies of deporting people out of the nation based on their ethnic and religious backgrounds.

During the same period, Sudan government-instigated conflicts broke out in areas across the new border with South Sudan. Auxiliary Bishop Daniel Adwok of Khartoum described how in the Sudan's Blue Nile state, entire villages and towns are deserted, their inhabitants having fled aerial bombardments. In one month, more than 25,000 people fled to Ethiopia to escape the fighting.

Already in November 2011, the bishops of Sudan had issued a warning that another full-scale civil war could be triggered. Reporting that "civilians are being terrorized by indiscriminate aerial bombardment," they said: "We have constantly warned of the danger of a return to hostilities if the legitimate aspirations of those areas [along the border] were not met." Condemning government corruption, the bishops also called on both Sudanese nations to be transparent and democratic in the development and execution of their policies.

Reports of Christian persecution and religious suppression continued to come out of the Republic of the Sudan. In Khartoum, in 2011 security forces ordered Christian communities to stop organizing biblical festivals. Many Imams in their Friday sermons were calling on Muslims not to greet Christians and to have no dealings with them.

A Presbyterian Church southeast of Khartoum was set on fire in January 2011. Six months later, in June, members of Sudanese armed forces looted four churches in the regional capital of Kadugli and then set them on fire. That same month, soldiers torched two Anglican church buildings and plundered and destroyed the bishop's residence.

After the Republic of Sudan's Ministry of Guidance of Religious Endowments in January 2012 threatened to punish Christian clerics caught praying in public, two leaders of the Church of Sudan were seized and beaten while in custody. Just days later, two Catholic priests were abducted from their parish in Rabak on the

White Nile south of Khartoum. Bishop Adwok insisted the abductions were not random. "The kidnappers would have known that these two men were priests," he said. The priests were released two weeks later with minor injuries after the Church refused to pay a ransom of 500,000 Sudanese pounds.

The Sudanese government officially announced in 2012 that new licenses to build churches were no longer being issued and gave orders to demolish a Catholic church and an Anglican one in Haj Yousif. The Minster of Guidance and Endowments said new churches were not needed because of the declining numbers of Christians and the increase in abandoned churches. Viewing the overall situation in Sudan, the Barnabas Team reported that since July 2011, "the persecution of Christians in Sudan has increased sharply . . . churches are demolished, Christian institutions and schools closed, Christians arrested, foreign workers expelled and Christian publications seized."

In 2012 and 2013, the Sudanese army was focused on ridding the Nuba mountain area of Christians. One humanitarian worker told CDN, "The Islamic North sees Nuba Christians as infidels who need to be Islamized through jihad. . . . This war is ethnic cleansing—a religious as well as a political war."

In *Persecuted: The Global Assault on Christians*, the authors describe this conversation with Bishop Macram Gassis, the Catholic bishop of Nuba:

> [He] leads a church that remains active in the war-wracked area. He told us the attacks now underway amount to ethnic cleansing and that Khartoum is now bringing the Janjaweed—the same genocidal militias that ravaged Darfur—to this diocese from across the border in Chad and Niger. He went on to say the government is preparing to import mercenaries from among Somalia's Al-Shabab terrorists.

Sudan armed forces in November 2012 attacked and destroyed 26 Nuba mountain villages in a 54-mile square area. Attacks continued into 2013 and in March bombs dropped from an Antonov plane, destroyed church buildings in Christian communities.

The Sudanese militias were also abducting young men and forcing them to join their ranks. Bishop Daniel Adwok of Sudan reported that there had been an upsurge of abductions in 2011-2012 of young men who are often snatched from their homes. He said that they are being forced to fight in South Sudan against that country's government. "The situation with the militia groups is becoming difficult. . . . The militias seem to have the upper hand. They can do whatever they want and the government will not stop them or oppose what they are doing," he said.

In July 2014, Bishop Eduardo Hiiboro Kussala, in a meeting with Aid to the Church in Need, gave this prescient assessment of the legal situation of Christians, particularly clerics in the Republic of Sudan:

> In Sudan bishops and priests have been living de facto as illegals since South Sudan's independence. . . . When we confront those in charge with this they emphasize that Christians have the same rights as their compatriots, but this changes nothing in legal terms. Bishops and priests are not granted passports and they do not have legal status. They are able to leave the country but re-entry may be refused. Priests have already been expelled; and the bishops are condemned to remain silent. . . . Because the Church has always called on those with political responsibility to respect the dignity of the people, their freedom and also their vote in favour of the independence of the South, it is now being made responsible for the South's break-away. But the Church does not pursue any political aims. We only call upon politicians to respect freedom of religious faith and conscience.

Part Three
Christian Perspectives on the Middle East

CHAPTER 11
ROUNDTABLE ON THE PLIGHT OF CHRISTIANS IN THE MIDDLE EAST

A list of key questions surrounding the fate of Christianity in the Middle East was put to a distinguished panel of experts with great experience in the region and deep knowledge of all the issues at hand—three prelates, a scholar of Islam, and a Church official in charge of caring for Christian refugees. Their answers shed light on a most complex situation that defies easy answers and solutions.

The panelists are:

Melkite Archbishop Jean-Clement Jeanbart of Aleppo, Syria—named to his current post in 1995, he leads a community scrambling for survival in a devastated city that not long ago was the thriving commercial hub of Syria. His biggest concern is to assist local Christians in finding ways to make a living, creating the conditions that will allow his flock to stay put rather than emigrate.

Archbishop Louis Fitzgerald, M. Afr.—from 2006 until his retirement in 2012, the archbishop served as papal nuncio in Egypt and as the Vatican's delegate to the Arab League. From 2002–2006, he was President of the Pontifical Council for Interreligious Dialogue, the successor to the Secretariat for Non-Christians, where Archbishop Fitzgerald served as Secretary for a number of years.

Bishop Camillo Ballin, M.C.C.J.—he is the Apostolic Vicar of the Apostolic Vicariate of Northern Arabia, with responsibility for a massive Catholic population—most of them guest workers—in Saudi Arabia, Qatar, Kuwait and Bahrain. In a remarkable development, the king of Bahrain in 2013 gave the bishop a piece of land destined to become the setting of the brand new Cathedral of Our Lady of Arabia.

Bishop Gregory Mansour—heading the Maronite Eparchy of St. Maron in Brooklyn, NY, Bishop Mansour is in charge of the Maronite Church in the entire Eastern U.S. Engaged in efforts to call the U.S. Christian audience's attention to the suffering of Christians in the Middle East, he also serves as secretary of Christian Arab and Middle Eastern Churches Together (CAMECT), the umbrella group for the leadership of Middle Eastern Churches in the U.S.

Father Samir Khalil Samir, S.J.—based at the Pontifical Oriental Institute in Rome, a much-heralded center for the study of Eastern Christianity, Egyptian-born Father Samir is considered one of the world's premier scholars of Islam. A regular visiting professor at universities in Europe and North America, he is the author of numerous books in Arabic, French and English, including "111 Questions on Islam."

Father Paul Karam—a Lebanese Maronite priest, Father Karam was appointed president of Caritas Lebanon in January of 2013. In that role, he oversees Church efforts to come to the aid of more than 1.5 million refugees in Lebanon, including hundreds of thousands of Christians. He also is the National Director of the Pontifical Mission Societies in Lebanon.

CHRISTIAN SURVIVAL IN THE MIDDLE EAST

Can Christianity survive in the Middle East?

Archbishop Jeanbart: Christians can survive in the Middle East if they are supported and helped by the West.

Archbishop Fitzgerald: It is important that Christianity survives in the Middle East. Many Muslims recognize this and want Christians to stay. Cooperation with Muslims should be encouraged. Greater unity among the Churches would help. Support from other parts of the world is important, but it is really the Churches themselves that have to maintain their vitality.

Bishop Ballin: They can survive if Christians are considered citizens like the others. Very often, especially in Egypt and in Sudan, they are considered second-class citizens, or even worse. How can they get by? The constitutions of the various countries should not make any distinction between Christians and Muslims.

Bishop Mansour: The Church has survived for 2000 years and it will continue to survive. When we began, we were up against even worse odds. How did we survive? Through works of charity: the eventual establishment of hospitals, nursing homes, rehabilitation centers, schools, universities, and a variety of other Christian service agencies. I will never forget the off-the-cuff 45-minute address by Pope Benedict XVI in 2010, to open up the Synod for the Middle East. He gave an outline of the struggles of the early Church in the Middle East, when there were persecutions on every side—how no one thought then that they would survive, let alone flourish. Today, we have so many priests and bishops, women and men religious, and institutes of charity. The sad thing is that we had so much more—and we lost it over the centuries. Today, we must find the same zeal as the early Christians.

Father Samir: The Church in the Middle East can survive if there can be an egalitarian system of citizenship. But that presumes that Muslims renounce the Salafist and fundamentalist dream of a return to the time of Muhammad and the first caliphs—which is considered to be the era of paradise, though the era is, actually, rather poorly understood! Muslims have to accept a form of statecraft that is in accordance with the Universal Charter of Human Rights; a concept of citizenship that is independent of sex, race, or religion;

the equality of all men and women without discrimination—all being subject to the rule of law as applied equally to all. And, of course, there has to be support for the poor and the weakest members of society—which is a principle inherent in Islam as it is in Christianity, but which is rarely put into practice.

Father Karam: Of course, Christianity can and must survive in the Middle East. Christians are not guests in this region but owners and the builders of several civilizations; they were there 600 years before the birth of Islam. What's needed is the commitment of the international community to keep them there and protect them—rather than doing everything to remove them from harm's way and trigger waves of emigration, this exodus, as is the case in Iraq today.

It began with the civil war in Lebanon, when boats were held at the ready to take Lebanese Christians to other countries; it continues today for Iraqi Christians, for whom emigration is held up as practically the only alternative to the tragedy they are living through.

It is important to understand that, fundamentally, the problem is not between Christians and Muslims, who, in general, are not intolerant of each other: There are external factors in play—with political, economic and strategic stakes. Even as our main goal, as Christians, is to guarantee the future of Christians in the Middle East and elsewhere, we also have to take into account that the three religions today—Christians, Jews, and Muslims (who are divided among themselves)—are threatened by major political and economic rivalries.

Men and women, no matter where they are and no matter their religion or beliefs, only want to live in peace and prosperity. No one wants to live in fear and anxiety. That requires true democracy which must, above all, respect religious freedom.

Besides persecution, are there other factors that threaten Christianity in the Middle East?

Archbishop Jeanbart: What worries Christians in the region more than their current misery are their prospects for the future. They worry that a fanatical Muslim regime will establish itself in their particular country and that they and their children will be reduced to living as inferior, second-class citizens, subject to the whims and the arbitrary policies of extremist leaders.

Bishop Ballin: There is also the division among the Christians themselves—not only between Catholics and Protestants and Orthodox, but also with the Catholic Church, which happens especially when the fundamental laws of the Church are not respected.

Father Samir: First, as regards persecution: Though it is an aberration, ISIS is terrible, barbaric. This is really the barbarians coming back: They first attack non-Muslims, then Shiites, then Alawites. It is typical of the Sunni fundamentalist movement. This is *takfir*, excommunication—to consider those who do not abide by their creed as *kaffirs*, inferiors. It recalls the situation of the Arabs when they were first confronted by Muhammad—everyone had to become a Muslim. There are the believers; then the pagans, unbelievers—in the middle are the "half believers," Christians and Jews, who must be humiliated, forced to pay the double tax. Submission can take different forms—being forced to kneel before Muslims, being forbidden to ride a horse, or being barred from employment.

ISIS is an exception, because normally a Muslim does not behave this way; many Muslims are shocked by the movement. Yet, ISIS does everything according to Sharia—with a mufti who gives a *fatwa*, stating that it is correct to kill this or that person. So you cannot say that ISIS has nothing to do with Islam; they imitate what Muhammad did, for example, when he ordered the killing of 600 Jewish men in Medina, with the women and children taken as slaves. It is not a normal Muslim reaction, but it cannot be excluded, as these extremists are applying Sharia in the form that it developed in seventh-century Bedouin culture. Of course, this is totally unacceptable.

I am sure that ISIS will be defeated, but it will take time. Many Muslims are afraid, though, of engaging in any form self-criticism; they protest against actions by Israel readily and angrily, but why not against ISIS? They should protest the funders of ISIS—organize rallies in front of the embassies of Saudi Arabia and Qatar. But a kind of cowardice is involved.

That said, in a more general sense, one cannot really speak in terms of the persecution of Christians in the Middle East. If it takes place, it is occasional and the work of extremists. It is, however, a matter of discrimination against Christians in Muslim countries. Christians are not treated legally as the equals of Muslims—and that is a very serious thing in modern society.

The Christian is no longer treated as a *dhimmi,* someone subjected to Muslim rule, as was the case in preceding centuries. The Christian is no longer required to pay a special tax or a tax on land, respectively *jiziyah* and *kharaj.* But there is no full equality with Muslims.

Hence, in the workplace, certain professions are still off-limits for Christians. In Egypt, a Christian cannot teach the Arab language under the pretext that he or she cannot properly explain the Quran, the foundation of the Arab language. A Christian cannot be a gynecologist because, for reasons of purity by sharia standards, Christians cannot touch Muslim women. In the army, a Christian man can never attain a superior rank, even if he deserves to. In that case, he is sent into retirement early, even at age 50. In courts of law, the witness of a Christian only counts for half of that of a Muslim. In general, Christians have a hard time finding work, even in cases when he or she is clearly more qualified for a particular job than other, Muslim applicants. The fact that one's a Christian is clearly indicated on identity cards.

All of this causes a sense of insecurity, which has material consequences for families as well as psychological ramifications. Surely, a Christian in Muslim societies feels like a second-class citizen— even though he or she knows full well, as does every Muslim, that they are authentic citizens of a particular Middle Eastern country. A good example is Egypt, where Christians call themselves *giptis* (or Copts), which is none other than the transcription of the Greek *Aegyptoi* (pronounced *Egipti,* Egyptians).

That state of subordination in many professions causes many

Christians to suffer economically. This is frequently the case, even as Christians often have a higher cultural level than Muslims, but they have to fight harder than most people to get anywhere. This is all part of what encourages Christians to emigrate to the West.

On the religious level, there is a latent form of oppression evident in social life, due to the growing Islamization of all the countries in the Middle East. Hence, since before dawn, mosques are loudly, invasively broadcasting verses from the Quran throughout the day. That happens even if the law forbids it (like in Egypt), but that regulation is never enforced. Five times a day, Christians have to hear the call to prayer and the proclamation of the Quran, which is a kind of latent form of brainwashing. During Ramadan, all of civilian life is affected: Work hours change, festivities go on late into the night and often the restriction on eating and even drinking water in public during the day is also applied to Christians—who even risk jail time if they refuse. All of that weighs on the conscience of Christians and can prompt some to become Muslims and others to emigrate.

Another particularly odious aspect of living in a Muslim country is the constant exhortation to become a Muslim, on all radio and television programs, especially during Ramadan; teachers of Arabic do the same in the public schools.

The treatment of marriage under the law is the worst example. A Christian man cannot marry a Muslim woman unless he becomes a Muslim himself. That situation often presents itself these days, given the sociological mix of contemporary life, in universities as well as in the workplace. The Christian is pushed to become a Muslim, even though he is told it is only a formal matter and that he can continue to practice his Christian faith discreetly. In fact, though, he will never be able to openly practice his faith again, and the children from such a marriage are automatically Muslims, even if they are secretly baptized (which is practically impossible).

What's more, if a man or woman from a Christian family becomes a Muslim, the children automatically belong to the Muslim parent or to the Muslim in-laws—not to mention the fact that those in the family who remain Christian no longer even have the right to inherit.

}175{

In the end, this subordination, in daily life as under civil law, in a general atmosphere of extreme Islamization—made worse by extremist and Salafist trends—is stifling to Christians. They are driven to emigrate toward freedom. They feel caught in a mentality that is outdated and retrograde, in sharp contrast to the rest of the world where freedom and liberalism are on the rise.

Father Karam: Lebanon is the only country in the Middle East where the president, according to the National Pact and the Constitution, has to be a Christian, a Maronite. Lebanon has defined a mode of equitable cohabitation that gives every religion its place and the respect of the other faiths. Still, when Lebanon was founded in 1943, Christians were in the majority (forming 54 percent of the population compared to 36 percent today). That decline in our share has brought about a predominance of Muslims in certain civil services, causing frustrations for Christians.

Is the conflict in the Middle East a "clash of civilizations"?

Archbishop Jeanbart: We don't think it's a "clash of civilizations." Just consider that certain groups and countries most marked by Muslim civilization are the Christians' closest allies, along with countries of West—together they are confronting nations and systems that also bear a strong imprint of the culture and civilization of the West. Everything is mixed together. The ongoing conflict has political roots, while displaying all kinds of outward signs that have nothing to do with its deepest causes.

Archbishop Fitzgerald: Arab Christians are part of the same civilization as Arab Muslims.

Bishop Ballin: Yes, Christians and Muslims have been living together for centuries. Their civilizations are very similar, despite the different traditions. The main reason for the conflict is fanaticism.

Bishop Mansour: There is a clash of attitudes—but not necessarily civilizations. Christians are more open to others. This attitude must be at the heart of future dialogue. There seems to be a war being waged within Islam. The vast majority of Muslims are moderate and sincere in their faith. These are the Muslims that President Abdel Sisi of Egypt is trying to appeal to when he urges Muslims as a whole to reject violence and fundamentalism. This is something that all people of good will can work on with their Muslim brothers. A clash of civilizations is not inevitable.

Father Samir: One can speak of a shock of civilizations. In fact, Islam, as has been true from its beginnings, wants to be a global project and envelop all aspects of human life—not only the spiritual dimension, but also the realm of politics, economics, social life, culture, etc.

Islam presents itself as a fully integrated way of life. It penetrates (and would like to govern) all the details of human life: as concerns food—with the distinction between *halal* (licit) and *Karam* (illicit)—the clothing of men and women; and also the relationship between men and women (in Cairo there used to be separate seating areas for men and women, not to mention the obsessive compartmentalization in Saudi Arabia and elsewhere). There are even efforts to forbid non-Muslims to use certain terms, like Allah, which non-Muslims might soon be barred from using in Malaysia, for example. Everything is being divided into Islamic or non-Islamic categories. In January 2015, ISIS killed a dozen adolescents in Mosul who were watching a soccer match between Iraq and Jordan on television!

Finally, an Islam that wants to control everything becomes totalitarian. Nothing can escape Islamization, at least according to the formulas of the Salafists. Islam is not a simple faith that consists of "believing in the One God and in Muhammad as his prophet," as the Muslim's profession of faith proclaims, the *chahadah*. As the Salafists or extremist movements seek to define Islam, there is no compromise possible between the Islamic manner of living and thinking and the ways of other countries or civilizations, especially not those of the West, whose very logic opposes the Islamic enterprise, thus defined. That explains the growing impression that there is this shock if not clash of civilizations—the perception that, more and more, Islamic civilization is incompatible with that of the West. That is true if one understands Islam by fundamentalist and Salafist standards. But I think—and hope—that Islam as a whole does not identify itself with that kind of Islam. Still, it must also be acknowledged that "this particular" Islam, this Salafist Islam, is also a legitimate form of Islam—not an aberration or a heresy. It is up to Muslims themselves to bring about reform by rethinking Islam in such a way that is not opposed to a well-conceived modernity and the principles enshrined in the Universal Declaration of Human Rights.

Father Karam: The conflict in the Middle East is principally an expression of the clash between the economic and strategic rivalries of the great powers; they are using the instrument of "religious extremism" to create chaos and achieve their objectives. It is these rivalries that we are seeing played out—it is not a clash of civilizations.

Is hatred of Christians in the Middle East directly linked to hatred of the West?

Archbishop Jeanbart: No, at least in Syria, the feelings of Muslims toward the West are generally not bad at all; that hatred has come from Salafist currents which have penetrated the countries of the region in recent years. The great majority of Muslims in our country have always respected Christians and loved socializing with them.

Archbishop Fitzgerald: Some Muslims in the Middle East suspect Christians of being linked to the West, which they consider to be a source of oppression. There is a love-hate relationship with the West, particularly as regards the U.S.

Bishop Ballin: Many identify the West with Christianity. We have Christians in the West—but not Christian countries; we have secular countries. But this is not understood by many in the Middle East—especially not by the extremists.

Father Samir: I would not say that Christians are hated in the Middle East or that Muslims hate or detest Christians. That is not the case, and it would be contrary to the spirit of Islam. In fact, for Muslims, Jews and Christians are believers, as they both believe in the One God, Allah, and that way they have the right to live with Muslims. But because they do not believe that Muhammad was the Emissary of God and, even less, that he was the greatest prophet— as the Quran affirms (33:40), considering Muhammad to be the one who received the final divine revelation, which, moreover, corrects the content of previous scriptures and excludes the possibility of any further revelation—Christians as well as Jews do not have the same rights as Muslims. They are situated in-between true believers—Muslims—and non-believers or misbelievers, pagans.

The problem is that Muslims consider the West to be Christian. That does not reflect reality, including political reality. But in the eyes of many Muslims, Christians Arabs are linked to the West. And because Muslims think of religion as being pretty much part of the national identity, they consider Arab Christians to be partners of the West and thus supporters of particular political positions. This perception has no basis in reality. Christian Arabs are first of all linked to their country—they do not think of Christianity as an *umma*, or a global community (as is the case for Islam). Arab Christians' bond with Christians in the West is a spiritual one, which does not involve a political relationship at all. This confusion of politics and religion is one of the evils of Islam, which many liberal Muslims would like to overcome . . . but without success.

Father Karam: It is not about a hate for Christians of the Middle East, but the execution of a plan to chase them out of the region. Those in the Middle East and elsewhere who "hate" the West make that very clear in their actions— such as attacks on European and U.S. interests; taking Westerners hostage in Africa, etc. But even on that front, it is not so much a matter of hate as it is an expression of frustration, resentment, and disappointment about feeling manipulated and exploited. Furthermore, Muslims, be they moderates or extremists, have a better overall knowledge of the West than the West has of them.

Can someone be both Christian and Arab in the eyes of a Muslim Arab?

Archbishop Jeanbart: In Syria, Christians are considered fully Arab by their fellow citizens. They are also recognized as having preceded the Arab renaissance. The same is true in all the countries bordering Syria.

Archbishop Fitzgerald: It is difficult for the Muslims of North Africa to conceive of Arab Christians, because they have no or little experience of them. In the Middle East, however, Muslims are used to living with fellow Arabs who are Christians.

Bishop Ballin: It is difficult. For the Arabs, an Arab is Muslim. Many "Arab" Christians don't accept being called Arabs, because for them also "Arab" means "Muslim."

Bishop Mansour: In the eyes of any discerning person, one can see that Christians were present in the Middle East even before Muslims, and they deserve to be considered as the original civilization— not as outsiders, as some mistakenly think of us. We are allied to both the East and the West. We have contributed so much to the Arab world and will continue to do so—even if our numbers are diminished.

Father Samir: In the majority of countries in the Middle East, Muslims know that Christian Arabs consider themselves to be part of the Arab world. The difference is that Arab Christians are more open to Western culture than Muslims.

What's more, it is wrong and absurd to identify Muslims with Arabs. Arab Muslims account for between 15 percent and 20 percent of the world's total Muslim population. Of course, the liturgical prayer of all Muslims is in Arabic (even as a majority of Muslims understand only little of what is being said). But most Muslims are not Arab at all, culturally or ethnically.

In Lebanon, Syria and Palestine, Christians are culturally Arabic. Only certain small groups—basically Armenians and Assyrians—do not consider themselves to be Arabs, having preserved their ancient languages in contemporary life.

Father Karam: That is not always clear for a Muslim, but, on the whole, at least in Lebanon, Christians are certainly not considered to be non-Arabs. Nonetheless, the regular upheavals that punctuate life in the Middle East and which sometimes particularly affect Christians, makes Christians wonder about their future in this region. What's more, the failure of ideologies—such as Arab nationalism—that transcend religious affiliation has also weakened the hope of Christians of being part of the same future as their Arab compatriots.

Could there be an autonomous Christian enclave in the Middle East?

Archbishop Jeanbart: We don't think it would be good to create a Christian enclave in the region. It will be much easier and a thousand times better to push for tolerance and the protection of pluralism and social harmony here in Syria when Christians are living among the general population.

Bishop Ballin: I don't think so. It will be continuously attacked by the extremists, who will constantly accuse Christians of everything.

Father Samir: There is no one in the Christian community today who can envision a Christian enclave in the Middle East. Such an idea arose during the 1975–1990 civil war in Lebanon among certain political parties with Christian roots, who were encouraged by Israel and strongly supported by U.S. Secretary of State Henry Kissinger.

Christian Arabs are native citizens of the Middle East. They belong to different linguistic and cultural traditions, notably Syriac and Coptic. They welcomed the Muslim invaders despite themselves, belonging politically still to the Roman Empire of the East (the Byzantine Empire), but which had abandoned them. Christians have rarely mobilized an army capable of defending themselves.

The creation of a Christian enclave in the region would, very quickly, lead to the demise of Christianity. A Copt is more connected to his Egyptian Muslim brethren than to his fellow Christians in Iraq or Lebanon. What's more, Christians want to be the yeast in the flower, as the Gospel puts it (Matthew 13:33). That is their vocation. To enclose themselves in order to form a Christian "nation" would run contrary to the ideal of Christian evangelization and would make no sense. Of course, there will always be Christians who would wish to establish a small Christian state in the Middle East. They have the right to dream if that brings them comfort!

Father Karam: There could be one, if that is a decision taken internationally, but what would be its benefit? What good is it to live alone, isolated? The Middle East is a blend of religions and civilizations and must remain so. Christians and Muslims, the West and the East, we need one another. We must promote what is proper to the Middle East—that is to say tolerance and coexistence.

Who really "owns" the land of the Middle East?

Archbishop Jeanbart: The countries of the Middle East belong to the citizens who are there and who have lived there for generation after generation.

Bishop Ballin: Practically speaking, the land is owned by the Muslims. But, again, it all depends on the level of fanaticism in a particular country.

Father Samir: The land belongs to those who live there.

In the Christian vision, religion resides in the heart of the believer and has no connection with a race, nor with a culture or a specific language or territory. It involves an act of faith, not a political, social or cultural act, even as it is true that faith can engender or orient a culture.

Unfortunately, Islam, like Judaism and like Hinduism, closely links religion with territory, hence faith with politics. That can only lead to conflicts.

Father Karam: The Middle East belongs to all its inhabitants, whether they be Muslims, Christians, or Jews. If there would not be international stakes driving one or the other from the land, there would not really be a reason to take what belongs to another.

ISLAM

To what do you attribute the rise and appeal of radical jihadist Islam?

Archbishop Jeanbart: Jihadist as ISIS is in its essence, it could also be an instrument of war used by certain powers to destabilize the countries of the region, to dominate and even destroy them. This pan-Islamic movement cannot distinguish between the conquest of territory and the conquest of souls. For fundamentalist Muslims, this war is a religious duty and a praiseworthy endeavor, waged as much for the growth of the Islamic faith as for political domination. For them, Islam is both religion and state, a belief and a governing regime.

Archbishop Fitzgerald: Positively, there is the attraction of a religion with definite rules, the following of which perhaps does not require much reflection. There can be a sense of exaltation in feeling that one is fulfilling God's will. Negatively: Despite the wealth of the Gulf countries, there is a feeling that Islam is not given due consideration in the world.

Bishop Ballin: Especially the extremists feel that Islam is attacked not primarily by other religions but especially by modernity. TV, videos, etc. can penetrate everywhere and at any time. Islam is no longer protected by its borders—there are no borders. In the past, the Church used to protect herself through expulsions or excommunications. But after Vatican II, the Church entered into dialogue with the world. Islam is afraid of modernity and not able to entertain a dialogue with modernity. It seems to have come down to either following modernity blindly or to attack the modern world.

Bishop Mansour: Anger and hatred towards others is the appeal. Poverty and corrupt political regimes feed this anger. Israel, the West, and Christianity are often scapegoated. That is not to say that these parties have not contributed to the worsening of the situation in the Middle East. However, this is not the whole story. There is a war going on for the soul of Islam, and radicals seem to be winning. But we hope that more moderate voices will arise among Christians, Muslims, and Jews.

Father Samir: There are a number of reasons, both immediate and at a greater distance, behind the appeal and rise of radical Islamic jihad. I will focus on three factors:

One: the military, political and diplomatic defeat of the Arab countries, heart of the Muslim world, in confrontation with the small Israeli state revealed the degree of degradation of the Arab-Muslim world. This triggered a movement of Islamic awakening—religious, political and military—which is still ongoing under different names and in different forms.

Two: A return to the golden age of Islam. The Muslim world saw a fantastic surge at its birth. First of all, with the conquests organized by Muhammad himself; the *ghazawat*, plural of the world *ghazwa*—which became the term *razzia* [wars of expansion] in many Western languages—helped him rally the majority of the Arab tribes in the north of the Arab Peninsula. The first biography of Muhammad, written by al-Waqid around 790—the *Book of the Ghazawat*—gives an account of more than 60 *razzias* between 624 and 632.

After the death of Muhammad, the first caliph, Abu Bakr, brought all the tribes that had left when Muhammad died in 632 back into the fold of Islam. These were the wars against the apostates—the *Hurub al-Riddah*. In 636, the conquest of neighboring countries began: Syria and Palestine; Egypt and Persia. In less than a decade, an immense territory in North Africa and Asia fell under the power of Islam.

The extremists the Salafists, the Muslim Brotherhood, etc — are conscious of the current decadent state of Islam, an Islam that is contributing nothing to world civilization, a far cry from its glorious history. The explanation that is offered is that Islam has strayed from its origins, having followed or imitated Westerners. The remedy for this decadence is to distance Islam from Western civilization and to return to the ways of the first Companions (the *Salaf*)—the literal application of the teachings and traditions of Islam just as it happened when Muhammad was still alive.

Today, the leader of ISIS, with its self-proclaimed pseudo-caliphate, Abu Bakr al-Baghdadi, claims to be returning to this mythical age. The anagram of ISIS and the surname of its leader evoke the Abassid Empire or Caliphate (750–1258). As to Abu Bakr, it is a reference to the first successor of Muhammad, the caliph Abu Bakr al-Siddiq (632–634).

Three: The Quran, so to speak, fell from the sky onto Muhammad, and literally applies to all times. The Quran is not the product of a human author. It is written by God, who brought it down to Muhammad his prophet, who transmitted it literally. This concept (which we would consider mythical) is affirmed by the majority of imams and considered official doctrine. Commentaries of the Quran are grammatical and linguistic explanations, with allusions to what are considered to be historical events in the life of Muhammad. The Quran, being of exclusively divine origin, cannot be touched or interpreted. The text must be taken as is, and applied as is.

This conception of the Quran paralyzes the thinking of Muslims today. But it has not always been this way. In the Middle Ages, for example, many thinkers interpreted the text and brought it to life in accordance with the thinking of their time. In our day, some hundreds of Muslims have spoken of the necessity of "rethinking the text," but the traditional formation of imams continues to be very rigid. This of course reinforces the thrust of the extremist and Salafist trend.

Father Karam: The rise of radical and jihadist Islam is due to the rivalry between the great powers. No human being logically and reasonably aspires to live in the shadows. What's involved is a very carefully studied and mounted manipulation to cause maximum damage. The way jihadist movements operate is strangely similar to that of religious sects, who go about recruiting with the most subtle means—treacherous and Machiavellian—all in the service of achieving diabolical objectives.

As is the case for sects, the appeal of jihadist movements is due to the fact that recruits are shown a mirage of a better way of life and a better world. Judging by what is going on around the world today, no one is safe from this mode of recruitment: Muslims, Christians, middle-class people, the poor, Westerners and Easterners. Just like with the sects, recruits are often confused and miserable people who are looking for structure and a place to belong. Once caught in the net of the jihadists, they are trapped and cannot get back out. They are stuck in the gears of a machine that brainwashes them and makes them commit the worst atrocities.

Has ISIS expanded the battle from territorial cleansing to conquest of souls?

Father Samir: ISIS is only supported by a minority of fanatics. The group wins over—above all online—a certain number of young people who find themselves on the margins of society, often already in revolt against society; then there are those who are simply aimless and let themselves be spellbound by the notion of heroic action that will grant them access to paradise and bring revenge for Islam. Surely, should ISIS succeed in creating Islamic states that are strong in all aspects, there is the risk that they will win over feeble souls.

Bishop Ballin: In my view, ISIS is the true expression of the incapability of Islam to dialogue with the world. They have closed in on themselves in an Islamic state, to protect themselves from the world, to save their soul from hell—which is the world. Some monastic Christian communities have the same mentality.

Bishop Mansour: They believe in both conquering territory and souls. The ISIS agenda is complete dominance. They are harshest on Muslims who do not accept their plans. But they are brutal towards everybody.

Father Karam: The exact role of ISIS is hard to define: It engages, on the one hand, in territorial conquest and on the other in the capture of souls. It is part of a plan to destabilize the planet, with a violent campaign beyond its frontiers and the spread of terror—again, to serve objectives other than those officially declared.

What are the tenets and basis of moderate Islam?

Archbishop Jeanbart: Moderate Islam needs an actualization of its way of seeing the world. The world today is more than ever pluralistic. Our contemporaries no longer support totalitarian systems. The indispensable condition for Islam to attain moderation is to irrevocably accept the fundamental human right of freedom of conscience and to respect the beliefs of all men and women.

Archbishop Fitzgerald: Moderate Islam accepts that not all the members of the community need to be Muslims. It therefore accepts pluralism. This includes accepting fellow Muslims who do not necessarily follow all the teachings of Islam. Moderate Islam is against *takfir* [ex-communication]. Moderate Islam accepts that the basis of the sharia law is the Quran and the *Sunna* [elaboration of Islamic law based on words and deeds of Muhammad], yet holds that the elaboration of sharia is a human construct—and that, therefore, there can be changes.

Bishop Ballin: Muslims should apply the verses of the Quran which call for respect of the Christians and the Jews.

Bishop Mansour: The Quran and the *Hadith* [the sayings of Muhammad] form the basis of all Islam. It depends on how they are interpreted. Imams and other preachers of Islam are very important in the interpretation and sometimes can make all the difference for the average Muslim.

Father Samir: In my view, there are four characteristics of a moderate Islam:

One—it is an Islam that opposes all violence committed in its name, and which favors dialogue and diplomatic means to solve conflicts;

Two—it is an Islam that supports the notion of citizenship, extolling the equality of Christians and Muslims, men and women;

Three—it is an Islam that embraces a modernity that is reasonable, non-revolutionary, and respectful of commonly accepted ethics and norms. This Islam is embarrassed by the novelties introduced in the West in the realm of sexuality (same-sex marriage, libertinism, exhibitionism, etc.). Overall, one could say that moderate Islam would stand for an understanding of morality that is rather close to that of classical Catholicism.

Four—it is an Islam that supports exchanges with the West.

Father Karam: There is no moderate Islam, just as there is no moderate Christianity or Judaism. There is Islam, Christianity, and Judaism. Religious extremism cannot be considered to be an extension of any given religion—it is the utilization of its principles in a radical, illegitimate manner.

Is there a moderate Islam in practice? How is it defined politically, socially, culturally and spiritually?

Archbishop Jeanbart: There is a moderate Islam in certain countries of the Middle East, particularly in those who have benefited by an ancestral Christian presence and which have been able to give their citizens a secular and modern academic education. This Islam must learn how to make its way among groups with a religious stamp and those with a political orientation. This necessarily requires the promotion of a spirit of tolerance and a culture of socio-political harmony and partnership. In other words, in order to thrive, a moderate Islam requires a positive form of secularism.

Bishop Ballin: There are moderate Muslims. But it is difficult to define a moderate Islam because there are contradictory verses in the Quran and there is no authority which can give an official and clear interpretation. Islam will become moderate when reason can be applied in the studies of the Quran, i.e., to make it possible to study the historical context of the so-called "revelation" of the Quran.

Bishop Mansour: Yes. It needs to be promoted by Muslims, Christians and all people of good will together. President Sisi of Egypt is urging a rethinking of Islam on this basis. I pray that more voices like his will be raised.

Father Samir: Moderate Islam is politically egalitarian; socially concerned about and open to the needs of the poor; culturally open to modernity and the West; and spiritually open to other religions— even open to non-militant atheism.

Father Karam: No normal human being could live in the realm of extremism. The moderate Muslim lives with respect for his religion. But, like everyone else, he has to live and work, evolve, and wants to educate his children in a world that is open and at peace. He is interested in what goes on around him. He gets involved in politics, social action and society at large, as well as culture—and then, of course, the spiritual realm.

Can "Mosque and State" ever be separated in Muslim societies?

Archbishop Jeanbart: In a society that pursues a fundamentalist form of Islam, the Mosque is inseparable from the State.

Archbishop Fitzgerald: Given the foundational experience of Islam, which was a political as well as a religious community, it is difficult to separate these two dimensions.

Bishop Ballin: Yes, when there will be a critical study of the Quran.

Bishop Mansour: Yes. It depends on interpretation, and on support for this interpretation in Muslim and Christian circles.

Father Samir: The clear separation between religion and politics, between mosque and state, is very difficult to conceive, because there is no tradition of this kind. But moderate Islam wants it, up to certain point—not, certainly, in the sense of a combative secularism, such as is the case in France, but rather along the lines of what Benedict XVI called "a positive secularism." The Lebanese model, its openness to all religions, is well regarded by moderate Islam. The model has very positive aspects, despite the risk of confessionalism.

Father Karam: There are certainly Muslims who are strongly in favor of secularism. Will that ever come about? If it does, it would certainly neutralize religious extremism, restore stability and make it possible to move forward. Christians are strongly in favor of secularism, often at their own expense, meaning in favor of not always honorable causes. Confronting extremism, Christians have to insist on their rights as well as the respect of other religions.

How is Christian persecution carried out in the Middle East?

Archbishop Jeanbart: Christians in Syria, Lebanon, Jordan and Iraq were not particularly persecuted all through the past century. That started happening only in the last decade, with the rise of extremist Islam. In Christians' long history of living close to Muslims, there have been highs and lows. Under Ottoman domination they suffered many hardships of all kinds, including savage persecution at the beginning of the twentieth century that produced many martyrs and uprooted peoples.

Bishop Ballin: Persecution and discrimination are carried out in many ways, almost always in an underhanded way: delays in granting documents, blocking their delivery; not respecting Christians' identity; "persecution" in the administration of exams in higher education; voluntary negligence and delays when it comes to authorities responding in case of fire or attacks, etc.

Bishop Mansour: There is terrible persecution But it also exists for anyone who is not part of the Muslim majority—Kurds, Yazidis, Bahais, non-believers, Shiites in Sunni countries, Sunnis in Shiite countries, etc.

Father Samir: It is more a matter of discrimination than persecution. It is manifested especially in the workplace—it is hard for Christians to find work—but also in the small things of everyday life. This discrimination also shows up in religiously-motivated attacks against churches and Christian institutions (schools, convents, community centers, etc.); it is evident in the media which uses injurious terms in referring to Christians (such as "idolizers of the cross," Nazareans, etc.). The most serious consequence is this push toward emigration toward countries where equality is recognized, which basically means the West; but those who leave are often disappointed to discover how weak Christianity is there.

Father Karam: Persecution of Christians takes the form of attacks on and ransacking of churches, as happened in Egypt, particularly in 2011, and in Iraq, as happened last summer. It also takes the form of the ban on practicing the Christian faith, as is the case in Saudi Arabia. By contrast, other countries in the Gulf have created an opening toward Christians, granting permission for the construction of churches. Then, in a less violent manner, in certain countries, there is the treatment of Christians as second-class citizens, and their inability to have access to certain public benefits or enjoy certain privileges.

How did Christian communities survive the waves of persecutions in the past?

Archbishop Jeanbart: The Christian communities have been able to survive thanks to their regrouping in the heart of the Church, gathered around their pastors who were community leaders as much as religious leaders. These men tried to protect them with all their means, helping them face adversity and encouraging them to cope with both moral and material difficulties. The solidarity among Christians, their mutual support, made this suffering bearable and less painful; it helped them get through periods of great unhappiness and to keep going despite all the obstacles.

Archbishop Fitzgerald: The development of a strong monastic trend in Egypt certainly seems to have helped the Coptic Church to survive. The monasteries gave refuge for Christians and also provided spiritual resources. This may also be true of Ethiopia.

Bishop Ballin: The Christian communities survived, but not everywhere. In the Gulf, *all* the Christians became Muslims. The same happened in North Africa and in Nubia (northern Sudan). The remaining Christian communities suffer a continuous erosion of faithful, many of whom, for various reasons, embrace Islam.

Bishop Mansour: Some survived by emigrating, others by strong and patient long suffering.

Father Samir: In the past, Christians had to put up with humiliations without being able to push back: being barred from important positions; being forbidden to ride horses; having to give up one's seat to a Muslim, etc. That was not a general phenomenon, however; it was something that happened during certain periods of intolerance. Christians did not have a choice; they had to put up with these vexations, while hoping for better times. In the modern era, starting in the nineteenth century, extreme forms of discrimination disappeared.

Father Karam: Many Christians survived by emigrating to faraway countries in America or Africa, or to ones closer by, like Egypt. Others stayed, braving the turmoil, waiting for the storm to pass

THE CHRISTIAN CONTRIBUTION

The Western perspective points at the role of Christians in Arab societies as contributing to the good of all. Are Christians perceived that way by Muslims too?

Archbishop Jeanbart: That perspective is held above all by the Church and by people of good will in the West—this expectation that Christians make important contributions to the progress of the Arab societies they are part of. Many Muslims think of us in the same way. Numerous political leaders in Syria, Lebanon, Jordan, Egypt and Iraq often expressed themselves in this way, wishing we would stay among them to enrich the society and the country, paving the way for greater openness and tolerance.

Archbishop Fitzgerald: The Quran recognizes Christians, particularly monks, as people of prayer. It is important that the communities give witness as praying communities. At the same time, the contribution of Christians to education, the care of the sick and the elderly is greatly appreciated. The various national associations of Caritas are generally well respected.

Bishop Ballin: That seems not to be the case. Many Christians have left their country of origin because they got tired of not being considered equal to the others.

Bishop Mansour: Most reasonable Muslims know that Christians add so much value to Middle Eastern culture. One can look at Lebanon and see—because of freedom of the press and because of the vibrant arts—that many voices of the Arab world are freely expressed there. However, it is a sad thing for me personally to see how some Christians use their freedom in Lebanon—for some, it is a license for immorality. This is counterproductive to our witness to Christ and to our fellowship with Muslims.

Father Samir: Among sophisticated Muslims, this fact is acknowledged. In fact, Christians have greatly contributed to the renaissance of Arab culture and to its opening up to Hellenism (philosophy, the sciences, medicine, astronomy, etc.) between the ninth and the twelfth century, as well as to the modernization of the Muslim world from the middle of the nineteenth century onward, across all fronts. The Christian contribution in the modern era is well known, while the public at large is less aware of Christian accomplishments in the Middle Ages.

Father Karam: Yes, of course, Muslims are very much aware of the role Christians played in the creation of their countries and they are committed to their presence. They are concerned about the mass exodus of their Christian fellow citizens with whom they have lived rather peacefully for centuries, even if appearances and certain events give a different impression.

What have Christians in the Middle East accomplished, in terms of peace-making, healthcare, education?

Archbishop Jeanbart: Middle Eastern Christians, both as individuals and as an ecclesial community, have done a lot in this regard, from the Muslim conquests of the seventh century until the present day. During the first centuries of Islam, Christians served as educators and administrators in the Muslim state. They transmitted arts and culture to the Muslims who occupied their country, inculcating in them civility and knowledge of the sciences. They translated the Greek philosophers into Arabic; Christians themselves wrote a great number of works on medicine, philosophy and a variety of sciences.

In Aleppo, the commercial hub in the region—where, in those days, there lived a great number of Christians—brought the East and the West together thanks to trading. Since the seventeenth century the city and region developed a way of life and a culture that was enriched by a Christian soul, which also stood for an openness to Europe. It allowed many Muslims to evolve and to open themselves up to the modern world.

To give an example, we can call attention to the presence in Aleppo in those ancient times of a number of European colonies—Venetians, French, British, Dutch, Austrians, Italians, Germans, Greeks—who had come for business and lived there in complete tranquility and in close proximity to the townspeople. There were many people in Aleppo who spoke more than two languages. Some locals of that era learned four or even five languages.

Clergy that had come from Europe to minister to their countrymen, in unison with the local bishops, set up courses of religious and moral instruction for the children. From the seventeenth century onward, these developed into small schools that in time also took in plenty of Muslim children, who, later on, along with Christians, worked toward the Arab renaissance. A number of Arab-language books were printed in Aleppo in this period and many European authors were translated in Arabic.

The Arab renaissance owes much to Christians. They were in the forefront of this very important movement that introduced modern Western thought into the region. It gave birth to a number of liberation movements, as well as Islamic-Christian partnerships and collaboration. Christians founded a number of political parties that supported pluralism and secularism. From the nineteenth century onward, the printed press got off the ground at the initiative of distinguished Christian journalists and generous Christian funders. They were responsible for the launch of most of the first Arab newspapers. It is important to remember that the first print shop in Aleppo was set up by the Church; it was subsequently moved to

Lebanon, far from the interference of Ottoman Muslims which was quite strong in those days in a city so close to Turkey.

Despite everything, it has to be acknowledged that Christians, helped by their brethren in the West, from the beginning of the nineteenth century onward offered the Muslim countries where they lived a number of services of enormous importance: medical care, thanks to the hospitals they built throughout the region; schools and universities; modern political parties; and sports, cultural and recreational clubs thrived wherever there were Christians present. All of this, in time, contributed greatly to the evolution of mentalities, the acceptance of the "other" thanks to mutual acquaintance, which allowed for the development of well-established social interaction between Christians and Muslims in this very eventful part of the world.

Bishop Ballin: If we look at the initiatives of the Catholic Church, we must recognize that the Christians have for centuries supported peace-making, health care and education. Thousands of missionaries (priests and sisters) gave their lives for that, without any compensation.

Father Samir: Christians have played and continue to play an important role in maintaining peace and understanding. They have been doing so on the international plane, notably by way of diplomatic relations, or in the relationship with Israel, in standing up for the rights of Palestinians, for example; Christians help maintain the Arab world's relationships with the West—without identifying the West with Christianity, but taking in everything that is positive in Western culture.

Father Karam: Christians have played a very important role for centuries in the building up and strengthening of the Arab nation, on the political as well as the economic plane, and in both the cultural and intellectual realms. The presence of Christians in academia, as well as culturally and economically, has made for an impact on society far out of proportion to the Christian share of the population. As Prince Hassan of Jordan has put it: "The numerical inferiority of Christians in the modern Arab world is compensated by their very positive social, economic, cultural and—in some cases—political presence."

Especially in the nineteenth century, the educational efforts of missionaries made the massive education of Christians possible, even as these institutions were also open to non-Christians. The phenomenon brought about the emergence of an intellectual elite and a large Christian middle class that gained affluence notably through commerce, especially in Syria (Aleppo) and nearby cities in Lebanon.

Christian intellectuals exiled themselves to flee Ottoman rule and came in contact with revolutionary and liberal European movements. Some settled in Egypt where the *Nahda* emerged, a movement of the Arab renaissance that would serve as a counterweight to Turkish occupation and Europe's growing intrusion in the Near East. That dynamic brought about, among other things, the modernization of the Arab language, which rediscovered its elasticity, its depth, and secularism. To boost greater freedom of the press, Lebanese Christians launched three major newspapers in Egypt: *Al-Ahram* (the biggest daily in the country to this day), *Al-Hilal* and *Al Mokkatam*.

During the first half of the twentieth century, Christians got heavily involved in the social, cultural and political life of their countries, working hard for their independence. They even supported nationalist parties, such as the Ba'ath Party, which were strongly wedded to secularism; there was pan-Arabism, pan-Syrianism, Egyptian nationalism (embodied by the Wafd party that saw the active involvement of Copts) and Lebanese nationalism (which would lead to the establishment of Greater Lebanon in 1920). Christian government leaders reached positions of the greatest responsibility in each of the countries of the region—for example, Boutros Ghali, grandfather of the previous U.N. Secretary General, became prime minister of Egypt in 1910.

But the situation changed drastically in the wake of the defeat of the Arab nations in their wars with Israel; in many cases, Christians had to withdraw from political life, limiting their activities to business, education or social and charitable work. Still, Christians remained at the forefront in important ways.

In Lebanon, the president of the Republic and the commander-in-chief of the army have to be Christians, and 128 seats in Parliament are equally divided among the different Christian communities. In Palestine, the presence of Christians on Hamas ballots helps improve the image of the party and boosts the chances of a Christian candidates being elected. In Iran, elected Christians are sworn in on the Bible and in Egypt the president appoints a number of Christians as deputies.

Why is Christianity vital for the region? Can you imagine the region without Christianity?

Archbishop Jeanbart: The Middle East we know today would have been unimaginable without the presence of Christians. In the past, Christians allowed the region to evolve and become what it is today. As to the future, Christians will make it possible—thanks to the Christian values they embody—for the region to soften, to not explode in turmoil, to continue to be a peaceful and friendly place of welcome—rich in the diversity of its social components, and its varied and pluralistic community life.

Archbishop Fitzgerald: Christianity contributes to a more open society. Moreover, it is important that there be Christian communities to keep alive the spirit of the Gospel.

Bishop Ballin: If Christians should disappear, there will be more violence among the Muslims themselves. There will be always an aggressive Muslim who will say to another Muslim: "Why are you not like me?"—and such a confrontation often has violent consequences. The presence of Christians makes for an element of balance and peace.

Bishop Mansour: The region without Christians would be a disaster, because we are the "other" and, without us, those who are of the majority in the Middle East will never learn to live with the "other" in the East or the West. When a majority is monolithic, the mosaic presented by other, different communities does not challenge the prevailing thought of the day. A certain cross-fertilization that comes from engaging with different cultures and religions is vital for society.

Father Samir: Christianity is open to the world, something that is often lacking among Muslims. On the religious level, Christianity offers a positive view of other religions, while Islam, in theory, only acknowledges Judaism and Christianity, looking upon all other faiths as superstition or paganism. As regards freedom, Christianity fundamentally defends religious freedom—the right to change religion, or to be agnostic or atheist—as well as the freedom of speech or the written word, provided it does not attack or lack respect for others. On the social plane, Christians have introduced into the Muslim world, as much as they have been able to, the notion of equality between Muslims and non-Muslims, between men and women, between the races. Christians do not identify religion with race and therefore opposes all forms of racism. Finally, in the political realm, Christians insist on the separation of the political and the religious.

Father Karam: Christianity is essential for the region. The presence of Christians was not imported. It was there that it was born, and where it has a natural role and purpose. As Pope Francis put it in November 2013: "We don't resign ourselves to a Middle East without Christians, who, for two thousand years, have been professing the name of Jesus, and have been citizens taking part in the social, cultural and religious life of the countries to which they belong." In December of 2014, the Pope wrote to Christians in the Middle East: "Your presence is precious for the Middle East. You are a small group, but with a great responsibility in this land where the faith was born and from which it spread. You are the leaven in the yeast."

INTERRELIGIOUS DIALOGUE

What is interreligious dialogue from the Christian, Muslim perspective?

Archbishop Jeanbart: In the present circumstances, both from the Christian and Muslim perspective, dialogue is limited to the social and humanitarian sphere: human rights, right to life, abortion, marriage, bio-ethics, care of the vulnerable, etc. A theological dialogue remains very difficult, as it must deal with the content of the Christian faith with, at its foundation, the mysteries of the Trinity, the Incarnation, the Resurrection and the divinity of Christ. For Islam, God, the Most High, only communicates with human beings through the prophets—some of them venerable chosen men, but all of them ordinary human beings. At the front of the line is Muhammad, to whom God dictated his Revelation in the Quran, of which the content and meaning is immutable because they are the *ipsissima verba*, the "very words" of the Most High.

This dialogue, if it is limited to exchanges of good will and cordiality, will always be beneficial and useful in achieving a way of living together in friendship in a society that is mixed and pluralistic. What's more, this way of proceeding may one day lead to a more profound exchange, which will touch upon a joint reflection on fundamental facts of religion. But for that to happen, it will be indispensable that Islam come to accept a less rigid interpretation of Quranic verses. Otherwise, from the start, there is nothing to discuss, as everything is already said and defined from the very start.

Archbishop Fitzgerald: The documents of the Catholic Church have distinguished different forms of dialogue:

Dialogue of life—people with different religious convictions living in peace and harmony;

Dialogue of action—cooperation in the service of humanity;

Dialogue of discourse—formal meetings to discuss questions which may or may not be specifically religious;

Dialogue of religious experience—sharing of a spiritual nature.

Muslims have no specific teaching on dialogue, apart from certain principles given in the Quran, but Muslims can be found engaged in all the types of dialogue mentioned above.

Bishop Ballin: Christians must learn to understand the feelings of the Muslims. As to the Muslim approach, it depends on who is organizing sessions of dialogue. Is the purpose just to create peace between Christians and Muslims, or is the goal to achieve political ends through dialogue?

Bishop Mansour: Hearing the other, and coming to truly love him or her. I always have to learn more.

Father Samir: For Christians, dialogue is an exchange between two or more people (or groups) to get to know each other and to understand each other better, while avoiding all preconceived notions and clearing up misunderstandings. The goal is to get to know and understand the other as she or he understands him or herself—not as we understand our dialogue partner. This happens with the help of the sources of the other (the partner's written works) and the partner's own explanations.

For Muslims, dialogue is most often used to project onto the other what he or she thinks of the dialogue partner and to present Islam in a form he or she thinks the other will understand—rather than in the form in which Islam defines itself. There is always an apologetic dimension, more so than the communication of rigorous information, featuring both the positive and the negative.

The difficulty of dialogue with Islam is the fact that, having come after Christianity and speaking of Christ and Christianity in the Quran, the Muslim believes he knows Christ and Christianity already and does not attempt to gain knowledge according to what the Gospel and Christians say about themselves. What makes things still harder is that the Quran implies that the Gospel has been modified, along with the fact that the Quran presents itself as the "final revelation" of God to humanity. Muslims therefore don't feel the need to investigate the Gospel or ask questions of Christians.

Father Karam: For both Christians and Muslims, dialogue means being open toward the other and accepting and respecting his or her values. Dialogue does not imply the cancelling out of one of the two partners. Dialogue means the one AND the other—not the one OR the other.

In Lebanon, Christians and Muslims know each other very well, and they know how to treat each other and how to arrive at a *modus vivendi* that meets the need of all. When one of the two communities is affected or hurt, there is a spirit of solidarity and a strengthening of ties. As in every family, not everyone agrees on everything and there are disputes, but common cause is made when needed. The problem happens on the level of interference from the outside.

In October 2007, in an open letter to the Pope Benedict XVI that was signed by 138 Muslim theologians, the point was made that, given the fact that Muslims and Christians account for 55 percent of the world's population, peace between the two is essential. "No single party can win unilaterally in a conflict that involves more than half of all the people on the planet. Hence, our common future is at stake. The very survival of the world itself may be at stake."

What is the calling of the Church in the Middle East, in our time?

Archbishop Jeanbart: The Church's calling today is one of promoting peace and reconciliation between warring factions. In all the countries where they live, Christians want to see a clear separation between nations' external policies and strategies, on the one hand, and their internal politics, on the other—to ensure Middle Eastern citizens' freedom of choice in recognition of the fact that the social fabric is very rich and complex and that it has been created in the course of centuries, from time immemorial. It has to be recognized that, despite all that is happening today, this pluralism remains deeply rooted in the mentality and customs of the people of the region.

Bishop Ballin: The Church is called to promote unity and mutual understanding.

Bishop Mansour: That calling is to be the light of the world and salt of the earth—to witness to Jesus and his unconditional love and mercy for all people.

Father Samir: The Church is called to strengthen the faith of Christians and to support them, intellectually and spiritually, in giving witness to the Gospel in public life and among Muslims; the Church is called to call on Muslims to discover the true Christ—not the one as presented by the Quran and even less the one presented by Muslim tradition—through the reading of the Gospel; finally, the Church is called to help our countries build a more just society, one that respects human rights, particularly religious freedom, and that cares for the poorest among us. And the Church is called to do so through the engagement of the laity in social and political life.

Father Karam: The calling of the Church in the Middle East today is to ensure the maintenance of the Christian presence in the region; the protection of Christians; and the promotion of dialogue and coexistence between Muslims and Christians.

What are the Churches' biggest needs today?

Archbishop Jeanbart: The most urgent needs of our Church in today's circumstances are finding the means to help the faithful survive, to be safe, and to continue the education of their children. The funding we receive from our friends in the West is indispensable for the Church to be able to respond to the people's biggest needs in Syria. They are lacking so much and we feel called to prioritize material support.

Bishop Ballin: "My" Church is in the Gulf. Here it depends on the country in which we live. There are countries that are very open, while others are very closed. In the Gulf, we need more space to receive our millions of Catholics. If our faithful are not given the right pastoral care, they will cause problems for both the Church and the government. They are human beings, and when a person is not helped spiritually he or she becomes unbalanced, which can have bitter consequences.

Bishop Mansour: There is a great need for financial and political assistance from the West—especially to resolve some of the long-term problems in the Middle East. The Christians in the Middle East must continue their faithful devotion to God and neighbor in the Middle East.

Father Samir: Our biggest needs today are to find ways to help the very poorest, the disenfranchised, and the refugees. We must help them gain access to the very minimum they need to escape poverty and be able to lead a life with a minimum of dignity. That requires education—at the very least the defeat of illiteracy—giving people a chance to learn a trade, and to provide them with healthcare.

In addition, it is very important to build up the Christian community, the parish community, to get involved with those who have lost everything—not to avoid or humiliate them, but to find ways to give them back their dignity.

Father Karam: Our Church has a real need for international support—concrete action to effectively protect Christian Arabs in order to guarantee their presence in the region and their coexistence with Muslims. Christians want to remain in their lands, in their homes, and they are heartbroken by the prospect of having to leave their environment.

What's happening, though, is that Christians are encouraged to seek exile, given the facilitation of emigration; then there is the lack of pressure by the international community to provide Christian refugees with humanitarian aid just as it supports the bulk of the Syrian refugees in Lebanon, most of whom are Muslim.

CHALLENGES FOR THE CHURCHES

What are the main challenges that your Church faces?

Archbishop Jeanbart: There are three key obstacles today: There is a lack of security that frightens many families who feel exposed to dangers of all kinds. Second, there is great unemployment—so many factories, workshops and business have disappeared, leaving citizens with no options to find work. Third, as a result of all this, many people, and particularly the younger generation, are trying to leave Syria. Emigration is a challenge—it poses a great danger to the future of our Christian community. It calls into question 2000 years of our presence here, in this country where the Church was born in order to evangelize the world. In fact, for us disciples of Christ in the Middle East, witnesses of the birth of the Church, this outcome would be very dramatic and deal a huge blow to our apostolic mission in the country, where so many need to know Christ and are awaiting the coming of the Savior into their lives.

Bishop Ballin: In the Gulf we have Catholics from every rite and from more than 100 countries. The main challenge is that we have so many Catholic Churches side-by-side, as it were, rather than one Catholic Church. By "one" I don't mean uniformity—especially in the Liturgy—but the unity of hearts and fellowship.

Father Samir: The Church faces the challenges of finding ways to battle fanaticism and Islamic radicalism; social injustice; and ignorance or the lack of formation of a large part of the population. For example, 40 percent of the Egyptian population is illiterate. When it comes to Christians, the challenges vary from country to country. In Egypt, for example, the Church must insist on the equality of men and women, and on raising the level of people's religious knowledge. What's needed everywhere is to help Christians find ways to respond to attack and objections from Muslims, how to highlight certain aspects of our faith, and how to concretely manifest love for Muslims and build friendships—despite the aggressive attitudes of some of them.

Father Karam: The greatest challenges facing our Church are all connected: the rise of religious fundamentalism and the departure of Christians from the region—and, not to forget, the humanitarian challenges.

How would you involve the laity?

Archbishop Jeanbart: Given today's circumstances it is obviously very hard to take on all these challenges. But, despite everything, and with God's help, we have the courage to call on our people to have patience; we are doing everything to let them know that we are at their side and that we will never abandon them or leave them without support. That said, and as we are awaiting calmer and somewhat less dramatic times, this is what we envision doing to stop the deadly flow of emigration:

Reawaken in our ecclesial communities the apostolic spirit and the missionary zeal to which all faithful Christians are called, wherever the Lord has placed them. We have to bear in mind that Providence has kept us safe amidst our Muslim brethren in order to testify among them of the love of our Lord, who has come for the salvation of all the nations. Only we can perform this sacred work, as asked for by the Lord and to which the Church has generously devoted itself since its birth. We must remind our faithful that it was precisely in our country that Christianity took its first steps—and it would be very sad to abandon and erase the traces of this unique history.

Against all odds and swimming against the tide, we must develop a culture of liberty, democracy and respect for the other in the context of a cordial atmosphere, one of harmony and generous solidarity. We must insist that we are living in a beautiful country, called to a future full of promise.

We must strengthen and build up our social, educational and charitable institutions. That also means instilling a spirit of initiative in our young people, and to encourage them to create competent business initiatives that can generate employment and substantial revenue.

We must confront the housing problem with courage and openness. That means both pushing the authorities to support semi-private cooperative initiatives as much as ourselves taking an entrepreneurial approach toward these social issues, particularly with an eye on the younger generation. We need to remind everyone that a family with a home is good for the country.

We must also launch a movement that will fight against emigration—an effort of committed groups of laity who are deeply grounded in an awareness of the importance of our presence in the country and the many advantages life here can offer us. "Building to Stay," for example, is a lay movement we launched in Aleppo before the civil war, precisely with that goal in mind. Such an effort, we realize, is today more urgent and important than ever in helping us cope with the current situation.

We have to support and encourage all those initiatives that seek to promote Islamic-Christian dialogue, and to help all believers to come closer together, even as people's private choices are respected. We have to manage to establish a forthright and friendly culture of citizenship. That will bring all citizens serenity, tranquility and the joy of living together.

Bishop Ballin: The laity are very much involved through parish councils, associations, advisory boards, etc.

Bishop Mansour: The laity are involved in all the Church-run institutions; in Lebanon, for example, there is a very mature laity, who are deeply involved in the life of the Church and all the charities.

Father Samir: The laity must be awakened to become active members in majority Muslim societies—to do so without fear and with the desire to be of service to all without any distinctions. That requires a good general formation, a capacity to love—despite the injustices one often suffers just for being a Christian—a good knowledge of the Gospel; and a solid Christian foundation in order to know how to respond to questions and criticisms from non-Christians.

Is there, as some charge, an absence of lay leadership in the Churches of Middle East?

Archbishop Jeanbart: There is no shortage of lay leadership for us, even though many of them have left in the past three years because of the fighting. We can still continue to count today on the generosity of the young and the not so young, who, with a bit of effort on their part and our support, can quickly form a network to lead the faithful and bring them along, with a view to promoting a greater participation in the life of the Church.

Bishop Ballin: Not in the Gulf, where lay people have a strong voice.

Father Samir: There is no lack of lay leadership in the Churches of the Middle East. Compared to the West, the faithful are strongly attached to their Churches and clergy. But because of discrimination that can go quite far at times, there are sometimes great obstacles to concerted action. But it is more often the clergy that sometimes needs a boost.

THE HUMANITARIAN CRISIS

What are the main aspects of the humanitarian crisis?

Archbishop Jeanbart: The crisis Syria is living through derives from the actions of certain foreign countries in coordination with political opposition to the regime—which has governed the country for 40 years. These players are pursuing a process of change such as took place in Tunisia, Libya, and Egypt, all under the umbrella of the "Arab Spring." In Syria, this process, which presumed the fall of the regime would occur in just several weeks, as happened elsewhere, did not come to fruition. Things worked out very differently. Thanks to a strong army, the regime has managed to resist for four years already the assault of a multitude of combatants who have come from everywhere. First, they came to support the opposition in its revolution, then it turned into a holy war, a jihad, and the establishment in Syria of the self-proclaimed Islamic State whose frontiers have been hard to figure out so far.

This is not the place for a political analysis, but it must be said that the causes of this war are much more complex than claimed by those belonging to revolutionary movements. It must be said that there are international, geo-strategic, energy-related and economic interests in play. The fact remains that Syria has been at war for four years and that the number of those killed are counted in the hundreds of thousands and that this poor country has undergone an incredible dismantling and unheard-of destruction of its vital infrastructure.

The humanitarian fall-out of this destructive war are many. To cite but the most important ones: The great number of dead, handicapped and disappeared, leaving so many families in mourning, bitterness and poverty; the enormous destruction that has ravaged the country, depriving the people of their homes and businesses, their workshops and factories. This has led to a number of problems: displacement, unemployment, poverty and the enormous movement of refugees to safer regions or camps. All of this has brought misery to many families, rendering them totally dependent on outside help, depending on what part of the country they are in.

The pursuit of emigration and the possibility of a massive and destabilizing exodus is on the forefront of the minds of Christians, leaving them anxious and depressed. The disappearance of a great number of young people, who may be dead, or who have disappeared or emigrated, has caused great social and economic problems. Many families are left behind without the support of husbands or the support of their children; many young women are left behind on their own, without partners.

Bishop Ballin: Problems occur when people don't receive their salary, or are beaten up.

Father Samir: The crisis first of all affects the Muslim population more than the Christians. In the same country, Christians are often more open-minded and dynamic than the Muslims. Christians have often taken the initiative, not only when it comes to education, healthcare, social services or cultural activities, but also when it comes to working for socio-political reforms.

In those countries where there is a certain freedom and equality with Muslims—notably in Lebanon and Syria—where there is, in other words, a degree of secularism, Christians are not suffering from any particular systemic crisis. Again, they generally tend to be more open to the world than Muslims, but more reserved in their thinking and in their behavior than Westerners.

What are the practical solutions that will alleviate the humanitarian crisis?

Archbishop Jeanbart: First of all, people need the war to stop—meanwhile, they depend on a lot of help of all kinds: food, medicine, medical care, hospitalization for very serious injuries; help to find a place to stay if their home has been destroyed; education. There must be support for parents who no longer have the means to pay for the necessary expenses of their families; help for refugees in the camps and for the displaced. A campaign has to be put in place to inform and encourage people, giving a bit of optimism which allows them to think of the future, in a less defeatist and negative way; we must launch programs of ethical formation and promote a sense of solidarity and resilience in the face of adversity and chaos.

Bishop Ballin: In the Gulf, there is a great need for laws to protect workers.

Father Samir: Given the present circumstances, Christians are suffering from a serious crisis everywhere, proportionate to the pressure and violence aimed at them by fundamentalists, be they ISIS militants, Salafists, or members of the Muslim Brotherhood. This crisis affects their economic, social, and spiritual life—and over and above it all, their interior freedom.

Most of them are tempted to emigrate to the West (Europe, the U.S., Canada, Australia), especially if they have parents or friends who have emigrated already. That is surely the greatest danger, not just for Christianity in the Middle East, but also for the social life, the economic, political, cultural and spiritual well-being of the

Middle East and the Muslim people. Massive Christian emigration will only worsen the extremist currents and hold back the development and evolution of Muslims in all domains. That is why many enlightened Muslims are asking Christians not to leave the country.

How is the Church managing the crisis?

Archbishop Jeanbart: First of all, the Church has been present amidst the faithful, standing by them in this great adversity. To help them, the Church, through the voices of its pastors, has spoken words of consolation and great encouragement. The Church has mobilized to link action to these words—action on the part of bishops, clergy and laity to help those among them who are in distress and in need. Not for a single day have these pastoral ministries come to a halt, despite the fact pastors face great danger in currently very dangerous circumstances.

Bishop Mansour: Caritas organizations in almost every country of the Middle East are doing the work; then there are organizations like the Catholic Near East Welfare Association, Catholic Relief Services and Aid to the Church in Need. Plus, local communities who are doing the best they can to accommodate so many people in need. In some parishes throughout Lebanon, Jordan and Syria, entire congregations have become charitable institutions in the service of refugees.

Father Samir: The Churches are doing their utmost to manage the crisis as best they can, by supporting Christians as much as possible, making sure that pastors stay very close to their flock—which is all greatly helped by material and spiritual aid provided by Christians in the West.

But this situation can't go on indefinitely. A great number of Christians have left Syria to find refuge in neighboring countries (Turkey, Jordan and especially Lebanon). In Iraq, the situation is even more dramatic in regions occupied by Islamic terrorists.

Christianity will not survive if Christians don't stay in their land and return to their villages and towns as soon as possible. But they can only do so if two conditions are met: There must be peace and security, on the one hand, and, on the other, they must find the financial and material means to rebuild what has been destroyed or, worse, what has been stolen. In both areas, these Christians are totally dependent on the West, especially Christians in the West.

How is the crisis specifically affecting women, children, and the elderly?

Archbishop Jeanbart: This war has had a great impact on the citizens of the country in general and particularly on the faithful of our Church community—women, children and the elderly worse than most. On the positive side, this hardship has reawakened many people from their spiritual torpor and re-focused them on the essential, on prayer and on God. We have witnessed a great rallying of people around their pastors who have mobilized to be at their disposal during these very hard times. The Church has newly become a family community. Priests and laity have rediscovered a spirit of solidarity that unites them.

Father Samir: The crisis affects everyone, but especially those who are weakest—physically or morally—and who cannot defend or take care of themselves. That is especially true for children and the aged. It is true for women as well; they are most often the victims of terrorists, especially if they have no men to physically protect them—there have been thousands of cases of rape, leaving the victims with physical and psychological scars for life. Women also suffer in everyday life, which has become very difficult, forcing them to rely basically only on themselves.

What are the expectations of the refugees from the Church?

Archbishop Jeanbart: Refugees and the displaced count on the Church's help to return to their homes once the war is over. They hope to get help to repair their houses which in many cases have been damaged by fighting or vandalized by combatants or thieves. Then there are those who wish to be able to access some modest financing so they can re-launch their business and set up their workshops again.

Bishop Ballin: Material help. However, there is the danger that people come to think of the Church as a humanitarian organization. Even though the first necessity is the provision of material help, the Church must never forget that her mission is to transmit the faith. Faith is the first and the best help that we can give to people in distress.

Father Samir: The Churches are doing what they can to help the refugees. By the grace of God, support from Christians in the West is an enormous help. Their response has been very generous, not just in terms of money, but also in the form of coming to live among the refugees, to lend moral support. The numerous visits by patriarchs, bishops—even some from the West—and the presence of men and women religious, priests and lay volunteers all has boosted the strength and spirit of the refugees. The problem is that no one knows when it will all be over and how much longer the refugees have to persist in their struggle.

What's most important: on the one hand, to tackle the most pressing problem, that of Islamic terrorism; next, we must find lasting solutions that will allow Christians to make new beginnings, be it in their own environment or in other acceptable settings.

THE INDIVIDUAL

Please tell us any individual stories of hardship.

Archbishop Jeanbart: Toward the end of October 2012, the 19th of that month to be precise, a bus carrying civilians coming from Beirut was stopped at Sarakeb, a small village near Aleppo that was then occupied by the armed opposition. Eleven passengers, all Christians, including seven Armenians, were kidnapped and a large ransom was demanded for their release. The victims have not been heard from since. Two of our faithful, though, Georges Rabbath and his father Béchara, were released after their kidnapping, after the family came up with a large sum. To raise the money, they had to sell their house and go into debt. Georges and his father reported that they had been treated very badly, and that the group of hostage-takers forced Georges, despite his surname of Abdullah, to renounce his faith and declare himself a Muslim. These jihadist combatants belonged to Jabhet Al-Nusra [Al-Nusra Front], an off-shoot of al-Qaeda, and included a number of nationalities—Syrians, Turks, Libyans, Chechens and even Belgians and French, with the Europeans treating their prisoners the worst.

What is the emotional toll of this crisis? Please touch upon the despair, the loss of dignity and other aspects of this suffering.

Archbishop Jeanbart: Unfortunately, this terrible war that has held Syria in its grip for four years has now found its hottest theater in Aleppo. At a certain point, hundreds of dead were strewn along the city streets and those of the suburbs; the scene was rendered more sickening and somber by the sight of hundreds of destroyed buildings, including socio-cultural institutions, schools and numerous hospitals. Tears readily came to our eyes in watching all this misery hit the people of Aleppo who, for months at a time, lived night and day under the threat of bombing raids. They lost loved ones, they have seen their businesses destroyed and their factories ransacked and looted.

Factory workers no longer have jobs and trades-people are no longer working. People are in distress and misery weighs on so many of them. Such a situation is afflicting us, saddens us and makes us deeply unhappy. What makes us sadder still are the executions of people who have surrendered, the assassinations and kidnappings of innocent folks. Three young priests from Aleppo were kidnapped as they left the city. Everyday anguished parents turn to me for help in finding their kidnapped children or those who have simply disappeared, we know not how. Several times, a woman in total despair has come to me in tears, pleading with me for help and support. She is the mother of six young children; her husband has been kidnapped by the rebels; she has received no word on his fate; she is without any means and does not know how to feed her large family on her own.

The story of the misfortune of the Syrian people can perhaps be well illustrated by way of what has befallen Aleppo because of this sad war. In fact, this town has been stricken materially and economically, its population humiliated and degraded. The denizens of this great metropolis—with local evidence of at least 7,000 years of human settlement—find themselves now four years into a senseless war, trapped in a disastrous situation. The prosperity that set Aleppo apart among the most famous cities in the region has lost its sheen. Its factories and once flourishing industries have been destroyed, along with its infrastructure, its social and administrative institutions, its trade and its legendary marketplaces, its ancient homes, its schools and hospitals.

All this splendor has been brought to ruin, its population impoverished in dramatic fashion—and Syria has been robbed of its main sources of economic wealth. Is it really necessary to mention all the difficulties confronted by the people of the city as the city continues to suffer an unprecedented siege laid by the rebels?

Have you, personally faced evil?

Archbishop Jeanbart: In June 2012, our archdiocesan chancery was attacked by a group of rebels, who invaded, vandalized and ransacked my personal office and the offices of my staff. Thanks be to God, I was providentially away from the city at that time and only material damage was done. We lost money, computers, electronic equipment and cameras. In October that same year we were hit by two bomb shells, which caused major damage; one of the priests who sought to help me was gravely wounded—he had to be transported to Beirut where he underwent several rounds of very delicate surgery; he had to convalesce for several months. Thanks be to God, he is fine now, but he nevertheless lost an eye.

In October 2014, en route to Beirut, a group of armed men attacked my car and tried to hurt my driver and myself; at least a dozen shots were fired at us. I asked the Virgin for help and I don't know how she saved us, because the car turned over and skidded on its side, almost blocking the emergency door. That attempt on my life left me only a bad memory and a small cut on one of the fingers of my left hand.

In fact, though, we are constantly in danger, in the archdiocesan compound, where I am every day. It sits not much more than 300 feet from the eastern front in the city. Still, I consider my presence in the mother house of our Christian community important—to help protect this centuries-old precious ecclesial patrimony as well as to give courage to the people of the neighborhood, to lessen the fear of Christians and boost their morale.

A pain that makes me suffer a lot, and which I experience every day, is when parents come to me, when I hear their plaints and sometimes see them cry as they talk to me about their very difficult situation, their intense misery as a result of the war. It is painful to watch all the hardship they put themselves through to help their young children, making sure that they receive at least the very absolute minimum they need.

How do you think this time of adversity has affected people's faith?

Archbishop Jeanbart: First of all, the war has awakened the Christians and reminded them that they are not alone. The war has brought them back to prayer and to participation in different liturgical celebrations and at Mass. The war has brought clergy and laity together, to rediscover the fraternal bond that unites them and brings them together, gathered around the bishops of the Church. The latter has been well typified by St. John XXIII in his famous encyclical *Mater et Magistra:* first *Mater*, and then *Magistra*—first Mother, then Teacher.

Chapter 12
"Voices" on Christianity & Islam

The Fate of Christians in the Middle East
By Bishop Elias Sleman

Introduction
Middle Eastern Christians began their history with persecution—first by the defenders of Jewish law; then by the Romans; then by emperors of all kinds; next by authorities belonging to other Christian communities who called them heretics or schismatics or gave them other labels; and, finally, by a new religion that appeared in the first third of the seventh century—namely Islam.

Politics
The Middle East was the birthplace of Christianity. Between the start of the Christian era and the appearance of Islam, there were many persecutions against Christians, and then many tensions between the different Christian communities, and there were many martyrs of inter-Christian warfare. With the appearance of Islam, the Christians had to live in a world dominated by the new Muslim religion, under the *dhimmi* regime (which consists of paying taxes for the supposed "protection" by Islamic authorities who run the state).

The Christians were never on an equal footing with Muslims, even until today, except in Lebanon, where a confessional regime reigns (consisting of power-sharing between the different religions: Christians, especially Maronites, Sunni Muslims, and Shiite

Muslims, and other religions with less important numbers, like the Druze and Alawites, among the Muslims and, among the Christians, Orthodox Christians of various kinds, especially the Greek Orthodox, the Greek Catholics, the Syriac Catholics and Orthodox, the Armenian Catholics and Orthodox, etc.).

In Islam there is no separation between religion and state, and, as a consequence, religion is always the state religion, and members of that religion are citizens of the first degree, while others are citizens of the second, third, or even lower degrees. There is no real equality among the citizens or freedom of conscience, which goes further than simple religious freedom. As a result, in the Middle East, it is religion that dictates law and not the citizens, unlike in the secular West. Even in Lebanon, every few years there is a war where one or another religion asserts itself, insisting on its due place because an increase in the number of its members or its importance.

The game of numbers always causes conflicts for the sociopolitical rehabilitation of the place of the community in society. One does not find oneself in a stable setting of inter-denominational harmony rooted in the very nature of a society on a cultural, political or socio-human plane. Christians have always been prey to persecutions, more or less violent or bloody. There are also other sorts of persecutions that take the form of segregation on the level of employment, public functions, and basic rights. Being second-class citizens, especially when you have been there for 2,000 years; and when we have welcomed the Muslims to be close to us; when we have built the countries of the Middle East with them; when we suffered the Ottomans together; when we have side-by-side liberated our countries from Western protectorates; and when Christians were the principal actors of the "Arab Spring," etc.—this all becomes heavy and wounding. We, the Christians, are suddenly marginalized by our compatriots in the name of religion! That is especially true today with this growing Islamist jihadism.

There are other reasons for persecution underlying everything that goes on in the region of the Middle East: there is the

Palestinian problem and the position of the West, especially the United States, dealing unequally between Israel and the Palestinians. This injustice is also a reason for persecution because the West is considered by the Muslims to be a Christian world. After my experience in France with French secularism, I discovered that French secularism is anti-Catholic, not anti-religious; it is pro-Jewish and pro-Muslim, but anti-Catholic. And so the West has played a role, even unconsciously, in working against Christians. There is in the West a poor comprehension of Middle Eastern Christians, even if Middle Eastern Christians have played an essential role in encouraging moderate Islam. Without the Christians, the Muslims of the Middle East become extremists. The presence of Christians in the Middle East is a Muslim necessity even before it becomes Christian necessity!

I do not see the conflict in the Middle East as a clash of civilizations. It is more of an anti-civilization conflict. That's what the *takfirists* [those who accuse other Muslims of apostasy] want, whoever they are—a clash of civilizations—to justify their violence and to nullify the rights of others to be different from them. They want socio-cultural and religious uniformity and conformity to be the normal way of life of people; they dictate their sharia so that everyone will submit to it. In Islam, a "believer," i.e., a Muslim, should not be governed by a non-believer, a non-Muslim. This principle is held by the jihadists even with regards to moderate Muslims who are considered by them as non-believers because they do not apply sharia law in the way extremists want it—in its most radical form. For them, that is the real Islam, and the rest is a betrayal of Islam.

Is that the clash of civilizations? Certainly not, because this current is anti-civilization where there reigns the law of desire and of *Houriyat,* the 70 women in paradise who await each of the believing Muslim men, especially those who engage in "Holy War," or jihad, from which we derive the word "jihadists." Everyone who is not like them should die, or disappear, so that Islam can reign—and what an Islam! They sow the terror of death everywhere without any sort of scruple! They film and distribute images of their horrors to sow terror everywhere, cleansing the land where they want to invade!

The Lebanese model proves that an Arab can be Christian and not only Muslim. But in the eyes of the jihadists, anyone who is not like them is not a Muslim. In reality, the movement of the "Arab Spring" was brought about principally by Christians. But for Muslims who have not known Arab Christians closely the idea of a Christian Arab is a curiosity, and even bothersome. I remember, when I was at the Institute Catholique in Paris between 1982 and 1988, there was a Tunisian Muslim working as a security guard; when he heard me speak Arabic, and found out that I was a seminarian, he got very angry and did not even want to speak to me. That is why the presence of Christians in the Middle East is also a Muslim necessity—it pushes Muslims to be open and moderate. The nature of Christianity is always against being closed off. The nature of Christianity is to hold a position that is always critical vis-à-vis all that is immoral, unjust, and inhuman. Christianity is against exploitation in the name of God. Jihadist Islam kills and commits horrors in the name of God. True, Catholic Christianity of a certain era engaged in activities that we no longer allow—that is no longer tolerated in the reality of the Church, especially in the post-Vatican II era.

It seems to me that the terrain of the Middle East is dominated in a new way, based on the refusal of the other in the name of religion, ethnicity and race! Why do we want to constitute countries on the basis of religion? Why, considering globalization, do we look to normalize the refusal to live with those who do not share the same religion? Where do we find inter-religious dialogue, the dialogue of civilizations? The Middle East is manipulated by many parties—and Christians are a target for everyone because they represent openness and moderation. Do they need to disappear from the Middle East for it to become the image of those who cry, "The New Middle East"? Why desire to prove that plurality and diversity are impossible? Why impose uniformity in a region where pluralism has been the norm for centuries and centuries? Must the imported idea that different religions are incapable of living together be imposed by force?

Unfortunately, the idea is in the process of becoming a conviction. Must the Middle East be emptied of Christians who are called minorities because of their number? Why not take as a yardstick the law of influence instead of the law of numbers? If criteria are based on influence, Christians become the majority in the Middle East—because by their presence they ensure moderation and openness!

Islam

We realize that the religious factor was once almost absent in its social impact. The West helped cause a revolution in Iran, helping to create the conditions that led to the ousting of the Shah and causing the religious leader Khomeini to be brought into power. Shiite Islam had been known for its moderation and openness. From that date, however, we see that tensions began to mount in both the Sunni and Shiite worlds. Why did the great powers want to play this game? In Islam, quite a few thinkers had become engaged in a current of tentative openness and began to open themselves to the application of the historical-critical sciences in the religious domain.

The principle of the shedding of blood over religious questions began to multiply in a way that demanded attention—but the West remained silent. It was not a common trend at first, but with time it became more common and familiar. The tension between the Sunni and the Shiite worlds began to grow, and hearts began to enter into the logic of a cold war, and, little by little, into the logic of hate. Reason began to retreat and the free reign of instinct advanced. The voices of ignorance began to drown out those of thinkers and moderates, and violence began to appear here and there. The ground became ripe for fanaticism. And, progressively, pro-secular currents retreated in the face of extremist currents. In this atmosphere the Iraq war was launched. With much tension accompanied by global media coverage, disorder began to be habitual. In Lebanon, an atmosphere of tension continues; between Palestinians and Israelis tension has never ceased.

During this time, the so-called "Arab Spring" began, and the explosion of rising Islamism took its toll with a shocking violence. The Muslim world was trapped and did not know how to free itself. It sank to the bottom of the abyss. The slogans of liberty and change for the better proved to be a means and a pretext to motivate the streets in Arab countries; and the Sunnis found themselves held hostage by jihadists and radicals of the Islamic State in Iraq and Syria. Today we find ourselves in lakes of blood flowing from the massacres in the name of Allah. Where is the place of Christians in all this? We are caught between leaving or violent death at the hands of terrorists who spread violence and horror everywhere! Is that the "Arab Spring?"

Christians, the so-called minorities, as well as moderate Muslims, are the victims. There are moderate Muslims, but they do not have voices strong enough to convince the people in the streets who are dominated by manipulators because of their ignorance. Moderate Muslims no longer have a place in this atmosphere; worse, they are on the hit list of the jihadists. Al-Azhar University in Cairo, the traditional reference point among Muslims, itself stands accused. There are moderate Muslims, but they are marginalized and abused by the fundamentalists.

In Islam there is not the possibility of the separation of Church and State. It is against the nature of Islam; for Muslims, the earth is the earth of Allah and the Quran is the foundation and the source of sharia. The sharia is found in the Quran, which is the source of the first law. In Islam, there is no supreme court, but only a single judge who must apply the law of Allah. And he is not to judge according to his own understanding; he should apply sharia as laid down literally by Allah. There is also no legislature in Islam. Rather, Allah is the unique legislator and the sharia law is the law of Allah. As a result, there is no question of separating Mosque and State.

Persecution

Christians are persecuted in the Middle East in a direct manner by this rising tide of Islamic jihadism. These are people who operate in the absence of reason and instinct drives all their actions. They kill with an unimaginable violence, and they take pleasure in torture, in making others suffer. Their knives are not sharpened, so that it must be very hard to cut off the head or neck. They cut the head by the neck from behind and leave the person to raise the head with a hand that supports the chin and walk. After a few steps, bathed in their own blood, the victims fall dead. Children are killed in front of their parents; women and girls are raped before being beheaded.

In times past, the atmosphere of war reigned everywhere, and Christians were persecuted for their faith; their stories of martyrdom show the atrocities they had to endure. The Lord intervened. There were also exterminations on a massive scale of people who refused to renounce their faith. Many emigrated; others apostatized.

The media actually allows us to know what happens in the world, pretty much immediately. Before, we did not immediately know what was happening apart from what was going on in one's own region, and as a result, we did not live in fear of advancing terror as is the case now. In the past, we were suddenly faced with attacks that confronted everyone; some got lucky, others quit their religion to join that of their persecutors. Today, so many Christians live in constant fear.

The Contributions of Christians

Moderate Muslims speak of the importance of the Christian presence in the Middle East. Such questions are dealt with in presentations with Christians present. We hear things about the positive role of Christians in the Muslim world. There is thus a discourse of truth and one that is covered, in part, by media. But few are those Muslims who hold a truthful dialogue among just themselves about the benefits of the presence of Christians in the Muslim world. In meetings and general assemblies, we hear a lot of the positive discourse, but when Muslims have meetings among themselves the same people express contrasting opinions.

Through their religious and moral principles, Christians are peacemakers. The talk of Christians is always a discourse of concord, calling for dialogue, encounter and the construction of a society worthy of humanity. But lately, most Middle Eastern Christians have only one main concern: to pack up and leave for whatever destination they can get a visa for. They gravely worry about their children. In the Maronite Eparchy of Latakia we are doing everything we can to support small projects for local Christians, to encourage them to remain where they are and to abandon plans to leave for foreign lands. Until now, we have not been able to secure any money for this objective.

For the sick, we try to procure medicine from several different sources, whether locally or from elsewhere. Catholic organizations always play a positive role in serving the poor, providing medicine, food, provisions of all kinds. In terms of education, we try to secure material support to students so they can continue their studies instead of having to work in order to be able to attend school or even to eat.

Inter-religious dialogue

Inter-religious dialogue with Muslims has no results if it is about theology, because, for Muslims, the Quran descended from heaven as it was and even in the Arabic language; all that opposes it is considered false. This is why dialogue is only possible on the socio-human or behavioral level, certainly not on the level of dogma and religious teaching.

For Muslims, dialogue is monologue. That is to say, they dialogue in the spirit of proselytism. They only want to convert Christians to Islam. Or they speak in public to show themselves as open, but they do not do so truthfully. There are certainly Muslims who become Christian by conviction; in that case, it is not a dialogue, but a common search for truth. These partners welcome with open arms, without even attempting to influence them. We answer their questions and we open our holy places for them; we listen to them and we help them to find the path of truth.

Leadership

The Church in the Middle East has a role of the first order. We have to educate our children about the principles of the faith and to be real witnesses of our faith in Jesus Christ. We also have a duty to live the joy of the Gospel as the Holy Father has described it—to be attractive in our faith. Our speech must be strong and convincing, making for a discourse of truth that is full of the warmth of divine and human love. The Church needs to be helped with resources for construction projects like farms, schools, dormitories for students, hospitals, universities, etc., so that our infrastructure can survive, particularly in the areas of education and healthcare.

Our dignity demands that our people can work for a living and that we do not remain dependent on aid from abroad. Those who help us are gratefully acknowledged, but it is important that we take charge of finding work for our people. We must launch projects so they can work and keep their dignity and spirit of solidarity—remaining attached to the land where work can be found. If we have offers of work, our dignity and our pride are saved, and we become unified and help each other in facing the difficulties of life. We also need permanent resources that will permit us to sustain our ongoing projects and develop new ones.

The laity are involved in all these questions that I have just touched on, in all these crucial matters of mutual aid and self-help projects. But they need to live. They cannot engage in a project full-time if they do not receive a salary for their work—and that is so hard to guarantee. Lay leaders are not absent in the Church; they are present and interested in all that touches the life of the Church and all its affairs, all that is in line with the mission of the Church.

The Humanitarian Crisis

The Church standing at the ready with baskets of aid carries the risk of turning our people into people living off of aid, without dignity and even solidarity and without attachment to the land. That attitude kills the conscience and promotes self-centeredness as well as a sense of rivalry. Poverty is rampant today. There are those who have gotten rich through the war, but they are not the Christians. The dangers blind the courage in many, and an unclear future destabilizes the young, and the fear of what menaces causes parents to be afraid for their children and their future. The Church is no longer able to take care of itself; and without work that generates resources, there is no way for the community to be autonomous. Construction and repair are not possible because we do not have the means. The horizon is far from being wide open in front of us! The crisis is truly severe for us on all levels!

The Church stands amidst its faithful. I assure them that, when I can no longer protect them, I will remain with those who remain—I will never leave Syria unless the authorities of the Church ask me to, for whatever reason. I always lead faith formation through a strong liturgical life; I encourage the faithful to be strong in their faith and stay on their land, to construct the country as best we can with the means we have, even if those means are reduced.

The women are afraid for their children, for their future, for their lives; they believe themselves to be the weakest members of society. They greatly fear being abused by Islamists, to end up like slaves and being sold like objects or animals! The children pay the greatest price. I think that all of them are in need of therapeutic treatment. They are victims of violence, either when the jihadists train them to be violent or when they are victims of violence themselves. They lack a healthy educational environment. Instead, they are plunged into the grown-up world and its problems even though they are still children! They are living the violence even in their games. The elderly are in horror! They see images in the media and close their eyes. They live with terrible concern for their loved ones. They live lives full of trouble and fear.

Who has not had crazy experiences in the course of these wars? Many questions arise, especially among the young—questions regarding God, the faith, humanity, existence, etc. To kill thousands of men and women, children and the elderly, in cold blood, in the name of Allah—as if one is praying or amusing oneself—is absolute evil. To train oneself to kill others, without even knowing whom one is in the process of killing, is absolute evil. To die in the expectation of going to paradise and have 70 women with which to enjoy oneself? Is this not absolute evil?

Many Christians have rediscovered the faith; and many

Muslims become Christians when they discover Jesus Christ—an experience that stands in stark contrast with what they are finding in their own religion—and when they reflect on the atrocities committed by Muslims who do it all in the name of Allah!

Bishop Elias Sleman has led the Maronite Eparchy of Latakia, Syria since 2012. Ordained a priest in 1987, he studied for the priesthood in Paris. Both a canon and civil lawyer, he holds several advanced degrees. The author of numerous books in both Arabic and French, he serves on the Maronite Appellate Court and teaches theology at Catholic universities in both Syria and Lebanon.

Meeting the challenges faced by Christians in the Middle East
By Bishop Angaelos

Indigenous Communities under Threat

Indigenous Christian communities have been a vital part of the identity, culture and heritage of the Middle East for over two millennia. These communities have been a stabilizing and reconciling element in the region for centuries and are an intrinsic part of the fabric of the Middle East. In their conduct and in their active role as peacemakers Christians continue to be "salt of the earth" and "light of the world" (1 Mt 5:13–16) in a region that is in desperate need of hope.

Despite their invaluable contribution and right to remain in their homelands, these indigenous communities are at risk because they have no place within the extremist narrative which is now more evident in the region. While Christians continue to suffer the brunt of these dangerous levels of exclusion and dehumanization, other religious and ethnic minorities, including many Muslims, also suffer the same fate. Innocent men, women and children face extreme persecution, torture and murder for their faith, sometimes in the most barbaric and medieval manner, which is unfathomable in the twenty-first century.

It is saddening to see the ever-spiraling levels of aggression and widespread brutality experienced by many in countries such as Iraq and Syria. The loss of these historic Christian communities, with their stabilizing and reconciling presence, will not only have a detrimental effect on their own countries but on the entire region as a whole. While this is the current situation, the longer-term concern is that the same dangerous model of intolerance and extremism will become legitimized and increasingly replicated throughout the Middle East and further afield if left unchallenged.

Despite the various challenges faced by Christian communities, they do not seek to be classified as minorities or anything other than legitimate citizens of their nation states, entitled to the basic human rights and freedoms afforded to all.

God-given Rights and Freedoms

The global community is founded upon the safeguarding of fundamental principles of freedom and equality, and as Christians we believe that these principles and rights are God-given and merely enshrined in international charters and conventions, such as Article 18 in the Universal Declaration of Human Rights. As Christians we believe that all humanity is created in the image and likeness of God, with that image intrinsic to our human nature (Gn 1:26–27), laying the foundation for the respect, love and value of all. Within this nature we believe that humanity has been given a reasoning spirit and entitlement to seek, accept, reject or be indifferent to God without compulsion or discrimination. This is central to our faith and indicative of God's respect for the humanity He created free, as explained in 2 Corinthians, "Now the Lord is the Spirit; and where the Spirit of the Lord is, there is liberty" (3:17). While this freedom of religion and belief is central to the lives of millions around the world, it continues to be widely violated. Subsequently, the entitlement to these rights of citizenship, justice and equality is often dependent upon a person's religious affiliation.

The Coptic Orthodox Church

The violation of these rights and freedoms is certainly not new to Christianity, and the experience of the Coptic Orthodox Church is one example of this historical reality. Coptic Christians are the indigenous people of Egypt and continue to form by far the largest Christian denomination in the Middle East, despite intense waves of persecution endured over centuries. The Coptic Orthodox Church is one of the most ancient in the world, founded in the first Century in Egypt by Saint Mark the Apostle and writer of the second Gospel of the New Testament. The word "Copt" is derived from the Pharaonic word "gypt" and the subsequent Greek word *Aigyptus* meaning "Egypt." Copts are therefore the indigenous Christian people of Egypt, the direct descendants of the ancient Egyptians, a people with perhaps the longest recorded history.

Historically the Coptic Church has been labeled the "Church of Martyrs," due to the fact that almost one million men, women and children were killed for their faith during the reign of Emperor Diocletian (284–305 A.D.). Further waves of persecution came with the entry of Islam in the seventh century, and the subsequent Arabization and Islamization of Egypt from the beginning of the second millennium.

Over the past 30 years there have been increasing attacks on Christians in Egypt, and a further escalation of violence and aggression following the popular uprising in 2011. This heightened level of persecution culminated in an unprecedented attack on more than 100 Christian Churches and places of ministry in a period of 48 hours following the forceful dispersion of Islamist protests in Cairo. In their peaceful response to these attacks, there was not a single act of retaliation from Christians, who on the contrary powerfully declared their faith by writing "We forgive you . . . we are taught to love our enemies" on the walls of their burned-out churches. To date, Egyptian Christians still face persecution for their faith, and continue to show resilience and commitment by following in the footsteps of our Lord Jesus Christ.

Holistic Approach to Meeting the Challenges

Religious persecution is by no means limited to Egypt, but occurs in many places around the world. For this reason a more holistic approach to safeguarding freedom of religion and belief at a more global level is needed. Rhetoric used to describe the atrocities in the Middle East must no longer remain within a religious framework, but rather deal with these events as unacceptable crimes against citizens of countries who are entitled to the basic rights and freedoms afforded to all. When speaking of alienation or marginalization, we must defend the rights to which every human being is entitled, and not focus on his or her religion, ethnicity or any other affiliation. It is within this context that the international community, religious leaders, and all those in positions of influence must commit themselves to providing, supporting, and advocating for Christians and others whose fundamental right to freedom of faith is denied.

Christ the Chief Advocate

As Christians we have a particular responsibility and calling to follow in the footsteps of our Lord Jesus Christ in advocating for all. He was an Advocate for the oppressed, marginalized, and outcast, as well as the chief Advocate for mankind as a whole (1 Jn 2:1). Out of His deep love and concern for His children, God cannot stand to see any of them suffering oppression or marginalization (2 Cor. 7:6) and through this love, He calls us to be ambassadors (2 Cor. 5:20), helping and supporting those in need. Based on this calling, it is the responsibility of Christians and the Church to imitate the life of their Shepherd. Advocacy in the Christian understanding is about speaking truth and upholding God-given principles such as love, justice, freedom and equality, and in doing so, being an example to the world, not only through the work of addressing injustice and oppression, but inherently through Christian witness.

Unified Efforts in Advocacy

As a result of the situation in the Middle East, greater humanitarian assistance and advocacy for a variety of people is continually needed and there has already been an immensely positive response from individuals and society as a whole. While reflecting on the darkness of these tragedies, we must also remember to give thanks for the light that shines through the good works of faithful organizations and individuals in their response, some of whom have sadly paid the ultimate price. Thankfully, there have been greater unified efforts across the ecumenical and inter-religious spectrums to express solidarity with, advocate on behalf of, and provide much needed aid to those suffering.

Religious and civic leaders have been challenged to speak out against violations of basic human rights, and in many cases have responded to that call with a greater sense of responsibility and commitment. This response however, is still disproportionate to the suffering, destruction and devastation that have been experienced, and much remains to be done. As individuals we should advocate for those who suffer gross violations of their basic human rights, realizing that when our efforts are expressed collaboratively in unity and solidarity with people across denominations and faiths, they are far more powerful and effective for all.

Hope and Reason to Give Thanks

It is increasingly difficult to be hopeful against the backdrop of those who continue to suffer for their faith, yet we are reminded through the powerful Resurrection of our Lord Jesus Christ, that in immense darkness, apparent death and defeat, there is an incredible light, witness, example, power and victory. We give thanks for our brothers and sisters, who despite the immense challenges, continue to live their Christian faith with extraordinary strength and resilience, and continue to advocate and pray for all who are denied their God-given rights and freedoms.

In seeking ways to meet these challenges we can find hope, comfort and reassurance in the words of Saint Paul, who says: "We *are* hard-pressed on every side, yet not crushed; *we are* perplexed, but not in despair; persecuted, but not forsaken; struck down, but not destroyed—always carrying about in the body the dying of the Lord Jesus, that the life of Jesus also may be manifested in our body" (2 Cor. 4:8–10).

Bishop Angaelos is the General Bishop of the Coptic Orthodox Church in the United Kingdom, a position he has held since 1999. A British citizen, he spent his childhood and early adulthood in Australia. In 1990, he was consecrated a monk by Pope Shenouda III. He specializes in working with youth.

Testimony of a Christian life in the Middle East
By Sister Marie Melhem, SSCC

I was born in a village, in the mountains in the north of Lebanon, along the famed "Route of the Cypresses," not far from Bécharré, the town where Gibran Khalil Gibran was born, the author of "The Prophet." In the winter my family would live in Tripoli, in the north, on the Mediterranean coast, where Sunnis are the majority. In Tripoli, I studied at a college that was run by the women religious of the Sacred Heart, an institution where Muslim and Christians rubbed shoulders without any problems. Up until age 18, I lived in that mixed milieu where believers prayed to the one God, in their respective churches and mosques in mutual respect—and in complete liberty.

In 1956, I entered the Congregation of the Sisters of the Sacred Heart, which was founded in 1853 by the Jesuits to educate girls in towns and villages, without distinction of religion or nationality, and with a preference for students from poor background or mixed environments where Christians and Muslims lived together.

In 1967, after my university studies, I was sent to Algeria, a Muslim country, at the request of Cardinal Leon-Etienne Duval of Algiers, who called on our congregation because our sisters were bilingual and Arab. He recommended that we wore civilian clothes so we would not be confused with the French women religious who had come to the country along with the settlers. We were responsible for the formation of teachers who would teach in Arabic in diocesan schools in the newly independent country.

Coming from the Middle East, this was a unique experience in my Christian life: there was great friendship and affection on the part of Algerian Muslims, both the leadership and ordinary people, with all of whom we very quickly established simple and fraternal bonds. For them it was the first time they met Arab Christians (who were not converts from Islam), who were praying in Arabic like they prayed the Quran which is written in Arabic. I spent seven years in Algeria and it was a time of consistent friendships.

In 1975, back in Lebanon to complete my religious formation, war broke out in the country, at first caused by the presence of Palestinian refugees driven out of Palestine. Lebanon, a welcoming, but weak country fast became the setting for the war of others; the civil war lasted for 15 years.

We had always lived together, Christians and Muslims, in the same villages, without any problems; we studied in the same schools and at the same universities; we were working together— thanks to ties that quickly strengthened again once the fighting was over. Muslims always tried to live in Christian neighborhoods and wanted to send their children to Christian schools.

It is another experience of living together that I experienced in Baalbek, a town with a Shiite majority where I was named to head a school run by my congregation. I was there also for seven years, at the height of the civil war—which meant no electricity, no telephone, explosions and kidnappings. The school was much sought after by the local population, which loved and also protected the Sisters. Militia leaders spontaneously lent protection to the school when they sensed that trouble was brewing in the city.

After Baalbek I was put in charge of the reconstruction of the Congregation's residences that had been destroyed during the war, serving at the same time as a "consultant" for the Pontifical Mission Society. I traveled throughout the country with staff of the Society in order to help people of all religious background. What was remarkable is that we were well-received everywhere, even though we came from a Christian institution, the Pontifical Mission Society.

From its beginnings, my congregation has worked in Syria, a country at war today, but which counts among its people and history a number of Christians playing crucial roles. For more than 50 years, my order has also worked in Morocco, teaching young people in a completely Muslim nation; we also were present in Chad, where we have worked in education, healthcare, and the promotion of Muslim-Christian dialogue. The local bishop asked us to live in Muslim neighborhoods in order to witness to Jesus Christ by way of our fraternal presence, discreetly, and with respect for our Muslim neighbors. There are so many examples to recount of living together in environments that were mostly Muslim: the Sisters always work while fully respecting the traditions of the country—for the betterment of all people, using all the means Providence has given them.

Exile

Christians in the Middle East have lived in those lands from well before the arrival of Islam in the seventh century. Many chose exile because of poverty—particularly at the end of the nineteenth century and at the end of World War I—and set out looking for work so their families could live in dignity. They found work in the West, in the U.S., where they discovered a certain humanism, science, culture, democracy, respect for human rights, and the dignity of work. In the U.S. today, many scientists, political leaders and even the very affluent hail originally from the Middle East.

Christians leave the Middle East because they have become a minority in countries with a Muslim majority who belong to a civilization that differs from that of the Gospel. Muslims also leave their countries in search of work, wealth and science.

Conflict

Anti-Western feelings stem in part from the support of the West for Israel—at the expense of the Palestinians, who, Christian and Muslim alike, are chased from their homes; and then there is poverty, ignorance and injustice, which all lead to violence and hate. War, violence and poverty have been pushing Christians of the Middle East to flee in search of a place where they can live in peace.

Christians and Muslims are citizens of the same countries.

Overall, they have lived in the same neighborhoods, but there are differences in cultural levels. For Christians the priority is to send their children to the best schools and universities, and even abroad for specialized studies, making great sacrifices in the process. That's why there are fewer children in Christian families and why Muslim families are bigger. But we both occupy the land that was inherited from our ancestors. The Christian is a full-fledged citizen. Creating a Christian enclave in the region would make no sense to us; we have always lived as good neighbors with Muslims.

Islam

The appeal of jihad stems from ignorance and exterior forces that use poverty to their ends and that want to sell arms. The principles of moderate Islam are based on education, living together, and respecting the rights of others in a democratic setting. In the U.S., there are a great many moderate Muslims. First they are citizens of the U.S., and only then Muslims. Everybody obeys the same laws in the U.S.. We have a similar culture in Lebanon, where Christians and Muslims have lived together successfully for centuries.

We have to work hard to develop democracies in this region, to build countries where the rights and duties of everyone are clearly defined. The Middle East is not just a source of oil or a market for arms dealers. In "The Joy of the Gospel" Pope Francis told us: "Social disparity sooner or later will engender violence that recourse to arms can never resolve."

The Church's contributions

The Christian Church, wherever she finds herself, has established educational institutions, universities, hospitals—all to help men and women flourish, regardless of their faith background. That is how the American university of Beirut has educated many leaders of countries in the Middle East from its founding until the present day. The same is true for St. Joseph University, founded by the Jesuits, which has contributed to the education of the elite. Christians and Muslims have received the same cultural formation, and many of them have continued their studies and research in the West, especially in the U.S.

A Middle East without Christians?

This notion is unthinkable. The Middle East is the cradle of Christianity. It is the land of Jesus Christ and the land that belongs to every Christian in the world. We are all in the same boat. The modern world is already an enormous village. We all are in solidarity with one another. We must work to develop and provide education to poor countries. That is less expensive than buying weapons and it is the only way to ensure the good of all.

Dialogue

This means living together in mutual respect, in democratic states. That is our experience in Lebanon, at least until external powers began using our "holy land" to wage their wars on our turf, taking advantage of our weak spots.

What's Needed

The Church here needs the solidarity of the universal Church to help Christians to stay in their countries. Rich Muslim countries are very present in the region with their generous resources. The Church has many charitable and educational institutions but we lack the resources to meet all the needs caused by this blind violence and war that have been introduced into the region.

Development is synonymous with peace, the Pope has said—and all human beings, especially the most fragile, deserve to be respected and treated with dignity. That is what Jesus tells us in the Gospel.

Where are all the weapons coming from? How can men become so savage? It is incredible—may God have mercy on us. But, despite everything, the suffering and tragedy, the faith of the people is stronger than ever. All are looking up at God, at the Church. People want to go back home in that sense. The pain of difficulties makes the faith more vivid. Our Churches are full at Mass, despite all the suffering.

The laity are close to the Church. The Church is in the heart of the Christian people. But everyone is hurting these days. There are no longer places to live in peace. People in the West get a glimpse through the media, but we, we live in the middle of this tempest of blind violence, the destruction of all places and people—without mercy! There are no words to describe the situation in the Middle East, the hardship of the people.

The stark reality becomes clear if one visits one of the many refugee camps set up in Lebanon where people have to live in the most inhumane conditions; and things are made worse this year by a bad winter, with fierce storms ripping away tents. How can one not pity these people overwhelmed by sorrow, and lacking food and basic supplies? In Lebanon today, one out of every two people is a refugee—without means! You only have to give them food and they will turn jihadist. That is the secret of the lure of terrorism: *poverty and violence suffered unjustly.*

Sister Marie Melhem is currently in charge of her congregation's motherhouse in Beirut, which is currently home to 17 women religious, including the congregation's Mother Superior. It serves as the order's administrative headquarters.

Violence in Islam and Christianity
By Father Wafik Nasry, S.J.

The greatest threat to Christianity in the Middle East today, as far as I can see, is ignorance. Many Christians in the Middle East today are ignorant not only of the secular sciences but also of their own faith. What is needed is good Christian education. Many Westerners think that they know Islam, but they do not. Worse yet, many of those who do have knowledge pretend to be ignorant and/or deliberately gloss over and/or distort reality lest they be drawn into the conflict.

Islam is a reality that is presenting itself in the clearest and strongest possible terms and is making its claim on power and control of the lives of people.

Meanwhile the Western democracies and many peaceful Muslims refuse to face reality. They pretend that the radical members of al-Qaeda and ISIS and many other Muslim militant political groups have nothing to do with the true Islam. As long as this erroneous position stands, neither the West nor the many non-violent Muslim peoples are going to solve the problem posed to the world today by the many different violent Muslim groups. Both the Western and peaceful Muslim leaders who advance such an erroneous understanding of Islam are not facing and/or dealing with reality, but with a figment of their own imaginations. They are dealing with a lie of their own making and live in the realm of wishful thinking. They either pretend not to know or do not really know.

Either way, their pretence and/or their ignorance is not going to make "this reality" go away. Both Muslims and Christians need to calmly face the reality of violence in Islam.

One of the ways that both Westerners and many Muslims have been evading any attempt to sit down and deal with the problem of violence within Islam is that for a long time any and every critique voiced about violence in Islam brings the response that "the same can be said of Christianity." The example of the Crusades is frequently cited as the proof of the place of violence in both faith traditions. No one has yet demonstrated if the source of violence in Islam is the same as the source of violence in Christianity?

One must also recognize that, although Islam has many faces and each has its own different varieties, Islam's basic inspirational texts are the uniting factors among its different groups, sub-groups, and institutions. The most important inspirational text in Islam is the Quran, which the Muslims believe to be the literal words of God that are valid for all times and all places. Another fundamental text for the Muslims is the biography of the messenger of Islam and his sayings due to their conviction of the authenticity and the finality of his message as the completion of the revelation about religion in history. As a result, Muslims feel, think, and assert a sense of obligation to spread Islam as well as a sense of superiority, and they act accordingly. Therefore, the call (*da'wah*) to Islam is seen in terms of Divine mandate and a human obligation, and the duty to fulfill it is a given. This is well demonstrated not only by the Quranic commentaries but also in practice. The Quran and the life of the messenger of Islam are the "measuring stick" for a Muslim to determine what is right and wrong.

Although the Quran calls both Christians and Jews "people of the book," the Christians are not a people of a book but of a "Person," namely Jesus, the Messiah. The main criterion, the single most important "measuring stick" for a Christian to judge what is right and what is wrong is Jesus, what He said, what He did, How He lived, how He died and how He rose from the dead. In fact, following Jesus and His teachings is the duty of every Christian. Accordingly, with regard to violence, if a Christian follows the words of Jesus literally, he will turn the other cheek. The violence present in the Old Testament has been placed in its right historical context in the light of the corrective of God's self-revelation in Jesus.

If a Muslim literally follows the words of the Quran and the messenger of Islam he would act in a specific manner. Let us take for example the concept of "terror." For a Christian, the word "terror" has a negative connotation. For a Muslim, it is something mandated by God in the *Quran*, as in the following texts:

> Against them make ready your strength to the utmost of your power, including steeds of war, to strike **terror** into (the hearts of) the enemies, of Allah and your enemies, and others besides, whom ye may not know, but whom Allah doth know. Whatever ye shall spend in the cause of Allah, shall be repaid unto you, and ye shall not be treated unjustly. Q. 8:60

In fact, in the Quran, God promises to terrorize the hearts of the infidels as a recompense of the infidels for their unbelief, as in the following verse Q. 3:151 "Soon shall We cast **terror** into the hearts of the unbelievers, for that they joined companions with Allah, for which He had sent no authority; their abode will be the fire; and evil is the home of the wrongdoers." Another example is found in Q. 8:12 "I will instill **terror** into the hearts of the unbelievers: Smite ye above their necks and smite all their finger tips off them." Hence for the majority of Muslims, who understand these verses literally, when they do that, they are simply following and executing God's wishes.

They do not see evil in terrorizing others who are not believers. In beheading a captured infidel, it is not an evil in their eyes, but pure obedience to God's command, as in the second part of the verse we have just seen, "I will instill terror into the hearts of the unbelievers: **Smite ye above their necks** and smite all their finger tips off them." Q. 8:12. The beheadings are to be numerous, a slaughter, and then they can hold captive the rest of the hostages as in Q. 47:4 that reads,

"So when you meet those who disbelieve [in battle], **strike [their] necks until, when you have inflicted slaughter upon them,** then secure their bonds, and either [confer] favor afterwards or ransom [them] until the war lays down its burdens. That [is the command]. And if Allah had willed, He could have taken vengeance upon them [Himself], but [He ordered armed struggle] to test some of you by means of others. And those who are killed in the cause of Allah—never will He waste their deeds."

As a result, Muslims who are acting violently, terrorizing non-Muslims and Muslims who do not share their understanding alike, draw the motives for their action directly from the founding Muslim texts. In fact, in his book *Quran wa Sayf* (Quran and Sword), on pages 137 to 139, the Egyptian Muslim thinker, Rif'at Sayyid Ahmad, who is a political expert and the founder and director of *The Yafa Center for Study and Research*, summarizes the aims of terrorism in Islam, as seen by the members of the radical Islamic movements as follows:

1. It is the recompense of the infidels for their unbelief. The divine power intervenes to terrorize the hearts of the infidels. This they base on Q. 3:151 "Soon we shall cast terror into the hearts of the unbelievers, for that they joined companions with Allah, for which He had sent no authority; their abode will be the fire; and evil is the home of the wrongdoers." The believers are required to arouse terror in the infidels. As far as they are concerned, this is based on a Divine mandate in Q. 8:60:

Against them make ready your strength to the utmost of your

power, including steeds of war, to strike terror into (the hearts of) the enemies, of Allah and your enemies, and others besides, whom ye may not know, but whom Allah doth know. Whatever ye shall spend in the cause of Allah, shall be repaid unto you, and ye shall not be treated unjustly.

Terror here is considered a good deed for which God rewards the individual who causes it. This is based on Q. 9:20 "The ones who have believed, emigrated and striven in the cause of Allah with their wealth and their lives are greater in rank in the sight of Allah. And it is those who are the attainers [of success]."

2. This terrorizing is done so that the infidels should keep their treaties with the believers.

3. Terrorism is considered a striking force and definitive tool in the battle; again, this is due to the intervention of Divine might using the weapon of terror. This is based on the verse we have seen twice before Q. 8:12 "I will instill terror into the hearts of the unbelievers: Smite ye above their necks and smite all their finger tips off them."

4. Terror is used as a psychological weapon with the infidels and hypocrites. It protects believers from the evil of the infidels, for if the infidels know that the Muslims are ready for the *jihad*, with all the weapons and apparatus, they would fear them. This fear is useful in more than one way. First, the infidels would not want to be neighbors with Muslims. Second, if the infidels' fear was great, then they might pay the tribute (*Jizya*) voluntarily. Third, this could be a motivation for the infidels to believe. Fourth, the infidels would not help other infidels. Fifth, there would be more embellishment in the house of Islam.

5. Finally, terror is used so there would not be *fitnah* (turning away and division) and the religion would be for God and the harm inflicted on the believers would stop, as in Q.2:193, "And fight them on until there is no more tumult or oppression, and there prevail justice and faith in Allah."

A number of reformers have attempted to contextualize the Quran and the life of the messenger of Islam with little or no success yet. In the eyes of the majority of Muslims, such reformers are declared infidels.

The example of the messenger of Islam is also used to provoke and inspire violence. The examples are too many to mention in the limits of time and space here. If we were to look at the many raids and invasions of different tribes and individuals, a Muslim can justify what ISIS is doing. One such raid was against a Jewish tribe known as Bani Qurayzah, in which, according to Muslim sources in the *Biography of the Messenger*, the messenger of Islam, after seizing the tribe, went to the market place, dug trenches and sent for the men of that tribe, and "struck off their heads in those trenches as they were brought out to him in batches. . . . There were 600 or 700 in all, though some put the figure as high as 800 or 900. . . . This went on until the apostle made an end of them."

Looking at the Muslim's sacred text, the Quran, the example of the founder, the history of the early Muslims as well as the present situation, we find them to be in harmony with violence, whereas if we look at the example of Jesus, the Christian sacred text, and the history of the first generation, we see something very different and very foreign to violence. We can use the Christian criterion, namely the example and the teachings of Jesus, and judge violent actions, of Christians and non-Christian alike, as wrong and sinful. If we use the Muslim criterion of judging right and wrong, as presented in their sacred text and the life of their founder, can we look at the violent actions of ISIS and say it is not of Islam? Is it true that one can say the same thing about Christianity? Is the source of violence in Islam the same as the source of violence in Christianity? Honest and well-intentioned Muslims and Christians of good will need to calmly face the reality of violence in Islam and realize that it is diametrically opposed to the teachings of Jesus.

Father Nasry, an Egyptian-born Catholic Copt, is an international scholar, expert on the Arab-Christian heritage, Islam and interreligious dialogue. He is a professor at the Pontifical Oriental Institute in Rome and teaches occasionally at the Jesuits' Pontifical University in Rome, the Gregorian. He has also taught at Loyola Marymount University in Los Angeles.

Why continue to pursue "dialogue" with Islam?
By Father Laurent Basanese, S.J.

Fifty years after Paul VI's October 28, 1965 promulgation of *Nostre Aetate* at Vatican II, "interreligious dialogue" is in trouble. At best, it runs the risk of being perceived as a trick or "hook" to convert people, or, at worst, it gives the impression, on the theological plane, that "all religions are equal." What's more, this new type of dialogue appears to be a waste of time and seems to be fruitless as the persecution of Christians around the world is only getting worse, especially in the countries in the Middle East where Muslims are the majority of the population. What good then is it to continue "to dialogue?"

I want to put the spotlight on the fact that the reasons for pursuing the "encounter" between people of different faiths are not obsolete, above all when everything seems to separate us. Nonetheless, the effort must not be pursued in a thoughtless or ill-considered way. The more obstacles there are, the more we have to work on making our encounters happen.

For starters, I insist that it is preferable to speak of "encounters" or "relationships" rather than "dialogue," as that term has been worn out and it does not correctly indicate all the dimensions of exchanges between people, highlighting principally the verbal aspect. "Encounters" do more justice to the richness, the diversity and the complexity of intersecting experiences, which promise the unexpected and are open, in general, to the future. The term also covers exchanges about ordinary preoccupations, such as collaboration on the human plane, such as charitable, economic, and social activities, as well as theological debates and the sharing of a life of prayer.

To persist in wanting to encounter "the other," "the enemy," is a profoundly Christian attitude. It is a characteristic of great souls. St. Francis de Sales, bishop of Geneva, doing battle with the Calvinists, said about St. Elizabeth of Hungary, whose devotion only grew amidst trials, pomp and vanities: "Great fires are stirred up further by the wind, but small fires are extinguished if they are not covered up." Hence, we must blow on the great fires, and protect the small ones. An encounter is like coals smoldering in a brazier. Those who take care of it with a generous heart will be set aflame themselves, but without getting burned.

Meeting with the Enemy?

We know that certain "sacralized" texts and traditions, on both the Christian and Muslim side, tend more toward rejection and defiance than to trust. On the Christian side, one only has to cite St. John:

"That one is the Anti-Christ, who denies the Father and the Son. Whoever denies the Son no longer has the Father; whoever confesses the Son also has the Father." (1 Jn 2, 22–23)

"Many false prophets are gone out into the world. Hereby know ye the Spirit of God: Every spirit that confesses that Jesus Christ is come in the flesh is of God; and every spirit that confesses not that Jesus Christ is come in the flesh is not of God: and this is that spirit of antichrist, whereof ye have heard that it should come; and even now already is it in the world." (1 Jn 4, 1–3)

On the Muslim side, it suffices to cite the Quran and Ibn Taymiyya (fourteenth century), with these writings widely distributed in the Wahhabi and Salafist milieus:

"Fight in the way of Allah those who fight you but do not transgress. Indeed. Allah does not like transgressors. And kill them wherever you overtake them and expel them from wherever they have expelled you, and associating [with them] is worse than killing." (Quran 2, 190–191)

"When God and his Messenger order us to confront our interlocutor because he transgresses and is hostile to the Book and to the Tradition, we have the order to confront him; we are not told to be gentle [. . .] Anyone who does not accept the ban on having as a faith—according to the direction of Mohammed [. . .] the religion of the Jews or of the Nazareans, and, rather, who does not consider [Jews and Christians] like miscreants and who does not detest them, is not a Muslim—he is below the Muslims." (Ibn Taymiyya, *Majmu Fatawa*, 3, 232 and 27, 464).

Nonetheless, Christians who want to remain faithful to their vocation must seek to behave the same way as Him Whom they confess. Christ, in fact, never tired of encountering people, especially sinners and those on the margins of society. To illustrate this attitude, we can meditate, first of all, on this famous passage from Paul VI's encyclical *Ecclesiam Suam* published during the Council:

> How truly wonderful is the inheritance of doctrinal riches bequeathed to Us by Our predecessors, and especially by Pius XI and Pius XII! Providentially they strove to bridge, as it were, the gap between divine and human wisdom, using not the language of the textbook, but the ordinary language of contemporary speech. *And what was this apostolic endeavor of theirs if not a dialogue?* As for Our immediate predecessor, John XXIII, he labored with masterly assurance to *bring divine truths as far as may be within the reach of the experience and understanding of modern man.* Was not the Council itself given a pastoral orientation, and does it not rightly strive to inject the Christian message into the stream of modern thought, and into the language, culture, customs, and sensibilities of man as he lives in the spiritual turmoil of this modern world? *Before we can convert the world— as the very condition of converting the world—we must approach it and speak to it* (ES 68).

Here the Pope speaks of the encounter of all men and women, cultures, all of society. Further on, he indicates the manner of conducting "dialogue," presenting it as a parallel to charitable work, such as described by St. Paul in his First Letter to the Corinthians, chapter 13:

> Dialogue, therefore, is a recognized method of the apostolate. It is a way of making spiritual contact. It should however have the following characteristics: *Clarity* before all else [then] *meekness.* [. . .] *It would indeed be*

a disgrace if our dialogue were marked by arrogance, the use of bared words or offensive bitterness. What gives it its authority is the fact that it affirms the truth, shares with others the gifts of charity, is itself an example of virtue, avoids peremptory language, makes no demands. *It is peaceful, has no use for extreme methods, is patient under contradiction and inclines towards generosity.* [Then] *confidence* [and] finally the *prudence* of a teacher who is most careful to make allowances for the psychological and moral circumstances of his hearer (ES 81).

Hence, the "encounter" is a dimension of the Church's mission. It is part of our identity and we cannot neglect it without denying who we are. It if is objected that this way of doing things is not "pure" because it includes—at least implicitly—the announcement of Jesus Christ, we can respond that we cannot hide and pretend that we are not Christians. We cannot conceal the charity of Christ as some would have us do, even in our social work. That is what Pope Benedict XVI affirmed in 2011 in his Apostolic Exhortation *Africae Munus*:

The Synod Fathers highlighted the complexity of the Muslim presence on the African continent. In some countries, good relations exist between Christians and Muslims; in others, the local Christians are merely second-class citizens, and Catholics from abroad, religious and lay, have difficulty obtaining visas and residence permits; in some, there is insufficient distinction between the religious and political spheres, while in others, finally, there is a climate of hostility. *I call upon the Church, in every situation, to persist in esteem for Muslims*, who "worship God who is one, living and subsistent; merciful and almighty, the creator of heaven and earth, who has also spoken to humanity." (*Nostra Aetate* 3) If all of us who believe in God desire to promote reconciliation, justice and peace, we must work together to banish every form of discrimination, intolerance, and religious fundamentalism. *In her social apostolate, the Church does not make religious distinctions. She comes to the help of those in need, be they Christian, Muslim or animist. In this way she bears witness to the love of God, creator of all, and she invites the followers of other religions to demonstrate respect and to practice reciprocity in a spirit of esteem.* I ask the whole Church, through *patient dialogue with Muslims,* to seek juridical and practical recognition of religious freedom, so that every citizen in Africa may enjoy not only the right to choose his religion freely and to engage in worship, but also the right to freedom of conscience. Religious freedom is the road to peace.

We cannot shirk the difficulties in our encounters, particularly those with Muslims—from dealing with our simple life in common to theological and social debates; we cannot gloss over the hardships, the misunderstandings, even the injustices, whether these come from the Christian or the Muslim side. It would be a greater scandal if we pretended all was well and that we were living a self-proclaimed happy co-existence. Sometimes what we call "harmony" is rather an embarrassed veil to cover up some confusion or a lie we dare not admit. On the contrary, we have to stand for justice, for the good of all: that is the only path toward peace, as John Paul II said in his January 1, 20012 message: "No peace without justice." And he added: "No justice without forgiveness."

We have to aim for truth and clarity. We have to talk and enter into relationships, up to the point of martyrdom, even at risk of becoming "martyrs of dialogue," "martyrs of encounter." That is to say, we have to be willing to forgive. The solution to conflicts is rarely a military or just a political one. Above all it requires a spiritual solution because it demands the leaving behind of the self, one's egoism and our private or community interests. If this attitude is not easy—even for a Christian who is even called to such an orientation permanently by the faith he or she professes—it is nonetheless never impossible. This leaving self behind, this encounter with the "other," hence overcoming hate, is never beyond our human capacity, with God's grace.

On this score, to illustrate that the word "impossible" does not belong in the vocabulary of someone who wants to imitate Christ and His words and acts, I will cite an example from an entirely different context than that of the Middle East; the example comes from a session of the "Truth and Reconciliation Commission" that was launched by Nelson Mandela and presided over by Archbishop Desmond Tutu:

> A frail black woman stands slowly to her feet. She is about 70 years of age. Facing her from across the room are several white police officers, one of whom, Mr. Van der Broek, has just been tried and found implicated in the murders of both the woman's son and her husband some years before.
>
> It was indeed Mr. Van der Broek, it has now been established, who had come to the woman's home a number of years back, taken her son, shot him at point-blank range and then burned the young man's body on a fire while he and his officers partied nearby.
>
> Several years later, Van der Broek and his security police colleagues had returned to take away her husband as well. For many months she heard nothing of his whereabouts. Then, almost two years after her husband's disappearance, Van der Broek came back to fetch the woman herself. How vividly she remembers that evening, going to a place beside a river where she was shown her husband, bound and beaten, but still strong in spirit, lying on a pile of wood. The last words she heard from his lips as the officers poured gasoline over his body and set him aflame were, "Father, forgive them."
>
> And now the woman stands in the courtroom and listens to the confessions offered by Mr. Van der Broek. A member of South Africa's Truth and Reconciliation Commission turns to her and asks, "So, what do you

want? How should justice be done to this man who has so brutally destroyed your family?" "I want three things," begins the old woman, calmly but confidently. "I want first to be taken to the place where my husband's body was burned so that I can gather up the dust and give his remains a decent burial."

She pauses, then continues. "My husband and son were my only family. I want, secondly, therefore, for Mr. Van der Broek to become my son. I would like for him to come twice a month to the ghetto and spend a day with me so that I can pour out on him whatever love I still have remaining within me."

"And, finally," she says, "I want a third thing. I would like Mr. Van der Broek to know that I offer him my forgiveness because Jesus Christ died to forgive. This was also the wish of my husband. And so, I would kindly ask someone to come to my side and lead me across the courtroom so that I can take Mr. Van der Broek in my arms, embrace him and let him know that he is truly forgiven."

As the court assistants come to lead the elderly woman across the room, Mr. Van der Broek, overwhelmed by what he has just heard, faints. And as he does, those in the courtroom, friends, family, neighbors—all victims of decades of oppression and injustice—begin to sing, softly, but assuredly, "Amazing grace, how sweet the sound, that saved a wretch like me."

(From: *Keep the Faith Share the Peace*, the newsletter of the Mennonite Church, Peace and Justice Committee, Vol. 5, Number 3, June 1999.)

Knowing Political Islam

Encounters should not be naïve, but frank, hence "virile." We have to know what we are dealing with. Muslims are not all "anonymous Christians," as Karl Rahner put it. This means we have to tackle political Islam, which presumes that it is called to govern all of society and all "the others"; this monochrome religion that is all over the media because of the odor of sadness and unhappiness it spreads around the world; this religion that seduces the youngest with its proclaimed ideals and which has older Muslims waxing nostalgic, believing that the "true Islam" is accessible. We have to be aware that all Salafists—heralds of this kind of Islam—reject all Western influences on their religion, especially such philosophical Enlightenment ideas such as democracy and secularism.

Democracy is theoretically rejected by this principle because democracy holds that political power belongs to the people and not to God. For Salafists, neither the people, nor the Parliament, nor the head of state can be sources of the law—sovereignty belongs only to God. What's also not possible, according to these ideologues of Islam, is the separation of religion and state—because religion envelops everything, ruling all aspects of the life of a Muslim. Hence, in short-circuiting the four traditional juridical schools of thought of Sunni Islam under the pretense of recovering the original Islam, Salafism rejects pluralism and diversity within the very bosom of the Islamic community in favor of doctrinal and theological uniformity. God being in essence One and Unique, there can be—in this vision—only one, unique way of adoring and worshipping him. On the cultural and social plane, "One and Unique" must correspond to a single type of religious practice in the service of a single worldview. Only this conception of Islam is considered authentic. According to the Salafists, other Muslims have given in to the mirage of modernity, of syncretism, secularism, hence atheism, and their fate is the same as that of non-Muslims.

Its religious thought formed in a polemical context, Salafism has always battled its theological enemies. Today, Salafist sheikhs draw their arguments from the thought of such figures as Ibn Hanbal (ninth century), Ibn Taymiyya (fourteenth century) and Ibn Wahhab (eighteenth century) each time they have to fend off approaches to sacred text that run counter to their own interpretations. Their primary targets are liberal Muslim intellectuals who want to examine Islamic scripture with the aid of the social sciences, hermeneutics, or linguistics. The Salafists also hope that by their individual and collective influence they can "convert" uninitiated Muslims, and even non-Muslims, to their form of religious practice and Islamic identity.

Yet, their politico-religious ideology is incompatible with modernity. Their power of attraction hinges nonetheless on the simplicity of the ideas their thinking develops: reducing the complexity of reality to elementary choices. Salafists describe the world in Manichean terms, opposing the pure against the impure, believers against the impious, the forces of the Good (the Salafists) against the forces of Evil ("lukewarm" Muslims, and non-Muslims). Salafists also give their followers an overall explanation of history, which goes hand-in-hand with their sense of superiority, as they see themselves as the chosen ones. Based on the evidence, they subscribe to an absolute knowledge, accepted by all, always true, and which can never be contradicted without flying in the face of common sense as shared by those who are in the know.

Today, with their thought elaborated upon and distributed by the main preachers of the modern state of Saudi Arabia, Salafists control a great part of Muslim literature. The internet undoubtedly also plays a large role in propaganda and the development of the international notoriety of this movement. This cyber-activism engenders a multiplication of sites creating a virtual *umma* in a globalized world, giving all members the sense that they belong to the same community. These sites also form the battleground for the various currents of Salafism fighting for a monopoly on the expression of legitimate Islam.

Encounters Yes, But Be Clear

On the Christian side, the door must always be left open, even for the most extreme Muslims. The self-proclaimed Islamic State in Syria and Iraq unfortunately resulted from a possible reading of the Quran that is supported by the majority of Muslim thinkers and widely distributed. Beyond demanding verbal condemnations, we must insist that "moderate" Muslims—in defiance of the ji-hadists in Iraq and elsewhere, who only want to hear from those who are just like them—firmly engage their co-religionists who broadcast this reading of Islam in their mosques and through their media outlets. Above all, they must revisit their texts and traditions, reconsider their sources in order to rethink the relationship of their religion to violence. All modern means must be utilized to penetrate these systems of thought: science, putting reality to the test, spiri-tuality. Only Muslims themselves can perform this crucial task, but Christians—in the course of their "encounters"—can encourage and help them. Humanity no longer supports this violence, among Muslims themselves or perpetrated against others. It is no longer tolerable today to reconcile the Figure of the Revealed God with violence.

The question of truth or the "real God" is in fact a central one that is always of interest and importance, as Benedict XVI, as well as Pope Francis, has ceaselessly reminded us: It is not because I be-lieve in a philosophy of life or in a "sacred text" that something is true: One always has to give an account of one's beliefs, to "prove" it to others, in reworking texts, traditions, legal instruments, etc. A believer today cannot be content to simply believe without effort and refuse to make an intellectual effort without the risk of falling into "bad faith," fideism or fundamentalism. That is because rea-son is one of the greatest gifts from God.

To separate ideology from "authentic religion," we must con-sider the fruits of our beliefs. Putting these the laws engendered by these beliefs into practice, do they help us live together more har-moniously, socially, and politically; do they help us construct a bet-ter world, or do they lead to discrimination? As to the spiritual challenge, if God is really God, one has to pay attention to prayer: Does the God I invoke listen to me and grant me fulfillment? Reli-gious formulations must pass the test of prayer and be subject to a reality test. That's the only way to verify if these formulations are "received" from God and that I am not led "astray" by adoring an idol, a system, and not the "real God" who would never demand to be obeyed by "force of the sword."

A guide to help the process of encounter: the document "Dialogue in Truth and Charity" by the Council of Interreligious Dialogue (May 2014)

This document was published on May 19, 2014 to mark the 50ᵗʰ anniversary of the establishment by Paul VI of the Secretariat for Non-Christians, and gives instructions and suggestion to help establish healthy relationships with other religions. What today is called the Pontifical Council for Interreligious Dialogue was put in place, according to its founding Apostolic Letter, to be attentive to those who are not Christians and to whom the following words of the Lord appear to be addressed: "I have other sheep that are not of this sheep pen. I must bring them also" (Jn 10:16). This dicastery clearly has a pastoral and missionary role, one that "pursues encounter in order to bring people together"—and not always from a theological point of view. The Council's declaration on the relationship of the Church with non-Christian religions (*Nostra Aetate*) has given it an entire program of reflections and initiatives.

After defining anew what the Church understands by "dialogue" and "proclamation," the document evokes various themes that can be utilized for interreligious encounters. Through the excerpts below it will be evident that these instructions, that this perspective on encounters, focuses on "what is clear." It is to be noted that, during the wished-for exchanges, nothing is said about more theological problems, such as those involved in questions about the Holy Trinity, Christology, prophecy. . . . Subjects tackled remain on the level of human dignity, social life, and justice:

* Defending human dignity and promoting the exercise of human rights
* Establishing bonds of trust and friendship among religious leaders
* Educating the youth for interreligious cooperation
* Interreligious cooperation in healthcare services
* "Mixed" marriages between Catholics and followers of other religious traditions
* Prayer and symbolic gestures

}253{

58. The right to religious freedom opposes any form of interference from outside the religion itself. It connotes the liberty, without any hindrance from outside, to practice one's own belief, individually and collectively; to transmit the teachings of one's religion to people of that religion and, with respect, to bear witness in the public square and also before followers of other religions. *Everyone has the right to invite others to an understanding of one's own religion, but such an invitation should never deny another's rights and it should take into account religious sensibilities.*

59. The natural right to civil freedom of religion also includes *the right to adhere to or not to adhere to a religion or to change from one religion to another.* This right is enshrined in the laws of many societies and in international charters. The Catholic Church fully respects such decisions of conscience, even as she laments the fact that in some regions civil and even religious authorities adopt a one-sided approach in this matter. *There are countries where Christians are pressured and sometimes coerced into adopting another religion. Besides, those who seek entrance into the Christian fold often face reprisals that include social marginalization, denial of civil rights, loss of job, jail, extradition, and even death. Such a lack of respect for the fundamental right to religious freedom deserves thoughtful and persistent reflection and discussion at the table of interreligious dialogue, resulting in joint action.*

60. [. . .] to build a peaceful society [. . .].

61. *All forms of religiously motivated violence are to be considered an attack against religion itself and the true good of human society.* Christians are called to work with followers of other religions to prevent instrumentalization of religion for political or other ends and to counter terrorism positively. As Pope Benedict XVI has affirmed: "No situation can justify such criminal activity, which covers the perpetrators with infamy, and it is all the more deplorable when it hides behind religion, thereby bringing the pure truth of God down to the level of the terrorists' own blindness and moral perversion."

63. [. . .] They must work together to defend the right *to display religious symbols in public places* as an aspect of religious freedom, insofar as such display is devoid of political manipulation, respects human dignity, and does not include any form of unjust provocation.

65. Proselytism in the biblical sense of bringing people to conversion is good, but the term can also be perceived with a negative connotation. It has been described in recent times as the use of unethical and unlawful means to win over another to one's religion by coercion, such as psychological pressure, spiritual and physical threats and violence, or fraud or enticements, without respect for a person's dignity and freedom. Such behavior undermines the good inherent in the pursuit of a religious path. *At the table of dialogue, this kind of negative proselytism must be recognized for what it is: an affront to conscience and a transgression of natural law.* Pope Paul VI reminds Christians that presenting Christ to the one who has not yet heard the Good News must never be an act of aggression, but *an act of respect*. The Christian proclamation of the Gospel is and should always be a service of charity on behalf of the human person who is called to accept in freedom the divine offer of life in abundance.

66. With regard to those who have converted to Christianity from other religions, they need assistance to grow in their knowledge and appreciation of the treasures of the Christian faith and, gradually transforming old ideas and habits inconsistent with the teaching of the Gospel. *The Catholic community is called to provide special assistance to all those who struggle after converting to Christianity*, because of greater physical, economic or social insecurity. The new converts are to be shown the love of Christ [. . .].

68. [. . .] *Relationships among local leaders begin and blossom when they share a common desire to meet and to listen to one another* in an atmosphere of respect and openness to the values that are found in their respective religions.

69. [. . .] According to Pope Benedict XVI, the religious leaders have their particular responsibility "to imbue society with a profound awe and respect for human life and freedom; to ensure that human dignity is recognized and cherished; to facilitate peace and justice; to teach children what is right, good and reasonable!" In periods of war, famine, or natural disasters, Catholic pastors need to frequently join hands with local leaders of other religions to offer relief to victims. *Even in times of tranquility, gestures of friendship, such as honouring invitations to attend a major religious feast, exchanging greetings during festivities, etc., help strengthen the bonds of trust.*

82. Often in the context of interreligious relationships, there comes a desire to pray together for a particular need of the society. It is important, however, to understand that being able to pray in common requires a shared understanding of who God is. Since religions differ in their understanding of God, *"interreligious prayer," meaning the joining together in common prayer by followers of various religions, is to be avoided.*

83. *On very exceptional occasions, people of different religions may come together to pray for particular needs in a "multi-religious prayer" service.* Practically speaking, this allows persons to be in each other's presence while praying, without actually praying in common. Pope John Paul II articulated an important principle regarding this after the first interreligious meeting at Assisi in 1986: "Certainly we cannot 'pray together,' that is, engage in a common prayer, but we can be present while others pray. In this way we manifest our respect for the prayer of others and for the attitude of others before the Divinity; at the same time we offer them the humble and sincere witness of our faith in Christ, Lord of the universe." Therefore, *such a service should be conducted with certain prudence, and the participants need to be of a human and spiritual maturity.* It is worth recalling the concluding moment of that historic meeting in Assisi, where the prayers of the representative of each religion, one after another, in a suitably distinct moment, were

recited, while all the others present assisted with a respectful attitude, both interior and exterior, of one who is a witness of the supreme effort of other men and women to seek God. *In preparing for occasions of "multi-religious" prayer, any practice that may give the impression of relativism or syncretism, such as the invention of "para-liturgical" services and the preparation and use of common prayers acceptable to all religions as well as compiling and reading excerpts from so called "sacred books" of different religions during public ceremonies are to be avoided.* Indeed, preference should be given to silence and personal prayer during such gatherings. Thus, it should be evident to all who participate that these occasions are moments of being "together for prayer, but not prayer together." Similarly, when representatives of other religions are invited to attend Catholic liturgies, they should not be invited to pray or exercise a ritual proper to their religion.

84. It is necessary for Catholic pastors to understand and explain to the faithful the implications of their gestures of friendship, hospitality and cooperation towards followers of other religions. Yet the duty of hospitality has its limits. *Offering a Church for use as house of prayer for people of other religions is improper and must be avoided [. . .].*

Father Laurent Basanese, S.J., is professor of Arab Christian theology and Islam at the Jesuits' pontifical university in Rome, the Gregorian. He specializes in Islamic fundamentalist thought and has worked with the Jesuit Refugee Service in Syria in 2011. He also teaches at the Pontifical Oriental Institute in Rome as well as the Jesuit Faculties (Centre Sèvres) in Paris.

EPILOGUE

Prayer for Peace
by Patriarch Louis Raphael I Sako, spiritual leader of the
Chaldean Church

Lord,
The plight of our country
is deep and the suffering of Christians
is severe and frightening.
Therefore, we ask you Lord
to spare our lives, and to grant us patience,
and courage to continue our witness of Christian values
with trust and hope.
Lord, peace is the foundation of life;
Grant us the peace and stability that will enable us
to live with each other without fear and anxiety,
and with dignity and joy.

Glory be to you forever.

† Louis Raphael I Sako

APPENDIX

Letter of His Holiness Pope Francis to the Christians in the Middle East

Dear Brothers and Sisters,

"Blessed be the God and Father of our Lord Jesus Christ, the Father of mercies and God of all consolation, who consoles us in all our affliction, so that we may be able to console those who are in any affliction, with the consolation with which we ourselves are consoled by God" (2 Cor 1:3–4).

When I thought of writing to you, our Christian brothers and sisters in the Middle East, these words of Saint Paul immediately came to mind. I write to you just before Christmas, knowing that for many of you the music of your Christmas hymns will also be accompanied by tears and sighs. Nonetheless, the birth of the Son of God in our human flesh is an indescribable mystery of consolation: "For the grace of God has appeared for the salvation of all people" (*Tit* 2:11).

Sadly, afflictions and tribulations have not been lacking, even more recently, in the Middle East. They have been aggravated in the past months because of the continuing hostilities in the region, but especially because of the work of a newer and disturbing terrorist organization, of previously unimaginable dimensions, which has perpetrated all kinds of abuses and inhuman acts. It has particularly affected a number of you, who have been brutally driven out of your native lands, where Christians have been present since apostolic times.

Nor, in writing to you, can I remain silent about the members of other religious and ethnic groups who are also experiencing persecution and the effects of these conflicts. Every day I follow the new reports of the enormous suffering endured by many people in the Middle East. I think in particular of the children, the young mothers, the elderly, the homeless and all refugees, the starving and those facing the prospect of a hard winter without an adequate shelter. This suffering cries out to God and it calls for our commitment to prayer and concrete efforts to help in any way possible. I want to express to all of you my personal closeness and solidarity, as well as that of the whole Church, and to offer you a word of consolation and hope.

Dear brothers and sisters who courageously bear witness to Jesus in the land blessed by the Lord, our consolation and our hope is Christ himself. I encourage you, then, to remain close to him, like branches on the vine, in the certainty that no tribulation, distress or persecution can separate us from him (cf. *Rom* 8:35). May the trials which you are presently enduring strengthen the faith and the fidelity of each and all of you!

I pray that you will be able to experience a fraternal communion modeled on that of the first community of Jerusalem. The unity willed by our Lord is more necessary than ever at these difficult times; it is a gift from God, who appeals to our freedom and awaits our response. May the word of God, the sacraments, prayer and fellowship nourish and continually renew your communities.

The situation in which are you living is a powerful summons to holiness of life, as saints and martyrs of every Christian community have attested. I think with affection and veneration of the pastors and faithful who have lately been killed, often merely for the fact that they were Christians. I think also of those who have been kidnapped, including several Orthodox bishops and priests of various rites. May they soon return, safe and sound, to their homes and communities! I ask God to grant that all this suffering united to the Lord's cross will bring about much good for the Church and for all the peoples in the Middle East.

In the midst of hostility and conflicts, the communion which you experience in fraternity and simplicity is a sign of God's Kingdom. I am gratified by the good relations and cooperation which exist between the patriarchs of the Eastern Catholic Churches and those of the Orthodox Churches, and also between the faithful of the different Churches. The sufferings which Christians endure contribute immensely to the cause of unity. It is the ecumenism of blood, which demands a trusting abandonment to the working of the Holy Spirit.

May you always bear witness to Jesus amid your difficulties! Your very presence is precious for the Middle East. You are a small flock, but one with a great responsibility in the land where Christianity was born and first spread. You are like leaven in the dough. Even more than the many contributions which the Church makes in the areas of education, healthcare and social services, which are esteemed by all, the greatest source of enrichment in the region is the presence of Christians themselves, your presence. Thank you for your perseverance!

Your efforts to cooperate with people of other religions, with Jews and Muslims are another sign of the Kingdom of God. The more difficult the situation, the more interreligious dialogue becomes necessary. There is no other way. Dialogue, grounded in an attitude of openness, in truth and love, is also the best antidote to the temptation to religious fundamentalism, which is a threat for followers of every religion. At the same time, dialogue is a service to justice and a necessary condition for the peace which all so ardently desire.

The majority of you live in environments which are predominantly Muslim. You can help your Muslim fellow citizens to present with discernment a more authentic image of Islam, as so many of them desire, reiterating that Islam is a religion of peace, one which is compatible with respect for human rights and favors peaceful coexistence on the part of all. This will prove beneficial for them and for all society. The tragic situation faced by our Christian brothers and sisters in Iraq, as well as by the Yazidi and members of other religious and ethnic communities, demands that all religious leaders clearly speak out to condemn these crimes unanimously and unambiguously, and to denounce the practice of invoking religion in order to justify them.

Dear brothers and sisters, almost all of you are native citizens of your respective countries, and as such you have the duty and the right to take full part in the life and progress of your nations. Within the region you are called to be artisans of peace, reconciliation and development, to promote dialogue, to build bridges in the spirit of the Beatitudes (cf. *Mt* 5:3:12), and to proclaim the Gospel of peace, in a spirit of ready cooperation with all national and international authorities.

In a special way I would like to express my esteem and gratitude to you, dear brother patriarchs, bishops, priests, and men and women religious, who accompany the journey of your communities with loving concern. How valuable is the presence and work of those completely consecrated to the Lord, serving him in their brothers and sisters, especially those in greatest need, and thus witnessing to his grandeur and his infinite love! How important is the presence of pastors in the midst of their flocks, especially in times of trouble!

To the young I send a paternal embrace. I pray for your faithfulness, your human and Christian development, and the attainment of your hopes and dreams. I repeat to you: "Do not be afraid or ashamed to be Christian. Your relationship with Jesus will help you to cooperate generously with your fellow citizens, whatever their religious affiliation" (Apostolic Exhortation *Ecclesia in Medio Oriente*, 63).

To the elderly I express my respect and esteem. You are the memory of your peoples. I pray that this memory will become a seed which can grow and benefit generations yet to come.

I wish to encourage all of you who work in the very important fields of charity and education. I admire the work you do, especially through *Caritas* and other Catholic charitable organizations in the different countries, in providing help to anyone who asks, without discrimination. Through this witness of charity you help support the life of society and you contribute to the peace for which the region hungers as if for bread. Education too is critical for the future of society. How important it is for promoting the culture of encounter, respect for the dignity of each person and the absolute value of every human being!

Appendix

Dear brothers and sisters, even though you may not be numerous, you play a significant role in the Church and in the countries where you live. The entire Church is close to you and supports you, with immense respect and affection for your communities and your mission. We will continue to assist you with our prayers and with every other means at our disposal.

At the same time I continue to urge the international community to address your needs and those of other suffering minorities, above all by promoting peace through negotiation and diplomacy, for the sake of stemming and stopping as soon as possible the violence which has already caused so much harm. I once more condemn in the strongest possible terms the traffic of arms. Instead, what are needed are plans and initiatives for peace, so as to further a global solution to the region's problems. How much longer must the Middle East suffer from the lack of peace? We must not resign ourselves to conflicts as if change were not possible! In the spirit of my pilgrimage to the Holy Land and the subsequent prayer meeting in the Vatican with the Israeli and Palestinian presidents, I encourage you to continue to pray for peace in the Middle East. May those forced to leave their lands be able to return and to live in dignity and security. May humanitarian aid increase and always have as its central concern the good of each individual and each country, respecting their identity and without any other agendas. May the entire Church and the international community become ever more conscious of the importance of your presence in the region.

Dear Christian brothers and sisters of the Middle East, you have an enormous responsibility and in meeting it you are not alone. That is why I wanted to write to you, to encourage you and to let you know how precious your presence and your mission are in the land which the Lord has blessed. Your witness means much to me! Thank you! I pray for you and your intentions every day. I thank you because I know that, amid your sufferings, you also pray for me and for my service to the Church. I do hope to have the chance to come to you in person and to visit and to comfort you. May the Virgin Mary, the All-Holy Mother of God and our Mother, accompany you and protect you always with her tender love. To all of you and your families I impart my Apostolic Blessing, and I pray that your celebration of Christmas will be filled with the love and peace of Christ our Savior.

From the Vatican, December 21, 2014,
Fourth Sunday of Advent
FRANCIS

Faith, Reason and the University—Memories and Reflections

Lecture by Pope Benedict XVI*
Aula Magna of the University of Regensburg
September 12, 2006

Your Eminences, Your Magnificences, Your Excellencies,
Distinguished Ladies and Gentlemen,

It is a moving experience for me to be back again in the university and to be able once again to give a lecture at this podium. I think back to those years when, after a pleasant period at the Freisinger Hochschule, I began teaching at the University of Bonn. That was in 1959, in the days of the old university made up of ordinary professors. The various chairs had neither assistants nor secretaries, but in recompense there was much direct contact with students and in particular among the professors themselves. We would meet before and after lessons in the rooms of the teaching staff. There was a lively exchange with historians, philosophers, philologists and, naturally, between the two theological faculties. Once a semester there was a *dies academicus*, when professors from every faculty

---

*   For an analysis of the lecture, see *The Regensburg Lecture* by James V. Schall, S.J. (St. Augustine's Press, 2007).

appeared before the students of the entire university, making possible a genuine experience of *universitas*—something that you too, Magnificent Rector, just mentioned—the experience, in other words, of the fact that despite our specializations which at times make it difficult to communicate with each other, we made up a whole, working in everything on the basis of a single rationality with its various aspects and sharing responsibility for the right use of reason this reality became a lived experience. The university was also very proud of its two theological faculties. It was clear that, by inquiring about the reasonableness of faith, they too carried out a work which is necessarily part of the "whole" of the *universitas scientiarum*, even if not everyone could share the faith which theologians seek to correlate with reason as a whole. This profound sense of coherence within the universe of reason was not troubled, even when it was once reported that a colleague had said there was something odd about our university: it had two faculties devoted to something that did not exist: God. That even in the face of such radical skepticism it is still necessary and reasonable to raise the question of God through the use of reason, and to do so in the context of the tradition of the Christian faith: this, within the university as a whole, was accepted without question.

I was reminded of all this recently, when I read the edition by Professor Theodore Khoury (Münster) of part of the dialogue carried on—perhaps in 1391 in the winter barracks near Ankara—by the erudite Byzantine emperor Manuel II Paleologus and an educated Persian on the subject of Christianity and Islam, and the truth of both.[1] It was presumably the emperor himself who set down this dialogue, during the siege of Constantinople between 1394 and 1402; and this would explain why his arguments are given in greater detail than those of his Persian interlocutor.[2] The dialogue ranges widely over the structures of faith contained in the Bible and in the Quran, and deals especially with the image of God and of man, while necessarily returning repeatedly to the relationship between—as they were called—three "Laws" or "rules of life:" the Old Testament, the New Testament and the Qur'an. It is not my intention to discuss this question in the present lecture; here I would like to discuss only one point—itself rather marginal to the dialogue as a whole–which, in the context of the issue of "faith and reason," I found interesting and which can serve as the starting-point for my reflections on this issue.

In the seventh conversation (διάλεξις—controversy) edited by Professor Khoury, the emperor touches on the theme of the holy war. The emperor must have known that *surah* 2, 256 reads: "There is no compulsion in religion." According to some of the experts, this is probably one of the *suras* of the early period, when Mohammed was still powerless and under threat. But naturally the emperor also knew the instructions, developed later and recorded in the Qur'an, concerning holy war. Without descending to details, such as the difference in treatment accorded to those who have the "Book" and the "infidels," he addresses his interlocutor with a startling brusqueness, a brusqueness that we find unacceptable, on the central question about the relationship between religion and violence in general, saying: "Show me just what Mohammed brought that was new, and there you will find things only evil and inhuman, such as his command to spread by the sword the faith he preached."[3] The emperor, after having expressed himself so forcefully, goes on to explain in detail the reasons why spreading the faith through violence is something unreasonable. Violence is incompatible with the nature of God and the nature of the soul. "God", he says, "is not pleased by blood – and not acting reasonably (σὺν λόγω) is contrary to God's nature. Faith is born of the soul, not the body. Whoever would lead someone to faith needs the ability to speak well and to reason properly, without violence and threats. . . . To convince a reasonable soul, one does not need a strong arm, or weapons of any kind, or any other means of threatening a person with death. . . ."[4]

The decisive statement in this argument against violent conversion is this: not to act in accordance with reason is contrary to God's nature.[5] The editor, Theodore Khoury, observes: For the emperor, as a Byzantine shaped by Greek philosophy, this statement is self-evident. But for Muslim teaching, God is absolutely transcendent. His will is not bound up with any of our categories, even that of rationality.[6] Here Khoury quotes a work of the noted French Islamist R. Arnaldez, who points out that Ibn Hazm went so far as to state that God is not bound even by his own word, and that nothing would oblige him to reveal the truth to us. Were it God's will, we would even have to practice idolatry.[7]

At this point, as far as understanding of God and thus the concrete practice of religion is concerned, we are faced with an unavoidable dilemma. Is the conviction that acting unreasonably contradicts God's nature merely a Greek idea, or is it always and intrinsically true? I believe that here we can see the profound harmony between what is Greek in the best sense of the word and the biblical understanding of faith in God. Modifying the first verse of the Book of Genesis, the first verse of the whole Bible, John began the prologue of his Gospel with the words: "In the beginning was the λόγος." This is the very word used by the emperor: God acts, σὺν λόγῳ, with logos. Logos means both reason and word—a reason which is creative and capable of self-communication, precisely as reason. John thus spoke the final word on the biblical concept of God, and in this word all the often toilsome and tortuous threads of biblical faith find their culmination and synthesis. In the beginning was the logos, and the logos is God, says the Evangelist. The encounter between the Biblical message and Greek thought did not happen by chance. The vision of Saint Paul, who saw the roads to Asia barred and in a dream saw a Macedonian man plead with him: "Come over to Macedonia and help us!" (cf. Acts 16:6–10)—this vision can be interpreted as a "distillation" of the intrinsic necessity of a rapprochement between Biblical faith and Greek inquiry.

In point of fact, this rapprochement had been going on for some time. The mysterious name of God, revealed from the burning bush, a name which separates this God from all other divinities with their many names and simply asserts being, "I am," already presents a challenge to the notion of myth, to which Socrates' attempt to vanquish and transcend myth stands in close analogy.[8] Within the Old Testament, the process which started at the burning bush came to new maturity at the time of the Exile, when the God of Israel, an Israel now deprived of its land and worship, was proclaimed as the God of heaven and earth and described in a simple formula which echoes the words uttered at the burning bush: "I am." This new understanding of God is accompanied by a kind of enlightenment, which finds stark expression in the mockery of gods who are merely the work of human hands (cf. Ps 115). Thus, despite the bitter conflict with those Hellenistic rulers who sought to accommodate it forcibly to the customs and idolatrous cult of the Greeks, biblical faith, in the Hellenistic period, encountered the best of Greek thought at a deep level, resulting in a mutual enrichment evident especially in the later wisdom literature. Today we know that the Greek translation of the Old Testament produced at Alexandria—the Septuagint—is more than a simple (and in that sense really less than satisfactory) translation of the Hebrew text: it is an independent textual witness and a distinct and important step in the history of revelation, one which brought about this encounter in a way that was decisive for the birth and spread of Christianity.[9] A profound encounter of faith and reason is taking place here, an encounter between genuine enlightenment and religion. From the very heart of Christian faith and, at the same time, the heart of Greek thought now joined to faith, Manuel II was able to say: Not to act "with logos" is contrary to God's nature.

In all honesty, one must observe that in the late Middle Ages we find trends in theology which would sunder this synthesis between the Greek spirit and the Christian spirit. In contrast with the so-called intellectualism of Augustine and Thomas, there arose with Duns Scotus a voluntarism which, in its later developments, led to the claim that we can only know God's *voluntas ordinata*. Beyond this is the realm of God's freedom, in virtue of which he could have done the opposite of everything he has actually done. This gives rise to positions which clearly approach those of Ibn Hazm and might even lead to the image of a capricious God, who is not even bound to truth and goodness. God's transcendence and otherness are so exalted that our reason, our sense of the true and good, are no longer an authentic mirror of God, whose deepest possibilities remain eternally unattainable and hidden behind his actual decisions. As opposed to this, the faith of the Church has always insisted that between God and us, between his eternal Creator Spirit and our created reason there exists a real analogy, in which—as the Fourth Lateran Council in 1215 stated—unlikeness remains infinitely greater than likeness, yet not to the point of abolishing analogy and its language. God does not become more divine when we push him away from us in a sheer, impenetrable voluntarism; rather, the truly divine God is the God who has revealed himself as logos and, as logos, has acted and continues to act lovingly on our behalf. Certainly, love, as Saint Paul says, "transcends" knowledge and is thereby capable of perceiving more than thought alone (cf. Eph 3:19); nonetheless it continues to be love of the God who is Logos. Consequently, Christian worship is, again to quote Paul—"λογικη λατρεία," worship in harmony with the eternal Word and with our reason (cf. Rom 12:1).[10]

This inner rapprochement between Biblical faith and Greek philosophical inquiry was an event of decisive importance not only from the standpoint of the history of religions, but also from that of world history—it is an event which concerns us even today. Given this convergence, it is not surprising that Christianity, despite its origins and some significant developments in the East, finally took on its historically decisive character in Europe. We can also express this the other way around: this convergence, with the subsequent addition of the Roman heritage, created Europe and remains the foundation of what can rightly be called Europe.

The thesis that the critically purified Greek heritage forms an integral part of Christian faith has been countered by the call for a dehellenization of Christianity—a call which has more and more dominated theological discussions since the beginning of the modern age. Viewed more closely, three stages can be observed in the program of dehellenization: although interconnected, they are clearly distinct from one another in their motivations and objectives.[11]

Dehellenization first emerges in connection with the postulates of the Reformation in the sixteenth century. Looking at the tradition of scholastic theology, the Reformers thought they were confronted with a faith system totally conditioned by philosophy, that is to say an articulation of the faith based on an alien system of thought. As a result, faith no longer appeared as a living historical Word but as one element of an overarching philosophical system. The principle of sola scriptura, on the other hand, sought faith in its pure, primordial form, as originally found in the biblical Word. Metaphysics appeared as a premise derived from another source, from which faith had to be liberated in order to become once more fully itself. When Kant stated that he needed to set thinking aside in order to make room for faith, he carried this program forward with a radicalism that the Reformers could never have foreseen. He thus anchored faith exclusively in practical reason, denying it access to reality as a whole.

The liberal theology of the nineteenth and twentieth centuries ushered in a second stage in the process of dehellenization, with Adolf von Harnack as its outstanding representative. When I was a student, and in the early years of my teaching, this program was highly influential in Catholic theology too. It took as its point of departure Pascal's distinction between the God of the philosophers and the God of Abraham, Isaac and Jacob. In my inaugural lecture at Bonn in 1959, I tried to address the issue,[12] and I do not intend to repeat here what I said on that occasion, but I would like to describe at least briefly what was new about this second stage of dehellenization. Harnack's central idea was to return simply to the man Jesus and to his simple message, underneath the accretions of theology and indeed of hellenization: this simple message was seen as the culmination of the religious development of humanity. Jesus was said to have put an end to worship in favor of morality. In the end he was presented as the father of a humanitarian moral message. Fundamentally, Harnack's goal was to bring Christianity back into harmony with modern reason, liberating it, that is to say, from seemingly philosophical and theological elements, such as faith in Christ's divinity and the triune God. In this sense, historical-critical exegesis of the New Testament, as he saw it, restored to theology its place within the university: theology, for Harnack, is something essentially historical and therefore strictly scientific. What it is able to say critically about Jesus is, so to speak, an expression of practical reason and consequently it can take its rightful place within the university. Behind this thinking lies the modern self-limitation of reason, classically expressed in Kant's "Critiques," but in the meantime further radicalized by the impact of the natural sciences. This modern concept of reason is based, to put it briefly, on a synthesis between Platonism (Cartesianism) and empiricism, a synthesis confirmed by the success of technology. On the one hand it presupposes the mathematical structure of matter, its intrinsic rationality, which makes it possible to understand how matter works and use it efficiently: this basic premise is, so to speak, the Platonic element in the modern understanding of nature. On the other hand, there is nature's capacity to be exploited for our purposes, and here only the possibility of verification or falsification through experimentation can yield decisive certainty. The weight between the two poles can, depending on the circumstances, shift from one side to the other. As strongly positivistic a thinker as J. Monod has declared himself a convinced Platonist/Cartesian.

This gives rise to two principles which are crucial for the issue we have raised. First, only the kind of certainty resulting from the interplay of mathematical and empirical elements can be considered scientific. Anything that would claim to be science must be measured against this criterion. Hence the human sciences, such as history, psychology, sociology and philosophy, attempt to conform themselves to this canon of scientificity. A second point, which is important for our reflections, is that by its very nature this method excludes the question of God, making it appear an unscientific or pre-scientific question. Consequently, we are faced with a reduction of the radius of science and reason, one which needs to be questioned.

I will return to this problem later. In the meantime, it must be observed that from this standpoint any attempt to maintain theology's claim to be "scientific" would end up reducing Christianity to a mere fragment of its former self. But we must say more: if science as a whole is this and this alone, then it is man himself who ends up being reduced, for the specifically human questions about our origin and destiny, the questions raised by religion and ethics, then have no place within the purview of collective reason as defined by "science," so understood, and must thus be relegated to the realm of the subjective. The subject then decides, on the basis of his experiences, what he considers tenable in matters of religion, and the subjective "conscience" becomes the sole arbiter of what is ethical. In this way, though, ethics and religion lose their power to create a community and become a completely personal matter. This is a dangerous state of affairs for humanity, as we see from the disturbing pathologies of religion and reason which necessarily erupt when reason is so reduced that questions of religion and ethics no longer concern it. Attempts to construct an ethic from the rules of evolution or from psychology and sociology, end up being simply inadequate.

Before I draw the conclusions to which all this has been leading, I must briefly refer to the third stage of dehellenization, which is now in progress. In the light of our experience with cultural pluralism, it is often said nowadays that the synthesis with Hellenism achieved in the early Church was an initial inculturation which ought not to be binding on other cultures. The latter are said to have the right to return to the simple message of the New Testament prior to that inculturation, in order to inculturate it anew in their own particular milieux. This thesis is not simply false, but it is coarse and lacking in precision. The New Testament was written in Greek and bears the imprint of the Greek spirit, which had already come to maturity as the Old Testament developed. True, there are elements in the evolution of the early Church which do not have to be integrated into all cultures. Nonetheless, the fundamental decisions made about the relationship between faith and the use of human reason are part of the faith itself; they are developments consonant with the nature of faith itself.

And so I come to my conclusion. This attempt, painted with broad strokes, at a critique of modern reason from within has nothing to do with putting the clock back to the time before the Enlightenment and rejecting the insights of the modern age. The positive aspects of modernity are to be acknowledged unreservedly:

we are all grateful for the marvelous possibilities that it has opened up for mankind and for the progress in humanity that has been granted to us. The scientific ethos, moreover, is—as you yourself mentioned, Magnificent Rector—the will to be obedient to the truth, and, as such, it embodies an attitude which belongs to the essential decisions of the Christian spirit. The intention here is not one of retrenchment or negative criticism, but of broadening our concept of reason and its application. While we rejoice in the new possibilities open to humanity, we also see the dangers arising from these possibilities and we must ask ourselves how we can overcome them. We will succeed in doing so only if reason and faith come together in a new way, if we overcome the self-imposed limitation of reason to the empirically falsifiable, and if we once more disclose its vast horizons. In this sense theology rightly belongs in the university and within the wide-ranging dialogue of sciences, not merely as a historical discipline and one of the human sciences, but precisely as theology, as inquiry into the rationality of faith.

Only thus do we become capable of that genuine dialogue of cultures and religions so urgently needed today. In the Western world it is widely held that only positivistic reason and the forms of philosophy based on it are universally valid. Yet the world's profoundly religious cultures see this exclusion of the divine from the universality of reason as an attack on their most profound convictions. A reason which is deaf to the divine and which relegates religion into the realm of subcultures is incapable of entering into the dialogue of cultures. At the same time, as I have attempted to show, modern scientific reason with its intrinsically Platonic element bears within itself a question which points beyond itself and beyond the possibilities of its methodology. Modern scientific reason quite simply has to accept the rational structure of matter and the correspondence between our spirit and the prevailing rational structures of nature as a given, on which its methodology has to be based. Yet the question why this has to be so is a real question, and one which has to be remanded by the natural sciences to other modes and planes of thought—to philosophy and theology. For philosophy and, albeit in a different way, for theology, listening to the great experiences and insights of the religious traditions of humanity, and those of the Christian faith in particular, is a source of knowledge, and to ignore it would be an unacceptable restriction of our listening and responding. Here I am reminded of something Socrates said to Phaedo. In their earlier conversations, many false philosophical opinions had been raised, and so Socrates says: "It would be easily understandable if someone became so annoyed at all these false notions that for the rest of his life he despised and mocked all talk about being—but in this way he would be deprived of the truth of existence and would suffer a great loss." [13] The West has long been endangered by this aversion to the questions which underlie its rationality, and can only suffer great harm thereby. The courage to engage the whole breadth of reason, and not the denial of its grandeur—this is the program with which a theology grounded in Biblical faith enters into the debates of our time. "Not to act reasonably, not to act with logos, is contrary to the nature of God," said Manuel II, according to his Christian understanding of God, in response to his Persian interlocutor. It is to this great logos, to this breadth of reason, that we invite our partners in the dialogue of cultures. To rediscover it constantly is the great task of the university.

Endnotes

[1] Of the total number of 26 conversations (διάλεξις—Khoury translates this as "controversy") in the dialogue ("Entretien"), T. Khoury published the 7th "controversy" with footnotes and an extensive introduction on the origin of the text, on the manuscript tradition and on the structure of the dialogue, together with brief summaries of the "controversies" not included in the edition; the Greek text is accompanied by a French translation: "Manuel II Paléologue, Entretiens avec un Musulman. 7e Controverse", Sources Chrétiennes n. 115, Paris 1966. In the meantime, Karl Förstel published in Corpus Islamico-Christianum (Series Graeca ed. A. T. Khoury and R. Glei) an edition of the text in Greek and German with commentary: "Manuel II. Palaiologus, Dialoge mit einem Muslim", 3 vols., Würzburg-Altenberge 1993–1996. As early as 1966, E. Trapp had published the Greek text with an introduction as vol. II of Wiener byzantinische Studien. I shall be quoting from Khoury's edition.

[2] On the origin and redaction of the dialogue, cf. Khoury, pp. 22–29; extensive comments in this regard can also be found in the editions of Förstel and Trapp.

[3] Controversy VII, 2 c: Khoury, pp. 142–143; Förstel, vol. I, VII. Dialog 1.5, pp. 240–241. In the Muslim world, this quotation has unfortunately been taken as an expression of my personal position, thus arousing understandable indignation. I hope that the reader of my text can see immediately that this sentence does not express my personal view of the Qur'an, for which I have the respect due to the holy book of a great religion. In quoting the text of the Emperor Manuel II, I intended solely to draw out the essential relationship between faith and reason. On this point I am in agreement with Manuel II, but without endorsing his polemic.

[4] Controversy VII, 3 b–c: Khoury, pp. 144–145; Förstel vol. I, VII. Dialog 1.6, pp. 240–243.

[5] It was purely for the sake of this statement that I quoted the dialogue between Manuel and his Persian interlocutor. In this statement the theme of my subsequent reflections emerges.

[6] Cf. Khoury, p. 144, n. 1.

[7] R. Arnaldez, Grammaire et théologie chez Ibn Hazm de Cordoue, Paris 1956, p. 13; cf. Khoury, p. 144. The fact that comparable positions exist in the theology of the late Middle Ages will appear later in my discourse.

[8] Regarding the widely discussed interpretation of the episode of the burning bush, I refer to my book Introduction to Christianity, London 1969, pp. 77–93 (originally published in German as Einführung in das Christentum, Munich 1968; N.B. the pages quoted refer to the entire chapter entitled "The Biblical Belief in God"). I think that my statements in that book, despite later developments in the discussion, remain valid today.

[9] Cf. A. Schenker, "L'Écriture sainte subsiste en plusieurs formes canoniques simultanées," in L'Interpretazione della Bibbia nella Chiesa. Atti del Simposio promosso dalla Congregazione per la Dottrina della Fede, Vatican City 2001, pp. 178–186.

[10] On this matter I expressed myself in greater detail in my book The Spirit of the Liturgy, San Francisco 2000, pp. 44–50.

[11] Of the vast literature on the theme of dehellenization, I would like to mention above all: A. Grillmeier, "Hellenisierung-Judaisierung des Christentums als Deuteprinzipien der Geschichte des kirchlichen Dogmas", in idem, Mit ihm und in ihm. Christologische Forschungen und Perspektiven, Freiburg 1975, pp. 423–488.

[12] Newly published with commentary by Heino Sonnemans (ed.): Joseph Ratzinger-Benedikt XVI, Der Gott des Glaubens und der Gott der Philosophen. Ein Beitrag zum Problem der theologia naturalis, Johannes-Verlag Leutesdorf, 2nd revised edition, 2005.

[13] Cf. 90 c-d. For this text, cf. also R. Guardini, Der Tod des Sokrates, 5th edition, Mainz-Paderborn 1987, pp. 218–221.

Encyclical of His Holiness Aram I on the 100th Anniversary of the Armenian Genocide

The year 2015 is the 100th anniversary of the Armenian Genocide. Therefore, the year 2015 must become a different year in its depth and meaning with its goal and message for each and every Armenian.

The Armenian Genocide has left an indelible imprint on the collective memory of the Armenian people. There is no Armenian in the world whose blood has not been forged, or whose life has not been engulfed by the Armenian Genocide. There is no Armenian on earth whose family has not experienced genocide, exile, homelessness, or dispersion.

For one hundred years we remembered with incense and prayers our million and a half martyrs, who were sacrificed in Western Armenia and Cilicia during the genocide planned and executed by the Turkish Ottoman Empire.

For one hundred years we remembered with lament and anger the destruction and ruins of our centuries-old cultural and religious sacred treasures—churches, monasteries, cross-stones, sacred sites, manuscripts, and innumerable spiritual intellectuals by the hand of the same genocidal perpetrator.

We remembered for one hundred years with eruptions and demands for the many thousands of national, religious, and individual properties that were confiscated during the genocide.

Truly, following the 1915 genocide and exile the beautified and flourishing cities and villages produced by the creative Armenian spirit in Western Armenia and Cilicia became a wasteland. How appropriate are the following words of the psalmist for the death and destruction of the Armenian genocide: "O God, the nations have come into your inheritance; they have defiled your holy temple; they have laid Jerusalem in ruins. They have given the bodies of your servants to the birds of the air for food, the flesh of your faithful to the wild animals of the earth. They have poured out their blood like water all around Jerusalem, and there was no one to bury them." (Psalm 79:1–3).

The criminal intent of the genocidal perpetrator was genocide, exile, and the destruction of the Armenian people, and with the dispersion to erase the Armenian people from the world map. . . .

Thereafter, the orphaned Armenian people—the children of the survivors—uprooted from their ancestral land never forgot the martyrs; did not forget their sacred legacy. They heard Christ's commandment, "Do not fear those who kill the body but cannot kill the soul" (Matthew 10:28). Girded with this faith and strengthened by the vision of the rebirth of the Armenian people, they reorganized their individual and collective life. They built churches and schools, established community institutions and organizations throughout the Diaspora. They also reminded the perpetrator and all humanity of the unpunished genocide and demanded justice for their people.

Truly, during the last one hundred years, our Church, our Armenian Cause, organizations, and for the past two decades our reestablished Armenian Republic, through advocacy, politics, relationships, and other means not only reminded the world about the Armenian genocide, but also continuously and tirelessly pursued recognition of the 20th century's first genocide that remains unpunished. In fact, today there are a large number of countries, churches, and organizations that have officially recognized the Armenian genocide. Along with Armenians, many non-Armenian scholars have published many works studying the many facets of the Armenian genocide and advocating its recognition.

The children of our people remained faithful, even during their most difficult times, to the legacy of the martyrs and made an oath, again in the words of the psalmist, "If I forget you, O Jerusalem, let my right hand wither! Let my tongue cling to the roof of my mouth if I do not remember you" (Psalm 137:5–6). For one hundred continuous years our people's brave children remembered and reminded others by knocking on the door of people's closed hearts and minds and making the recognition of the genocide the center of their struggle.

Dear Armenian People,

It is necessary to continue that same sacred struggle with pan-Armenian measures and renewed effort. The time has come for our people to give our demands new impetus and contemporary by bringing it into the judicial realm and in the light of international law pursue their violated rights.

Genocide and human rights declarations clearly state that genocide is a crime against humanity and therefore the criminal, be it an individual, an organizations, or a government, must come before the international court of justice. International law also emphasizes that recognition of genocide means reparation. Therefore, the recognition of the Armenian genocide must not be considered to be the goal of the Armenian people's demands. Recognition and reparation must be considered together, closely connected as one and indivisible entity and must become the strong foundation and clear goal of the Armenian people's struggle. It is possible that the current geopolitical conditions are not favorable for our demands. Perhaps, the genocidal perpetrator, with its diplomatic and economic effective means will hinder any attempts by our people toward this direction. However, in spite of this harsh reality our people are summoned to continue their demands with even greater faith and commitment.

The Armenian people in Armenia, Artsakh, and the Diaspora, are preparing to commemorate the centennial of the genocide with unified spirit and unified effort. This 100th anniversary is not, nor should it become, an ordinary anniversary. It is our duty to make this date a worthy event in our nation's life with a high level of zeal and purpose. The 100th anniversary must become a turning point in our people's struggle to regain our just rights.

Appendix

The collective sanctification of the martyrs that will take place on April 23, 2015, in Holy Etchmiadzin under the presidency of the Catholicoi, will most certainly be an important event in the 100th anniversary sphere.

It is also necessary to look beyond the 100th anniversary. . . . The ever-changing world conditions and priorities often need re-examination of approaches, way of acting, and emphasis so that the effort in the pursuit of the Armenian Cause becomes compatible with the reality that surrounds us. It is a duty for us to be alert and always united in our purpose. It is also necessary to properly read "the signs of the times."

The Armenian Cause is the cause of each Armenian and all Armenians. It is our martyrs' cause, the cause of our future generations. So every Armenian is called upon to contribute in our pan-Armenian efforts to regain our rights.

On the threshold of the 100th anniversary of the genocide, with this Pontifical Holy Encyclical, we call upon:

* Our Prelacies, for the extensive participation of our people at religious services, public meetings, and other events to keep the memory of our martyrs and to keep alive their eternal message.
* Our organizations working within the life of our nation, to make collective efforts and with a unified spirit organize and evaluate this important event in our lifetime.
* Our educational institutions, to be attentive to the formation of the students in human and Armenian values and give special attention to the 100th anniversary in our schools, teaching our students about the meaning and message of this anniversary.
* Our intellectuals, through their research and lectures, to focus on the imperative of recognition of the genocide and the demand for reparations.
* To all Armenians, to be full-hearted participants in the efforts on behalf of the Armenian Cause in general, and for the 100th anniversary events in particular.

May the memory of our one-and-one-half million martyrs always remain alive, and their legacy always resonate in our individual and collective lives.

Let us walk forward toward our bright future, renewed with our Christian faith and strengthened by our martyrs' message.

May you live forever in the Lord, be strengthened with the grace of the Holy Spirit and be forever blessed by us. Amen.

ARAM I CATHOLICOS OF THE GREAT HOUSE OF CILICIA
Encyclical delivered at the Catholicosate of Cilicia, in Antelias, Lebanon December 28, 2014, in the year of our Lord.

The ideology that justifies Islamist violence must be dismantled
By Patriarch Louis Sako I

Dear Sisters and Brothers,

Religious and national groups in Iraq are authentic ingredients; they are deep like the roots of the country, rather than being communities descended from another planet. These groups, which are seen as minorities, were once the majority, and they have contributed greatly to the building of both the Iraqi and Islamic culture. These communities are today marginalized, and dealt with harshly and brutally. This has happened in many cities of Iraq, and finally in Mosul and the towns of the Nineveh Plain. No more Christians actually remain there, not a single one. All this led them to seek emigration

Traditionally and historically, we have lived side by side with respect; we shared bread and salt, the sweet and bitter, but today we wonder why this immoral and uncivilized phenomenon is happening.

Sure, religious extremism and violence are driving the assault on Christians and other minorities; obviously we can't put the blame for all this on the 1.6 billion Muslims around the world and hold them responsible for this excess.

Dear Sisters and Brothers, the fact is that the biggest threat is not only the terrorism of ISIS or any other terrorist organization. It is the *takfiri* way of thinking [whereby one group of Muslims in excommunicates those Muslims who do not think and act like them] that is promoted by its preachers and promoter. It is also exploited by some of the competing great powers under the cover of religion.

This is the biggest threat that Iraqi people are enduring, as well as all the peoples of the region; however, the religious minorities are the principal victims.

We . . . call upon our fellow Muslims to take the initiative and lead a campaign of rejecting any sectarian discrimination.

We urge them to take part in a joint Islamic project having as its objective the dismantling of this ideology in a radical way. We suggest this to be implemented in the following ways:

1. Building op an open and enlightened Islamic opinion by thoroughly reviewing the texts adopted in the teaching of religion and history, as well as the very ethics of its teaching methods.

2. Adopting the appropriate interpretation of the texts; closing the door to those who are influencing the mentality of young people by encouraging the use violence in the name of religion. This would be accompanied by revising the preaching in mosques. In all this, adopting a centrist-moderate form of speech that is directed towards promoting humanitarian, national and spiritual solidarity among all people, as all are children of the same homeland and the same human family.

3. To promote a civilized culture of acceptance that acknowledges others as brothers and sisters, co-citizens and full partners; all support for the rejection and eradication of others must be rejected and eliminated. However, it is necessary to acknowledge that this process will take time and will require the healing of memory.

It is of the utmost importance that religious authorities and political leaders address the culture of hatred and all forms of violence that destroy human life and violate human dignity. It is a difficult task indeed! But it is not impossible if everyone cooperates in the promotion of a culture of peace and confidence. In the end, everyone would overcome the fear of coming together and building bridges between citizens.

The media must provide information that respects all religions. News coverage must not harm religious symbols and insult adherents of a particular religion. Let us all promote an open culture that dispels prejudices and strengthens confidence and exuberance.

At this point, there is no other future for us than one in which all of us will be able to live together in peace, harmony and cooperation.

Baghdad, January 17, 2015

This text is taken from an address given to the Iraqi Center for Diversity Management in Baghdad by Patriarch Louis Sako I, leader of the Chaldean Church. He was elected "Patriarch of Babylon" in January of 2013, having served from 2003 as archbishop of Kirkuk. The recipient of the International Pax Christi Award in 2010, he has been the most prominent Church leader from the Middle East to condemn Islamist violence and Western inaction.

Cardinal Timothy M. Dolan, Archbishop of New York, President of the U.S. Conference of Catholic Bishops Address to the USCCB General Assembly November 11, 2013

Just last August, I had the honor of concelebrating the Mass of Dedication for the Cathedral of the Resurrection in Kiev. A particularly moving moment came when Metropolitan Shevchuk asked the Lord's protective hand upon believers suffering persecution for their faith anywhere in the world. That such a heartfelt plea came from a people who had themselves been oppressed for so long made it all the more poignant.

This morning I want to invite us to broaden our horizons, to "think Catholic" about our brothers and sisters in the faith now suffering simply because they sign themselves with the cross, bow their heads at the Holy Name of Jesus, and happily profess the Apostles' Creed.

Brother bishops, our legitimate and ongoing struggles to protect our "first and most cherished freedom" in the United States pale in comparison to the Via Crucis currently being walked by so many of our Christian brothers and sisters in other parts of the world, who are experiencing lethal persecution on a scale that defies belief. If our common membership in the mystical body of Christ is to mean anything, then their suffering must be ours as well.

The new Archbishop of Canterbury has rightly referred to victims of Christian persecution as "martyrs." We are living in what must be recognized as, in the words of Blessed John Paul II, "a new age of martyrs." One expert calculates that half of all Christian martyrs were killed in the twentieth century alone. The twenty-first century has already seen in its first 13 years one million people killed around the world because of their belief in Jesus Christ—one million already in this still young century.

That threat to religious believers is growing. The Pew Research Center reports that 75 percent of the world's population "lives in countries where governments, social groups, or individuals restrict people's ability to freely practice their faith." Pew lays out the details of this "rising tide of restrictions on religion," but we don't need a report to tell us something we sadly see on the news every day.

While Muslims and Christians have long lived peacefully side-by-side in Zanzibar, for instance, this past year has seen increasing violence. Catholic churches have been burned and priests have been shot. In September one priest was the victim of a horrific acid attack. Nigeria has also been the site of frequent anti-Christian violence, including church bombings on our holiest days.

The situation in India has also been grave, particularly after the Orissa massacre of 2008, where hundreds of Christians were murdered and thousands displaced, and thousands of homes and some 400 churches were torched. Just recently, a Christian couple was recently attacked by an angry mob just because of their faith, their Bibles torn from their hands.

We remember our brothers and sisters in China, where Catholic bishops and other religious leaders are subject to state supervision and imprisonment. Conditions are only getting worse, as the government closes churches and subjects members of several faiths to forced renunciations, so-called re-education, and torture.

Of course, it's not just Christians who suffer from religious persecution, but believers in other faiths as well. Much religious persecution is committed by Muslims against other Muslims. Buddhists in Tibet suffer under government torture and repression. In Myanmar Muslims suffer at the hands of Buddhist mobs. All of us share apprehension over reports of rising anti-Semitism.

But there is no escaping the fact that Christians are singled out in far more places and far more often.

I don't have to tell anyone in this room that our brothers and sisters in the Middle East face particular trials. As Patriarch Bartholomew of Constantinople has observed, for Christians in the Middle East, "even the simple admission of Christian identity places the very existence of [the] faithful in daily threat. . . . Exceptionally extreme and expansive occurrences of violence and persecution against Christians cannot leave the rest of us—who are blessed to live peacefully and in some sense of security—indifferent and inactive."

The humanitarian catastrophe that continues to unfold in Syria has been particularly close to our hearts these past few months. We've prayed for and stood in solidarity with the Church and the people of Syria, and with Pope Francis and the bishops of the Middle East in their call for peace.

It's no surprise that this violent and chaotic situation has bred even more religious persecution. Of course we're all familiar with Syria's venerable history as the place from which our faith spread to the rest of the world, and Syria has long been home to a sizable Christian minority. Yet those Christians who have remained in Syria face ever-present, rising threats of violence.

Last April two of our Orthodox brother bishops were kidnapped in Aleppo by gunmen as they returned from a humanitarian mission. Their driver was shot and killed. And a little less than a year ago an Orthodox priest from Hama was killed by a sniper while helping the wounded. Similarly tragic violence against believers is now commonplace.

Just as Syrian Christians have suffered from the war raging in their land, the war in Iraq has devastated that ancient Christian community in that country as well. As Bishop Shlemon Warduni of Iraq tearfully told us during our spring assembly in 2012, remember, the situation of Christians there "became a tragedy of immense proportions after 2003," with many religious and lay faithful tortured and killed.

Violent attacks continue to terrorize the Iraqi people. Just a little over a year ago the war's worst massacre of Iraqi Christians occurred in a brutal attack on Our Lady of Salvation Church in Baghdad, where some 58 believers were massacred. Those martyred for their faith included their parish priest who died holding a crucifix, forgiving the gunmen and asking him to spare his people.

The situations in Syria and Iraq wrench our hearts, but the plight of Christians in Egypt is no better. This past summer saw the serious escalation of violence against our brothers and sisters there, as the ancient Coptic Christian community has been targeted. Dozens of Coptic churches have been burned; Christian-owned businesses and hotels have been attacked; and individual believers have been murdered.

To take one example, John Allen reports that in August, "hundreds of Muslim extremists stormed a school run by Franciscan sisters in . . . Upper Egypt, where they reportedly raped two teachers. Three nuns were paraded before the crowd as prisoners of war." It was only through the intervention of a Muslim lay teacher that other sisters' lives were spared.

We as bishops, as shepherds of one of the most richly blessed communities of faith on the planet, as pastors who have spoken with enthusiastic unity in defense of our own religious freedom, must become advocates and champions for these Christians whose lives literally hang in the balance.

Pope Francis recently invited us all to an examination of conscience in this regard during his General Audience on September 25:

> When I hear that so many Christians in the world are suffering, am I indifferent, or is it as if a member of my own family is suffering? When I think or hear it said that many Christians are persecuted and give their lives for their faith, does this touch my heart or does it not reach me? Am I open to that brother or that sister in my family who's giving his or her life for Jesus Christ? Do we pray for one another? How many of you pray for Christians who are persecuted? How many? Everyone respond in his own heart. It's important to look beyond one's own fence, to feel oneself part of the Church, of one family of God!

I am convinced that we have to answer those questions of Pope Francis, not merely as individual believers, but collectively as a body of bishops.

So you ask me, what can we do? Without any pretense of being exhaustive, here are some ideas I'd like to lay before you, with a nod to John Allen and his recent compelling work on this topic.

First, we can encourage intercession for the persecuted. Remember how the "prayers for the conversion of Russia" at the end of Masses over a half-century ago shaped our sense of what was going on behind the Iron Curtain? A similar culture of prayer for persecuted Christians today, both in private and in our liturgical celebrations, could have a similar remedial effect.

We can also make people aware of the great suffering of our brothers and sisters with all the means at our disposal. Our columns, our blogs, our speeches, and our pastoral letters can reference the subject. We can ask our pastors to preach on it, and to stimulate study sessions or activist groups in their parishes. We can encourage our Catholic media to tell the stories of today's new martyrs, unfortunately abundant. Our good experience defending reli-

gious freedom here at home shows that, when we turn our minds
to an issue, we can put it on the map. Well, it's time to harness that
energy for our fellow members of the household of faith hounded
for their beliefs around the world.

We know the importance of supporting organizations such as
Aid to the Church in Need, the Catholic Near East Welfare Association, Catholic Relief Services, and the Society for the Propagation of the Faith, who have done heroic work, while among our
Protestant brothers and sisters groups such as Open Doors make a
similar contribution. Writers such as Nina Shea, Paul Marshall,
John Allen, and Phillip Jenkins here in the United States help keep
the issue alive, as does our own Committee on International Justice
and Peace.

Finally, we can insist that our country's leaders make the protection of at-risk Christians abroad a foreign-policy priority for the
United States. We can also cajole political leaders to be more attentive to the voices of Christians on the ground, since those Christians will certainly feel the consequences of whatever the West does
or doesn't do. As Dr. Thomas Farr reminded us at our spring meeting a couple summers ago, the protection of religious freedom
abroad, and advocacy of oppressed believers, has hardly been a
high foreign policy priority for administrations of either party.

In general, my brothers, we can make supporting the suffering
Church a priority—not one good cause among others, but a defining element of our pastoral priorities. As historians of this conference know, speaking up for suffering faithful abroad has been a
hallmark of our soon-to-be-century of public advocacy of the
gospel by the conference of bishops in this beloved country we are
honored to call our earthly home.

Protecting religious freedom will be a central social and political concern of our time, and we American bishops already have
made very important contributions to carrying it forward. Now we
are being beckoned—by history, by Pope Francis, by the force of
our own logic and the ecclesiology of communion—to extend those
efforts to the dramatic front lines of this battle, where Christians
are paying for their fidelity with their lives. As the Council

reminded us, we are bishops not only for our dioceses, not only for our nation, but for the Church universal.

May all the blessed martyrs, ancient and new, pray for us, as we try to be confessors of the faith.

Praise be Jesus Christ!

MAY 7, 2014 PLEDGE OF SOLIDARITY AND CALL TO ACTION
On behalf of Christians and Other Defenseless Religious Minorities in Egypt, Iraq and Syria

FACTS

In the Middle East today, Christians collectively form the largest religious group that is not Muslim, numbering up to 12 million people. The majority of the Christian faith communities of today's Middle East, which include Orthodox, Catholics, Protestants, and evangelicals, suffer violence, abuse and injustice from radical Islamist forces simply by virtue of being Christian. Now facing an existential threat to its presence in the lands where Christianity has its roots, the Churches in the Middle East fear they have been largely abandoned by their coreligionists in the West.

In a siege that has accelerated over the past decade, Egypt, Iraq and Syria—three of only four Middle Eastern countries with Christian communities remaining of significant size—have seen scores of churches deliberately destroyed, many clergy and laypeople targeted for death, kidnapping, intimidation and forcible conversion, and hundreds of thousands of believers driven out. The Christian population in Lebanon, the fourth and only other indigenous Church community in the region numbering over 1 million, is being rocked by the instability across its country's borders and stands precariously on a precipice. While there is no apparent organization or coordination among the persecutors from nation to nation, their actions are leading to one conclusion: the very real possibility that Christianity may soon be extinguished in the region of its origin.

No Christian tradition is spared in this current wave of persecution. Pope Francis has called this the "ecumenism of blood," meaning that the persecutors do not discriminate among the Christians they are attacking. Ecumenical Patriarch Bartholomew has also spoken of the contemporary "crucifixion" of Christians. In these same three countries, other defenseless religious groups—Mandeans, Yizidis, Baha'is and others—suffer similarly.

It has become abundantly clear that the brutal campaigns of Islamist extremists are resulting in the eradication of non-Muslim religious minorities or, for those who remain, the prevention of them from having any influence or even basic rights within their society's political, social or cultural spheres. These assaults on religious minorities continue to occur despite rejection by the majority of Muslims and condemnation by prominent Muslim voices, such as Jordan's Prince Ghazi bin Mohammed and Iraq's Grand Ayatollah Sistani. Moderate Muslims also face grave threats from the extremist groups and forces that wreak destruction in the name of a political interpretation of Islam.

The current trajectory, marked by political violence and, in the cases of Iraq and Syria, full-blown war, cannot but result in a Middle East largely emptied of Christians, their millennia-old presence gone for good. Turkey offers an example of what the future may hold for the region as a whole: Turkey now has a Christian population that constitutes a mere 0.15 percent of the country's 79 million people, down from almost a quarter of the population a century ago. Turkey's Christian community, once the heart of Eastern Christendom, is near extinction.

Britain's Prince Charles has drawn attention to this crisis. A life-long proponent of building bridges between the Christian and Muslim faiths through dialogue, he warned last year: "We cannot ignore the fact that Christians in the Middle East are, increasingly, being deliberately targeted by fundamentalist Islamist militants. Christianity was, literally, born in the Middle East and we must not forget our Middle Eastern brothers and sisters in Christ."

Testifying about Egypt before the US Congress in December 2013, Bishop Angaelos of the Coptic Orthodox Church in the UK made similar observations. He stated that the attacks by "radical elements" are not merely targeting individuals, but "the Christian and minority presence in its entirety." Over three days in August 2013, Egypt's Coptic Christians who, numbering about 8 million, comprise the region's largest Christian community, experienced the worst single attack against their churches in 700 years. Both before and after that episode, the Copts have suffered other violence, including a mob assault on the Cairo Cathedral of the Coptic Pope during a funeral service and the bombing of the Church of All Saints that killed 85 people. Tens of thousands of Copts are estimated to have recently fled their homeland.

After more than a decade of political turmoil in Iraq, where Christians have been targeted and killed in their churches, school buses, neighborhoods and shops, the United Nations High Commissioner for Refugees estimates that 850,000 Christians in that country have fled. Canon Andrew White, the leader of Iraq's only Anglican Church, asserted that, "all the churches are targets. . . . We used to have 1.5 million Christians, now we have probably only 200,000 left. . . . There are more Iraqi Christians in Chicago than there are here."

In Syria, large segments of both the Christian and Muslim populations have already been displaced and many suffering horrific daily assault, forced starvation and unspeakable hardships are leaving the country. The Christians are defenseless, resisting demands to take up arms for either side, and thus are caught in the middle of a brutal war. But the Christians are also victims of beheadings, summary executions, kidnappings, and forcible conversions in deliberate efforts to suppress or eradicate their religious faith. Over 30 percent of Syria's Christian churches have already been destroyed. Recently, jihadists have driven out virtually all of the population from the Christian towns of Maaloula and Kessab. An entire convent of nuns was taken hostage and held for ransom, along with many others. Priests who have worked to build interfaith bridges and sought truces among the warring Muslim factions

Appendix

have been assassinated. Two Orthodox bishops, Metropolitans Mar Gregorios Yohanna Ibrahim and Boulos Yazigi have been held captive since April 22, 2013.

Baghdad's Chaldean Patriarch Louis Sako recounts: "For almost two millennia Christian communities have lived in Iraq, Syria, Egypt and elsewhere in the Middle East. . . . Unfortunately, in the 21st century Middle Eastern Christians are being severely persecuted. . . . In most of these countries, Islamist extremists see Christians as an obstacle to their plans." We take to heart his observation in an extended address last month that "it is sad to note that most Western Christians have no real awareness of the painful situation of Christians in the Middle East, even though they could actually highlight their real condition and raise awareness among politicians."

Egyptian, Iraqi and Syrian Christians are now leaving their countries in great numbers not simply to look for better economic opportunities. They are fleeing targeted campaigns against them, some of whose common elements include the following:

* Scores of churches—some while full of worshippers—monasteries, cemeteries, and Bible centers have been deliberately demolished and crosses on others have been removed.
* The building and repairing of churches has been curbed and prohibited.
* Private Christian homes, businesses and lands have been targeted for looting, confiscation or destruction because Christians are deemed not to have property rights.
* Christians, including some clergy, after being identified as such by their names, identity cards, or some other means, have been beheaded, shot execution-style or otherwise brutally murdered. Clergy have also been killed for their peacemaking efforts or simply as personifications of the Christian faith.
* Untold numbers of Christians, including bishops, priests, past ors, and nuns, have been kidnapped and held for ransom.
* Young women have been abducted and forced to convert to Islam and marry their captors.

}291{

* Christians have been told to convert to Islam or be killed and some have been forced to pay protection money.
* Christians have been forced to submit to medieval Dhimmi contracts under which their religious and other rights are suppressed and they are forced to live as second class citizens.
* Muslim apostasy and blasphemy codes and standards for dress, occupation and social behavior are being enforced for Christians, as well as for Muslims.
* Christians have been barred from practicing their faith publicly.

Such abuse and injustice is frequent and pervasive enough to form observable patterns in these three countries. Extremists and terrorist gangs are behind most of these incidents; they have been largely carried out with impunity, and sometimes with the acquiescence of state and local authorities. It is their cumulative effect that has triggered the current massive exodus of Christians.

American religious leaders have been markedly quiet about this human rights crisis. The sense of abandonment felt by the Middle Eastern Churches is reflected in the searing words of Patriarch Sako, last December: "We feel forgotten and isolated. We sometimes wonder, if they kill us all, what would be the reaction of Christians in the West? Would they do something then?"

PLEDGE OF CONSCIENCE

We, as Orthodox, Catholic, Protestant and evangelical leaders, have come together across lines of ecclesial distinctions in this joint pledge to speak up for our fellow Christians and other defenseless religious minorities in the Middle East. We invite other faith leaders and all men and women of good will who are concerned with the dignity and safety of all human beings to join us in this urgent task.

We are compelled to take this action by the grave dangers that confront the Churches of Egypt, Iraq and Syria, in particular. Christians have been leaving the Middle East for many years, and, in these three countries, members of all communities—including other religious minorities and Muslims—suffer from violence and political turmoil; the Egyptian, Iraqi and Syrian Christian communities, under the additional scourge of intensifying religious persecution, are experiencing a sudden, massive exodus of their members from the region. Since these communities account for most of the indigenous Christians in today's Middle East, Christianity appears doomed to extinction in the lands where it originated 2,000 years ago.

Recognizing the spiritual, humanitarian and geopolitical implications of this historic flight, we have joined together to affirm our moral obligation to speak and act in defense of religious freedom for all human beings.

As Americans, we believe that the ability to worship God, or not, and to freely practice one's faith, is a basic, inalienable human right, as recognized in our country's founding documents, and that it has universal application. We witness this right under assault today in Egypt, Iraq and Syria.

As Christians, we are also called to take to heart what Paul told the Corinthians, speaking of the Church as the Body of Christ, "If one part suffers, every part suffers with it," and the Hebrews, "continue to remember those in prison as if you were together with them in prison, and those who are mistreated as if you yourselves were suffering." We are aggrieved by the suffering in the Middle East today of our brothers and sisters in Christ.

In support of the persecuted Christians and other faith communities in Egypt, Iraq and Syria, we pledge our efforts for a nation-wide effort to call together our own congregations in sustained prayer, education and engagement in US foreign policy on behalf of the persecuted Christians and other religious minorities of Egypt, Iraq and Syria. All too clearly, we see the "tears of the oppressed" and cannot ignore them.

CALL TO ACTION

While the fate of Christianity in the Middle East is unquestionably important to Christians, it should be emphasized that the continued presence of Christian and other religious minority communities in that region is in America's national interest. We agree with President Obama's assertion before this year's National Prayer Breakfast that the right to religious freedom is an essential human right that "matters to our national security."

Cultural diversity provides the important experience of different faith communities living together. If the robust communities of Egyptian, Iraqi and Syrian Christians and other religious minorities continue to be driven out of the Middle East, pluralistic co-existence would be tragically diminished region-wide. Furthermore, the Christians of Egypt, Iraq and Syria have rejected violence as an acceptable response to oppression and, instead, by both word and action, have supported a message of peace and non-violence.

Though Christians are a fraction of the overall populations of these three countries, it is difficult to consider them minorities since they have long been an integral part the social fabric, and have contributed, alongside Muslims, to the construction of the Arab civilization. They have had an especially formative role in promoting modern education, literacy and learning that benefits society as a whole.

In addition, the area would suffer the sad loss of professional and entrepreneurial groups important for a dynamic middle class, as well as active intellectuals long committed to norms and practices of human rights, the rule of law, and the rights of individual citizenship, all essential for democracy and hence essential for making these counties partners in peace with the US and other Western nations.

Even as we pledge to do all within our power to alleviate the suffering of those persecuted for their religious beliefs in the Middle East, we also urgently appeal for action from our government, which, under both Republican and Democratic Administrations, has failed to recognize the unique plight of the religious minorities.

It is our conviction that American foreign policies can be more effectively used on their behalf. We welcomed President Obama's public remarks regarding his March 27 meeting with Pope Francis, specifically his reaffirmation that "it is central to U.S. foreign policy that we protect the interests of religious minorities around the world." As a matter of conscience, we, therefore, respectfully call for the following actions:

I. Appointment of the Special Envoy on Middle East Religious Minorities. A new special envoy post, filled by a prominent and knowledgeable citizen is needed for deep engagement in the issues and circumstances affecting persecuted Christians and other religious minorities in the region. Over 20 special envoy posts exist to protect a range of other groups and interests but none is dedicated to the plight of Middle East religious minorities. American policies, including military ones, continue to be formed without taking into account the impact they might have on these vulnerable communities. A high caliber envoy who has the ear of the President could ensure:

* The views and interests, including physical safety and equal rights, of the members of defenseless religious minorities groups are considered in any peace negotiations concerning Syria.
* Persecuted religious minority communities are not over looked in the distribution of American and international foreign assistance, and humanitarian and resettlement aid.
* Every diplomatic effort is made to press other governments to stop facilitating, harboring, and assisting any extremist groups and militias, and to foster respect for the defenseless religious minorities.
* Other policies to promote protections and respect for members of persecuted religious minority communities through out the Middle East are considered at the highest levels while there is still time to act.

It was just such a special envoy who helped draw attention to genocidal levels of religious persecution in Sudan and usher in a comprehensive peace agreement to end the north-south conflict there in 2005.

II. Review of Foreign Aid. As he has done in the interest of other stated administration priorities, President Obama should initiate an internal review to ensure that American assistance programs uphold American anti-discrimination policies and principles—specifically as they relate to religious freedom and pluralism. The review should include the region's national textbooks, local governmental broadcasting, statements by public officials, and national identity cards, where the inclusion of one's religious identity is often used to deny rights. U.S. government-sponsored broadcasting, legal and constitutional assistance, and educational efforts should promote religious tolerance and protect religious freedom, including for all religious minorities.

III. Refugee & Reconstruction Assistance. Our principal purpose in speaking out is to help Christian communities remain safely in the region. To that end, vulnerable religious minorities, including those who are refugees in neighboring countries or displaced within their home countries, must be provided their fair share of American refugee, humanitarian and reconstruction aid. Many will need assistance to be relocated elsewhere in the region and American help could be decisive. Above all, the US government must ensure that religious minorities are not discriminated against by local authorities from majority religious groups in the distribution of aid donated by the US government, as was reported to have occurred at certain junctures in Iraq, contributing to the wholesale exodus of its religious minority communities. It must also find new aid approaches to benefit Christians and other minorities who eschew UN refugee camps that they perceive to be dominated by majority religious groups and their militias. In some particularly tragic instances, we recognize that individual members of defenseless religious minorities will never be able to return to their homes, and urge that those individuals be given fast track asylum in the United States and elsewhere in the West.

CONCLUSION

A generation ago, American religious leaders successfully mobilized support for the International Religious Freedom Act of 1998. That law created the US Commission on International Religious Freedom and institutionalized regular State Department reporting on the status of religious liberty around the world. That legislation should be credited with helping to ensure, as President Obama acknowledged at the National Prayer Breakfast last February, that "promoting religious freedom is a key objective of U.S. foreign policy." Now, new action is desperately needed by our churches, our government and our institutions here in the United States, and by all people of good will to make that objective a reality.

This statement, signed by more than 300 Protestant, Catholic and Orthodox Christian leaders—lay and clergy (including the author)—was formally released on Capitol Hill May 7, 2014, under the auspices of now retired Rep. Frank Wolf (R-VA) and Rep. Anne Eshoo (D-CA).

SELECT BIBLIOGRAPHY

Algermissen, Konrad. *Christian Denominations*. Herder, 1945.

Allen, John L. *The Global War on Christians*. Image, 2013.

Armstrong, Karen. *Islam: A Short History*. Modern Library, 2000.

Attwater, Donald. *The Christian Churches of the East, Volumes 1 and 2*. Bruce, 1948.

Belloc, Hilaire. *The Battleground: Syria and Palestine*. Lippincott, 1936.

Berman, Paul. *Terror and Liberalism*. Norton, 2003.

Burleigh, Michael. *Blood and Rage: A Cultural History of Terrorism*. Harper, 2009.

Carroll, Warren H. *The Building of Christendom*. Christendom Press, 1987.

Carroll, Warren H. *The Founding of Christendom*. Christendom Press, 1985.

Cragg, Kenneth. *The Arab Christian: A History in the Middle East*. Westminster, 1991.

Crocker, H. W. *Triumph: The Power and the Glory of the Catholic Church*. Forum, 2001.

Daniel-Rops, H. *The Church of Apostles and Martyrs*. Dutton, 1960.

Daniel-Rops, H. *The Church in the Dark Ages*. Dutton, 1959.

Daniel-Rops, H. *Our Brothers in Christ*. Dutton, 1967.

Durant, Will. *The Age of Faith*. Simon and Schuster, 1950.

Durant, Will. *Caesar and Christ*. Simon and Schuster, 1944.

Eberhardt, Newman. *A Summary of Catholic History, Volume I.* Herder, 1961.

Eberhardt, Newman. *A Summary of Catholic History, Volume II.* Herder, 1962.

Hitchcock, James. *History of the Catholic Church.* Ignatius, 2012.

Hourani, Albert. *A History of the Arab Peoples.* Belknap/Harvard, 1991.

Hughes, Philip. *A History of the Church, Volume I.* Sheed and Ward, 1949.

Hughes, Philip. *A History of the Church, Volume II.* Sheed and Ward, 1949.

Huntington, Samuel. *The Clash of Civilizations and the Remaking of World Order.* Simon and Schuster, 1996.

Ibrahim, Raymond. *Crucified Again: Exposing Islam's New War on Christians.* Regnery, 2013.

Jenkins, Philip. *The Great and Holy War: How World War I Became A Religious Crusade.* Harper, 2014.

Jenkins, Philip. *The Lost History of Christianity.* Harper, 2008.

Johnson, Paul. *A History of Christianity.* Atheneum, 1979.

Joseph, John. *Muslim-Christian Relations and Inter Christian Rivalries in the Middle East.* State University of N.Y., 1983.

Karabell, Zachary. *Peace Be Upon You: The Story of Muslim, Christian and Jewish Coexistence.* Knopf, 2007.

Lewis, Bernard. *The Assassins: A Radical Sect in Islam.* Oxford University Press, 1967.

Lewis, Bernard. *The Crisis of Islam: Holy War and Unholy Terror.* Modern Library, 2003.

Lewis, Bernard. *Cultures in Conflict.* Oxford University Press, 1995.

Lewis, Bernard. *Islam and the West.* Oxford University Press, 1993.

Lewis, Bernard. *A Middle East Mosaic.* Random House, 2000.

Lewis, Bernard. *The Shaping of the Modern Middle* East. Oxford University Press, 1964.

Lewis, Bernard. *What Went Wrong?* Oxford University Press, 2002.

Laqueur, Walter. *The New Terrorism: Fanaticism and the Arms of Mass Destruction*. Oxford University Press, 1999.

Laqueur, Walter. *Terrorism*. Little Brown, 1977.

Laqueur, Walter. *Terrorism in the Twenty-First Century*. Continuum, 2004.

Malik, Habib. *Islamism and the Future of the Christians of the Middle East*. Hoover Institute Press, 2010.

Marshall, Paul, General Editor. *Religious Freedom in the World: A Global Report on Freedom and Persecution*. Broadman and Holman, 2000.

Marshall, Paul and Gilbert, Lela and Shea, Nina. *Persecuted: The Global Assault on Christians*. Thomas Nelson, 2013.

Marshall, Paul with Gilbert, Lela. *Their Blood Cries Out*. World Publishing, 1997.

Marshall, S. L. A. *World War I*. American Heritage Press, 1971.

Meyer, G. J. *A World Undone: The Story of the Great War 1914 to 1918*. Delacorte Press, 2006.

Reica, Walter, Editor. *Origins of Terrorism: Psychologies, Ideologies, Theologies, States of Mind*. Woodrow Wilson Center Press, 1998.

Robertson, Ronald. *The Eastern Christian Churches: A Brief Survey*. Edizioni, 1999.

Royal, Robert. *The Catholic Martyrs of the Twentieth Century*. Crossroad, 2000.

Samir S.J., Samir Khalil. 111 *Questions on Islam*, Ignatius, 2002.

Sennott, Charles. *The Body and the Blood: The Middle East's Vanishing Christians and the Possibility for Peace*. Public Affairs, 2003.

Shea, Nina. *In the Lion's Den: A Shocking Account of Persecution and Martyrdom of Christians Today and How We Should Respond*. Broadman and Holman, 1997.

Sookhdeo, Patrick. *Understanding Islamic Terrorism*. Isaac Publishing, 2004.

Wilmshurst, David. *The Martyred Church: A History of the Church of the East*. East and West Publishing, 2011.

Zakaria, Fareed. *The Future of Freedom: Illiberal Democracy at Home and Abroad*. Norton, 2003.

ABOUT THE AUTHOR

George J. Marlin is Chairman of Aid to the Church in Need-U.S.A., an agency under the guidance of the Pope that supports the persecuted and suffering Church around the world.

He served two terms as Executive Director and CEO of the Port Authority of New York and New Jersey (1995–1997). In that capacity he managed thirty-five facilities including the World Trade Center, La Guardia, JFK and Newark Airports, PATH Subway, and the four bridges and two tunnels that connect New York and New Jersey. In 1993, Mr. Marlin was the Conservative Party nominee for mayor of the City of New York. In 1994, he served on Governor-elect Pataki's transition team and in 2010 served on Governor-elect Andrew Cuomo's transition team. Mr. Marlin has been a member of the Governor of New York's Council of Economic and Fiscal Advisors and served as a Director of the Nassau County Interim Finance Authority (NIFA), a state fiscal oversight and control board (2010–2014).

Mr. Marlin is the author/editor of twelve books including *The American Catholic Voter: Two Hundred Years of Political Impact, Narcissist Nation: Reflections of a Blue-State Conservative, Squandered Opportunities: New York's Pataki Years, Fighting the Good Fight: A History of the New York Conservative Party, The Guidebook to Municipal Bonds* (co-authored with Joe Mysak), *The Quotable Chesterton, Quotable Fulton Sheen* and *Quotable Paul Johnson*. Mr. Marlin has also served as general editor of *The Collected Works of G. K. Chesterton*. His 450+ articles have appeared in over two dozen periodicals including *The New York Times, New York Post, Long Island Business News,* TheCatholicThing.org, *Newsmax, National Review, Newsday, The Washington Times* and the New York *Daily News.*